Silence in a Democracy:
Prisons for Profit

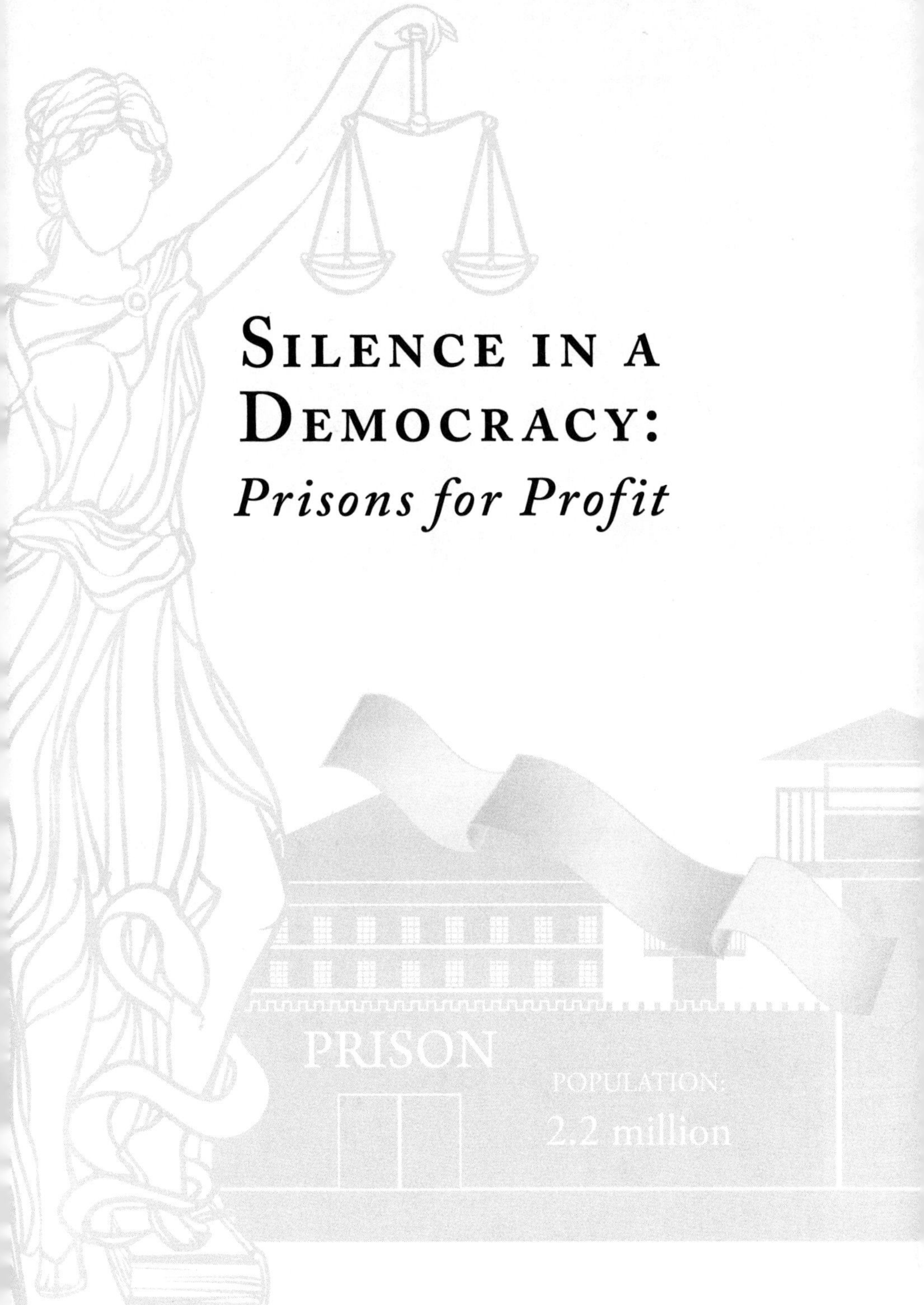

Silence in a Democracy: *Prisons for Profit*

But you have eyes only for greed and dishonesty!
You murder the innocent, oppress the poor, and reign ruthlessly.
Jeremiah 23:17

Prisons: 21st Century Modern Day Slavery

A Message America Never Learned:
The Evils of Human Bondage

Using humans as an economic product
to perpetuate a prison industry

Dorothy R. Swygert

Retribution?
The Lord will respond swiftly upon this nation
with an enlightening force who controls
all elements of this earth!

Silence in a Democracy: Prisons for Profit

Printed in the United States of America

ISBN: 978-0-9648737-8-0

Library of Congress Control Number: 2016933372

Book cover design by
Janee` Roberts
Hampton University senior
Communication and Graphic Arts,
Dr. Joseph F. Martin

Published by:
Rekindle the Heart
Post Office Box 219
Hampton, VA 23669

As we analyze the prison system in America,
we can see the crisis in American democracy.

This book is dedicated to
God, the Creator,
Who blessed this nation into being
and
to those who realize

The earth is the Lord's, and the fullness thereof;
The world, and they that dwell therein.
PSALM 24:1

Contents

PART II
THE AFRICAN AMERICAN LANTERN

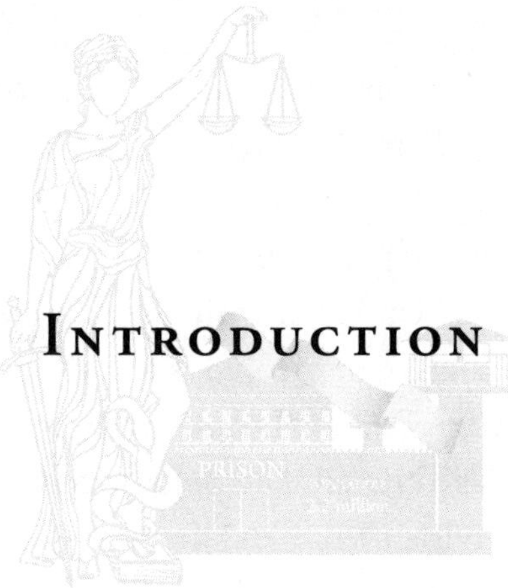

Introduction

Across the nation there is a consuming disease flourishing in America and she is the worst for hosting this germ in a democracy. The inception of slavery began in 1661 where it dominated the South. I am always spiritually uplifted to read the words of Abigail Adams, the wife of President John Adams. She was a political anomaly during the Revolutionary age. In 1774 *Abigail Adams* wrote to her husband: "It always appeared a most iniquitous scheme to me to fight ourselves for what we are daily robbing and plundering from those who have as good a right to freedom as we have."[1]

About the same time Thomas Jefferson wrote *A Summary View of the Rights of British America*, in which he said the abolition of slavery was the great object of desire in the colonies, but it had become increasingly difficult because Britain had consistently blocked all colonial efforts to put an end to the slave trade. As the British used the thirteen colonies as an economic labor force to grow her wealth and to enhance her power, so did the colonies in the South embrace this philosophy to use slaves as their economic tool. This ill seed was almost incurable and the germ led to the Civil War and almost annihilated the nation. The close of the Civil War in 1865 did not heal the soul of America. The spiritual reasoning of Abigail Adams did not resonate in the hearts of all Americans. One would think the lesson at the close of the Civil War would have healed the depraved economic soul of the nation but it did not. How many times do we have to fight the war for the same spiritual concept—that God made man and man made slaves?

The great African American warriors who orchestrated and continued in various forms of protest to steer the nation into realizing the African American, a citizen on par with others, were now dead and the voice to sway America has been silenced. From the pre–Civil War voices of Nat Turner, Gabrielle Prosser, Denmark Vesey, Frederick Douglas, David Walker, Harriet Tubman, and Sojourner Truth to the minds of the thinkers and activists of the 20th century—Stokely Carmichael, Fannie Lou Hamer, Martin L. King, Malcolm X, Roy Wilkins, A. Philip Randolph, H. Rap Brown, Huey Newton, and Herman Ferguson—all now belong to the Ages. Instead of taking heed to the voice quest for justice, our nation has sought to silence these voices. They fail to realize that in each generation God, Himself, raises up horns to apprise a people of their sins before he comes to destroy a nation. Will America take heed, or will America continue to rely upon her left-over scientific and technological industry inherited from Hitler's war machine to carry on an evil work in our times?

The focus of this book, in the 21st century, is the danger of exploiting human beings as economic products to enhance wealth for corporations in a democracy. The second focus of this book is the dire need of America to nurture her children.

After all the struggles, the deaths, fire burning, bombing, and terroristic tactics used to keep African Americans in a specifically defined status in this nation—and second-class citizenship across the board—one would think that our nation would have embraced the spiritual lesson of God. I, said the Lord, created my people in various shades to put upon this earth because I know they are beautiful. I wanted to spread these colors across the earth just as I painted the beautiful rainbow in the sky. But you have misconstrued my message and designated physiognomy to determine the value, place, and destination of my people. I AM no respecter of person. Did you not comprehend the lesson? Did you read my word in Numbers 12, when "Miriam and Aaron spoke against Moses because of the Ethiopian woman whom he had married: for he had married an Ethiopian woman"? To show He is not a respecter of person Moses's sister was punished by God.

> *And the anger of the LORD was kindled against them: and he departed. And the cloud departed from off the tabernacle; and, behold, Miriam became leprous, white as snow: and Aaron looked upon Miriam, and, behold, she was leprous.*
>
> *And Aaron said unto Moses, Alas, my Lord, I beseech thee, lay not the sin upon us, wherein we have done foolishly, and wherein we have sinned.*
>
> *Let her not be as one dead, of whom the flesh is half consumed when he cometh out of his mother's womb.*
>
> *And Moses cried unto the LORD, saying, Heal her now, O God, I beseech thee.*
>
> *And the LORD said unto Moses, if her father had but spit in her face, should she not be ashamed seven days? Let her be shut out from the camp seven days, and after that let her be received in again.*
>
> *And Miriam was shut out from the camp seven days: and the people journeyed not till Miriam was brought in again.*

God created people to live freely upon this earth and to enjoy the bountiful resources of His own creation. He did not create human beings first. God is an orderly God and He does everything in perfect order. His vision of His creation had an orderly and divine system. First He took care to create this world. He separated the darkness from light. He separated the waters from dry land. He enriched the dry land with seeds within itself for permanent perpetuation in the design of the seasons. He illuminated the earth and sky with a greater light and a lesser light. He placed the birds and fowls in the sky. He placed fish and whales in the seas. He placed animals and beasts upon the land. After He had prepared His earth and put everything in order, in His infinite wisdom He created humankind. He placed man upon this earth and gave him divine instructions on how to live upon this earth. Obedience would have led to unending peace upon the earth, but humankind defiled the instructions of God, and in their own disobedience sought *to be a god*, instead of obeying and following the instructions of God. Where are we today?

America, a nation which God blessed into being, has turned away from God's law and instructions on how to live and to let live on His earth. In Psalm 24:1, we are told, "*the earth is the Lord's, and the fullness thereof, the world, and they that dwell therein*." It is not that we, the inhabitants of this nation, have not been taught, because we know the Founders inscribed it into the United States Constitution. But an evil population, without a conscience of right and wrong based on the law of God, has devised a furtive plan to turn this nation in another direction. The entire climate of the nation has been changed to distort the minds and hearts of people to a philosophy of lust, greed, wealth, and immorality. It is this philosophy I address in this book. I address it, because, hopefully, the nation will have enough communicants with God to begin turning this nation around before God sends His destroyer.

A Spiritual Vision

As I slept on Sunday, July 20, 2014, the Spirit of the Lord came upon me and gave me instructions to research the prison system. Immediately, I got up to begin the work. What I found was an appalling sin—that my country had already re-enslaved the African Americans about forty years ago. God frequently uses the number forty. In my research, I came to realize how an insidious evil seed had been planted in America forty years ago. Before I continue to write this book, I will say I am so ashamed of my nation for permitting such an ugly, evil seed like this to grow in a democracy. I have already given you a capsule history of this seed planted for wealth and power at the expense of masterminding an economic system to incarcerate African Americans as a cheap labor force in the 21st century—a democracy.

Prisons have become a booming industry in the United States since 1983. In fact, this nation has the largest prison population in the world. Our nation has more prisons than China. China has twenty percent of the world's population and America has only five percent. What has happened to the structure and climate of America that a prison industry flourishes in a democracy? To understand this phenomenon, there is a need to analyze the design, origin, and founders of such a system. We must study the factors that have contributed to the expansion and growth of prisons in a democracy.

How can we understand the pattern of prison growth? How can we identify factors that contributed to the prison expansion within one decade from 1973 when the population was very low to 1983? Statistics from the Correctional Association of New York indicate, "In January 1973 there were 12,500 persons in the State prison system." Just a decade later, there were 58,000 in the prison system. Was this a natural growth pattern or a contrived pseudo-growth population? The true question is what caused such a swift growth in the prison population within one decade.

Were there tangible items that inflated the prison growth, or was it a normal pattern? To understand this, we would have to study the growth pattern and analyze factors that contributed to the cause of prison growth. This would bring us to understanding the design used to induce the prison population. We would need to question the methods used to swell the prison population. The next question to ask: Who are the people who wanted to increase the prison population? What would be their motive/purpose for propounding and expanding prison growth across the nation? The crucial question to ask is how does a democracy permit such an economic farce to thrive in the nation.

We will need to study this prison design to comprehend what caused such a geometrical/exponential growth in the prison system. First, let us provide a summary of the mood of the country in the 1970s.

Prisons: The Thinking of the 21st Century (Expansion of Prisons)

I worked in prison ministry in Brooklyn in the early 1990s. I knew the composition of the prison population, but I had no idea many of these inmates were lured to these cells with drugs as the enticing bait. My heart was touched to observe the different categories of the populace. The predominant population was black and Hispanic.

As a ministerial team, our work was to transform the lives of these inmates, give them courage, hope, and a desire to prepare themselves for a return to mainstream America. Members of my immediate team had organized to prepare some inmates to take the GED. This would be one step towards creating a means for them to re-enter society. Each member of my team specialized in one of the academic disciplines: English, math, science, and history.

As we worked with this group of inmates, I became very much aware of their stories, their talents, their love for their families, and their desire to return to their families and to their communities. Working with these young people opened a new horizon for me to become aware of their gifts and talents. There was the story of one who had experienced the loss of so many relatives that before she realized it, she had begun using drugs as a crutch to deal with the hurt and pain of losing so many loved ones. She had her own computer business, but there was no stability in her life, and with the loss of so many relatives, hope had taken a back seat.

I, especially, admired the poetry of one Spanish female who wrote beautifully. In her poetry, she expressed her life hopes, and dreams were revealed.

There was a young black female who took time to engage us in role playing. As a teacher, I was accustomed to professional techniques in my work. This young lady decided to do a simulation with me: "Rev. Swygert," she said, "no one is going to listen to you with that speech and that dialogue. You have to take on the demeanor of us. You have to get the mannerism, do the body language and the slouch as we do. You have to shuffle your body and give that slang-type street language. In this demeanor, they will know you, dig, and you will understand them." As she talked, she demonstrated everything she said. "You are a beautiful person and we thank you for coming to see about us. Now when you get this prison swag and mannerism, you will get their attention and Be able to do your work to help us." I burst into laughter and said, "Thank you, I will embrace what you have shared."

Now, to my book! I was appalled at so much life locked behind the prison bars with so much illiteracy, so much mental illness, and so many health challenges.

When the Spirit of the Lord awakened me on that third Sunday morning of July 2014, I got up and began research. I began reading articles by Elizabeth Kolbert, Eric Schlosser, Tracy Huling, Vicky Pelaez, and the Rose and Clear Report. First, I was very thankful for these writers of courage, tenacity, and desire to uplift humanity with the pen. Soon, my thoughts were flowing. I felt the burst of a whole new understanding of what truly was happening with the prison system. In a brief moment, my heart was broken. I was so sad to realize that in the 21st century, we had individuals in an American democracy who blemished humanity to enhance their wealth.

I am an African American, third generation from slavery, who lived during the Jim Crow period in our history. I can recall my history classes throughout my early childhood, high school, and college. I was blessed to have lived in the village of Fairfield, a segregated town. If there were ever a village, Fairfield was the model, during my growth year. There was a complete unity of the home, church, school, and community working together to form the character of children. We were taught by quality teachers who had a love for children and a care for building positive community. They knew the heritage of the community and used their talents to guide children to take their journey in life.

I mentioned this educational phase because we were taught African American history. I knew well the Civil War, the battles, the generals, and the role the African American played in bringing that war to an end. I could still hear the voice of Frederick Douglass. I could see Harriet Tubman sneaking through the southern boundaries to steal slaves and packed them on her train to victory. "Much obliged" to the Quakers and others who provided hiding spaces and places for them during the day where they traveled by night—one day at a time, following the North Star in quest of freedom. I was most impressed with the work of Senator Charles Sumner of Massachusetts and Representative Thaddeus Stevens. They were fiery white voices, who spoke vehemently against the slavery institution and played a vital political role to usher in the Civil War Amendments.

But back to my storyline, here in 2014–15, my heart was breaking to realize that lust, greed, and power would smother the hearts and minds of a small group of people to engage as a "think tank" to re-enslave a people right here in America, in a "democracy" for the sake of using human beings as a cheap labor force to enhance their wealth. America, *this* is why I write this book! Randall Robinson's *The Debt: What America Owes to Blacks* addresses this liberty issue. The nation has never compensated African Americans for more than two hundred years of slavery to enrich this nation and now another group of unwise, unscrupulous think tank individuals have sat down behind closed doors and devised a plan to re-enslave them without any concern for their children, their families, and their communities. I can ask just one question: What kind of soul rests in the body of such a people?

As my grandmother used to say, "The truth is the light." This is a reality and I will proceed with this writing for humanity. There was no need for prison expansion. A group of individuals sat behind closed doors and conjured an idea on how to grow and expand prisons as an economic market to create a means to enhance their wealth, power, and control.

Acknowledgments

Silence in a Democracy: Prisons for Profit has been a true spiritual journey for me. When I began my research, as guided by the Spirit of the Lord, I was so inspired by courageous writers as Eric Schlosser, Vicky Pelaez, Diano-La Prensa, and Elizabeth Kolbert. My heart was inspired because if there are no people to raise the bar on democracy, America stands in her worst measuring poll. Wherever these writers are, I send blessings to them and ask God to continue to bless them in their work to uplift humanity. These writers are to us as Thomas Paine and Patrick Henry were to the colonists when they spoke truth to power—inspiring them to rise up to fight for their independence. I salute the bastion of other writers in this field and encourage them to continue their work on the frontline. Our work is equated to America's fireside poets, William Cullen Bryant and James Russell Lowell—feed the pipeline of America to pursue truth, justice, and equality for all.

Now, I want you to know how grateful I am to the writers I have quoted, in large volume, because it was so apropos to accentuate the message and to make history come alive. This book is really a saga, a song, through the years in America, where the black man has been in constant search for freedom, justice, and equality. The most unique cruelty of it all is, because of his physiognomy, he has been deprived of his God-given gifts and talents and restrained from using them to do what the Creator has endowed him to do—that is, to use the same, to make this a better world. I have marveled at this weakness since my childhood years. As I taught school, my motto was to be fair across the board to the children of various nationalities because I had to pave the way for them to cultivate their gifts in a measure where they would come to know why they were placed on this earth—not about color and physiognomy, but about loving, caring, sharing, and forgiving. The question in the forefront of my mind is this: Why does this country deprive a people from developing their gifts and talents, whereas, if unharnessed, they could develop them in a manner to uplift humanity? The record, despite legal obstacles, has shown how the gifts of blacks, throughout the years of working, have built this nation (and we dare not mention the works of a few who have excelled in disciplines) across the study map. The question remains—why, then, do we seek to override the talents of individuals to make them a personal footstool—harnessed and suppressed, unable to realize God's purpose for one's birth. *Silence in a Democracy: Prisons for Profit* is such an egregious example.

I salute some willing workers in God's vineyard. Carolyn Andrew, a nurse, is one of the persons I referenced in the text, working in my prison ministry. I thank her for sacrificing time during the holiday season to read my manuscript. She supervised the prison ministry and the Prison Fellowship program in Concord Baptist Church. I am most grateful to my neighbor, Etta Ladson, a retired administrator in New York, who has spent her life working with youth and continues this work with middle school students to offer them incentives and scholarships. Special kudos to Andrea Morrison and the Writers House, LLC, 21 West 26th Street, New York 10010, management of the King's Estate, for permission to print Dr. Martin L. King's *Letter from a Birmingham Jail.* I felt this was most important because it reverberates the theme of how the black man has been in a continuous search for freedom from 1661 to the 21st century. It has been so long, until the Lord awakened me on a Sunday morning with this given assignment to sound the horn. He cannot destroy a people until they have received exceeding warnings to turn around.

This book tells the history of this great struggle—a struggle without compensation which is a "no-no" for God. Scripture echoes clearly, "a worker is worthy of his hire." (Luke 10:7). When you exploit a worker intentionally, you are accountable unto God.

Men of great courage like John Chisholm, District Attorney in Milwaukee County, Wisconsin, with "The Milwaukee Experiment" by Jeffrey Toobin, have embarked upon a great project in our times. In their astounding work, they realized "*in 2010 thirteen percent of the state's African-American men of working age were behind bars—nearly double the national average of 6.7 percent.*" This research showed how in Milwaukee County, "where more than half of African-American men in their thirties had served time in state prison." But the most profound question asked is the salient principle of this spiritual examination. It was his soul that guided him to ask this question. He could have been blindsided, picked up big bucks under the table, but his soul resonated with his being and he chose to listen. Chisholm did some soul searching: "How had the work of his own office contributed to these numbers?" When you work in high power positions, take your soul with you. It is your soul that has to give accountability to the Creator. Oh yes, we may live a century, but at the close of the day, we stand in the presence of the God who has a complete record of our lives. To read about this project, I direct you to *The New Yorker*, May 11, 2015, edition, "The Milwaukee Experiment" by Jeffrey Toobin. We can get busy using the gifts we have been given to uplift humanity.

Another superb writer is Jed S. Rakoff, author of *Mass Incarceration: The Silence of the Judges*. I cannot believe this writer spoke such bold truth. *"For too long, too many judges have been too quiet about an evil of which we are a part: the mass incarceration of people in the United States today. It is time that more of us spoke out."* Rakoff has made a profound observation. He says, even though the number of violent crimes has steadily decreased over the past two decades, the number of prisoners serving life sentences has steadily increased, so that one in nine persons in prison is now serving a life sentence. Can you analyze his statement? If not, when you complete your reading of *Silence in a Democracy*, you will review the thirteen stages on how to grow a prison industry in chapter six. Take time to broaden your knowledge on prison exploitation of human beings as an industry. Read Rakoff's article in the *The New York Review of Book*s, May 21, 2015/Volume LXII, Number 9.

I am most grateful to the work of the Justice Policy Institute. You may retrieve a copy of the eleven-page policy report, *Too Little, Too Late, President Clinton's Legacy* by accessing the internet: justicepolicy.org. For statistics, use The Sentencing Project, 1705 DeSales Street NW, 8th Floor, Washington, DC 20036.

I had completed my manuscript July 2016 when I received a copy of Paul L. *Williams' Operation Gladio*. This book affirms my *Silence in a Democracy: Prisons for Profit*. What the spirit of the Lord revealed to me in 2014 was to research the prisons. God never assigns anything without an affirmation. *Operation Gladio* was my affirmation. I am most grateful for this publication. Williams' speaks of *Ghetto Gold* in *Operation Gladio*. "Wild Bill had drafted plans to create a postwar central intelligence agency and knowing this, Helliwell came up with another brainstorm—a surefire means of gaining covert funding for Gladio and other security operations.9" According to *Operation Gladio*, the financial concept was derived from General Chaing Kai-shek, leader of the Chinese National Army. "The new agency, he realized, could obtain cold cash by adopting the same measures as General Chaing [Kai-Shek]. It could supply heroin to the black community in America's ghettos." (Paul L. Williams, *Operation Gladio*, p. 32).

Alfred McCoy, another and historian, earned his Ph.D in Southeast Asian history at Yale University. His scholarly work is a great contribution to humanity. The Chicago Review Press, published *The Politics of Heroin: CIA Complicity in the Global Trade.*

My final salutation is to Elizabeth Evans, librarian at Hampton University. I extend kudos to Ms. Evans for taking time to read my manuscript.

Now, let each of us, proceed to use our gifts and talents to do a work to uplift humanity. The work we do between birth and death, may contribute to determining our eternity. Hebrew 9:27 says, "It is appointed unto men once to die, but after this the judgment." Remember to reference my *Do the Research: The Flourishing Drug Market* page.

Dorothy R. Swygert

Part I

CHAPTER I

From Humanity in a Democracy to a Prison Economy

Peace Corps: A Good Idea in a Democracy

Ask not what America will do for you, but what together we can do for the freedom of man.
John F. Kennedy. January 20, 1961.

When a good idea thrives in a democracy, the people benefit from the positive seeds. Conversely, when an evil idea is planted, the basic principles of a democracy can be destroyed. John F. Kennedy designed the Peace Corps, a good idea in a democracy. Many college students and graduates joined the program to make a difference. Their philosophy of life differed from our times where the dollar is valued over humanity.

The 1960s climate still embraced an essence of something called love for God's creation. It was the decade when John F. Kennedy held great hopes for the nation and for humanity across the globe. As a teenager, he spent time in England, where he was groomed and shaped for military participation in World War II. He engaged in political bull sessions that set his mind on provocative thinking on détente and global peace.

> As an anxious Europe waited for the Nuremberg party rally on September 12, 1938, where it was thought that Hitler would clarify his intentions with regard to Czechoslovakia, Joe Kennedy prepared to return to the embassy. Jack was to sail from Southampton at the beginning of the month, so it was decided that he would accompany his father to London while Kick, young Joe and the rest stayed on in Cap d'Antibes with their mother. On August 28, Jack and his father flew to Paris, where the ambassador talked with other American diplomats, before continuing to London.[1]

Those sessions helped to shape his thoughts on war and peace and how to save humanity from destruction. From a teenager spending time in England to his military participation in World War II, John F. Kennedy exuded vigor and intellectual energy to envision peace in a global world.

The Peace Corps was John F. Kennedy's idea for building a global connection. He embraced this as an idea to foster the belief that every individual is an important person. This interconnection developed new ways of thinking, opened new horizons on how people could come together under the umbrella of humanity to find their worth, develop their dreams, realize their visions, and to cultivate greater pathways of learning in God's world.

This good idea is a reflection of the true values of a democracy. "The Peace Corps was established by executive order on March 1, 1961." President Kennedy's idea was a model and a hope for building bridges to humanity in Africa, Asia, or in other lands to improve living conditions, provide educational services and to use their talents in any way they could. This program would not only improve the image of America but would also fulfill a vital role in building peace and harmony through understanding and working to uplift humanity. It was not just giving; it was an exchange of ideas, gifts, and talents. I guess Margaret Mead, the anthropologist, would probably say it was a link for cultures to broaden new ways of living, caring, and sharing. In this sharing, there was the potential of growing international relationships to build a ladder to global peace.

A democracy's legislation and programs should be designed to benefit the citizenry and not just a minute group interested in self-aggrandizement. With the Peace Corps, college graduates were given reward bonuses for completing two years in the program. It was a two-way relationship. The youth shared their gifts and talents, and the government provided the finances for them to complete their graduate education. While in college, my sociology class read and discussed *Patterns of Culture,* an anthropological book, written by Ruth Benedict. This book was a study of race, environment, and the concept of culture. We also had the opportunity of sharing the work of Margaret Mead, cultural anthropologist, and Melville J. Herskovits, an American anthropologist who "firmly established African and African-American studies in American academia." He wrote *The Myth of the Negro Past*, where he "rejects the notion that African Americans lost all traces of their past when they were taken from Africa and enslaved in America." Herskovits emphasized race as a sociological concept, not a biological one. Some of my colleagues joined the Peace Corps. A two-way relationship between the youth and the government is the proper bond. This is how it should be. The youth develop their gifts and talents to make this a strong nation, and the nation provides finances for graduate work and providing employment. This type of relationship develops a bond and love between the youth and the nation.

The Peace Corps was just one example of inspiring youth to develop and to use their gifts to contribute to human development on a global order. This program had a natural concern about developing and nurturing children to realize the purpose of their being. The political leaders had created dedication and concern for inspiring positive human development. The laws they enacted in Congress had a humane impact upon society. Educators worked with legislators to keep them abreast of the needs of the nation's children. The unity of this bond overflowed with a sense of caring for our children—providing educational networks to foster educational development and designing programs that would not drain them financially but use creativity in molding great leaders and responsible followers.

John F. Kennedy developed a great idea to build our country. Some ideas are just the opposite of the late president's. The subject of this book is to explore how negative ideas can contribute to the destruction of our democratic principles. This book, *Silence in a Democracy*, will explore how an evil, nefarious idea is permitted to grow in a democracy as a furtive design to destroy, to exploit, and to abuse one segment of the population to the financial advantage of a think tank that has one purpose in mind—how to use human beings as a cheap labor force by growing a prison–industrial complex, prisons for profit at the expense of public taxation.

CHAPTER 2

America's Faith in Education

A Good Idea in a Democracy

Open the door of the schoolhouses to all the children in the land. Let no man have the excuse of poverty for not educating his offspring.
Daniel Webster

John F. Kennedy's Peace Corps reflects the heart of American democracy, when the nation cared for its children and was dedicated to equipping them with the best education possible. This faith in educating the children clearly defined the American heritage. It was internalized in the nation as a responsibility to educate their children and to invest in the future of America.

As we peer through history, we can access the origin of this value placed upon education in our nation. A pamphlet written in 1643 highlights the value Americans placed on education.

A review of this document illuminates the basic institutions that shaped the foundation for America to become a great nation. Reverend Timothy Flint, a frontier missionary who served from 1815 to 1840, said, "a minister, a church, and a school are words to flourish in an advertisement to sell lots." The community bond was the heritage foundation of the nation. First came the establishment of the home and the church, then came the school. The attitude of the first settlers towards school is evident from the view of a New England pamphlet.

> After God had carried us to New England And we had builded our houses Provided necessaries for our livelihood Reared convenient places for God's worship And settled the civil government One of the things we longed for And looked after was to advance learning And perpetuate it to posterity Dreading to leave an illiterate ministry To the churches when our present ministers Shall lie in the Dust (original spelling, "New England's First Fruits," London, England, 1643).[1]

The first public schools were established in 1635 in Massachusetts, along with Harvard College. A year later, the Massachusetts legislature passed the first compulsory education law in America. In essence, this law mandated "the selectmen in every town shall have power to take account of all parents and masters as to their children's education and employment... They [the selectmen] are to see that the children can read and understand the principles of religion and the capital laws of the country . . ."[2]

In 1647, the Massachusetts legislature enacted another law, the Old Deluder Satan Act, to correct some deficiencies in a 1642 piece of legislation. This law required "all towns having fifty or more families of 'householders' to provide an elementary school, and all towns having one hundred or more 'householders' to provide a secondary school in addition to the elementary school." Excerpts from this law gives evidence of the colonial settlers' interest and abiding faith in the education and well-being of their children:

> It being one chiefe project of that ould deluder, Satan, to keepe men from the knowledge of Scriptures, as in former times by keeping them in an unknown tongue,

> so in these latter times by perswading from the use of tongues that so at least the true sence and meaning of the original might be clouded by false glosses of saint seeing deceivers, that lerning may not be buried in the grave of our Fathers in the church and commonwealth, the Lord assisting our endeavors (original spelling).[3]

With the building of the school, these three basic institutions became the reality of community living in America. American governmental officials' top priority was centered on how well we educate our children.

Statesmen's Views on Education

Governor DeWitt Clinton served as governor of New York for nine years. He expressed his pride and the value in providing education for the nation's children.

> The first duty of government, and the surest evidence of good government, is the encouragement of education. A general diffusion of knowledge is a precursor and protector of republican institutions, and in it we must confide as the conservative power that will watch over our liberties and guard them against fraud, intrigue, corruption, and violence. I consider the system of our common schools as the palladium of our freedom, for no reasonable apprehension can be entertained of its subversion as long as the great body of the people are enlightened by education.[4]

Governor DeWitt Clinton valued education as the keystone to freedom—a necessary opportunity to provide for the growth and development of American children.

What did *Daniel Webster*, the great orator of his age, think about education? An eminent statesman and a lawyer, Daniel Webster was renowned for his orations in the lawmaking halls of Congress. What were his views on education and the impact it had upon a growing nation? In 1837, he propounded his views on education in an address at Madison, Indiana.

> Education, to accomplish the ends of good government, should be universally diffused. Open the door of the schoolhouses to all the children in the land. Let no man have the excuse of poverty for not educating his offspring. Place the means of education within his reach and if he remain in ignorance, be it his own reproach...On the diffusion of education among the people rests the preservation and perpetuation of our free institutions."[5]

Daniel Webster's views on education resonated with Governor DeWitt Clinton. In order for a democracy to grow and to flourish, freedom must reign and education is the key to open that door.

Congressman Thaddeus Stevens lived during the pre-post period of the Civil War. His vision, in a democracy, was to provide education for all the citizens. In 1834, the state of Pennsylvania enacted a Free School Law. But one year later, there was a proposal in the Pennsylvania Legislature to repeal the Free School Law. Congressman Stevens made known his voice in the legislature opposing such a change and expounded his views on the value of education for all children in a democracy.

> If an elective Republic is to endure for any length of time, every elector must have sufficient information not only to accumulate wealth and take care of his pecuniary concerns, but to direct wisely the legislature, the ambassadors, and the Executive of the Nation—for some part of all these

> things, some agency in approving or disapproving of them, falls to every freeman. If, then, the permanency of our Government depends upon such knowledge, it is the duty of Government to see that the means of information be diffused to every citizen. This is a sufficient answer to those who deem education a private and not a public duty—who argue that they are willing to educate their own children but not their neighbor's children.[6]

Congressman Thaddeus Stevens, throughout his political career, spoke out for liberty and justice where democracy is renowned as the blessing for all children.

The 20th century voice of *Governor Alfred E. Smith* of New York was known as a "friend to the public school." He placed the highest value on education. In 1928, Smith was a candidate for the Democratic Party. He publicized his views on education. During the darkest hours of depression, he said:

> Whatever may be the exigencies, whatever may be the reason for drastic reductions in appropriations, one thing must not happen. There must be no curtailment of educational facilities. The school systems for the education of our children in every state must be kept up to one hundred per cent efficiency. A state can afford to lose time on the construction of a road, a bridge, or a building and by speeding up construction at a later time possibly catch up, but education must be continuous."[7]

Governor Alfred E. Smith maintained an optimistic attitude about the value of education for the children of the nation. In his historical perspective, the sole purpose of a democracy is to teach, train, and nurture children to perpetuate the American heritage.

Providing quality education to its children was the American way from colonial times to the 1960s. The nation's priority was how they could prepare their children to perpetuate a strong democratic nation.

Teachers and administrators across the nation were dedicated to the cause of educating its youth. The value set on education was ingrained in the home, church, school, and community. The most important emphasis was seen in the White House Conference held each year with a theme to propel the nation's children on a proper course of learning to uplift the nation.

> In the language of the National Committee, the Midcentury Conference, bases its concerns for children on the primacy of spiritual values, democratic practice and the dignity and worth of every individual. Accordingly, the purpose of the conference is to consider how we can develop in children the mental, emotional and spiritual qualities essential to individual happiness and responsible citizenship and what physical, economic and social conditions are deemed necessary to this development.[8]

During this conference, Hugh Leavell, chair of the Executive Board of the American Public Health Association, led a 31-panel discussion with a theme, *Healthy Personality Development in children.*

"America's abiding faith in education—a faith that education, especially of the right kind, is necessary for the realization of the potentialities of the individual and for the stability and the progress of society."[9]

Along with the faith in education was a set of goals and objectives to serve as a guide to insure the students were acquiring the best education possible. The goal of education was to prepare the individual to become a responsible, efficient person to use his or her gifts and talents effectively in a democracy. "The most powerful urge and ambition of man have always been the desire to rear children who could successfully make their way in the world and to help others."[10]

The Impact of Communication on Educating Children

The Federal Communications Commission fulfilled a vital role in its design to monitor communication prior to the 1970s. During this period, there was still a concern for teaching, training, and nurturing children. All agents in the communication network were guided to fulfill its role in the positive nurturing of the nation's children.

A review of the communication system before the 1970s demonstrates this concept. The schools provided the bulk of a child's learning, but there were other agencies that influenced the learning of children

> Although the influence of the school has constantly increased, it is apparent that the modern person does not obtain his education wholly from the school. On the contrary, it is seen that most education comes from the "school of life"—from the home, the church, the radio, the newspaper and magazine, the library, the cinema, television, travel, work and play, and all environment—rather than from the school.[11]

The home, the school, and the neighborhood played a vital role in the growth style of youth, but we know there are other agencies that impact the lives of our children. Some of the non-school agencies that affect the lives of our children are the radio, television, and cinema. Among these include the press, radio, television, and cinema.

Has America neglected its responsibility to the children since the 1970s?

This White House Conference on Education began with precepts of their goal for existing as a body. Schools, colleges, and universities throughout the nation directed their attention to the proper growth and development of children. This immense responsibility was integrated in the institutions of the nation—home, church, and community. Our priority, as a nation, is to write and to design laws to benefit the growth and welfare of the nation's children. The media system, before the 1970s, united to realize this role. Besides the schools, the media was assessed as the second greatest influence on children, therefore, a communication agency was created to monitor what was printed and spoken. Before the 1970s, there was a tacit agreement that these co-partners in nurturing children would censor what they would blast to the public.

During the holiday season, human-interest stories were interwoven into Christmas, Thanksgiving, and holiday stories and vignettes. These programs were designed to impact the hearts and minds of the nation's children with a positive message to uplift humanity. There was always a human lesson to be learned. What has happened to our nation since the 1970s? The entire landscape of the nation has been unraveled. Instead of the stories to inspire people to seek changes in their lives, our television networks flourish with sex, drugs, and violence—a media system designed to destroy the hearts and minds of our children.

Mass Media Glorification of Violence

How can anyone seek to send out a message almost demanding gun control, when in reality, the media and Hollywood producers advertise violence that teaches and trains the minds of the young and old alike to engage in violent behavior—shooting, killing, and murdering in the worst vile manner. It is ironic that such a call can go out to the NRA about guns when no bulletin is sent out to television and Hollywood producers to turn from their scripts of sex, drugs, and violence. Why? My supposition is that the media is purchased with trillions of dollars and the poor little people of the nation must sit on the sideline where they are fed the rhetoric, "We need Gun Control!" What a great farce! What then is the role of the Federal Communications Commission (FCC)? There is a great need to require the FCC to fulfill their role beyond the commercialization and promotion of human destruction, killing, murdering, and immorality. Billionaires who value commercializing their programs for the dollar are in direct conflict with nurturing the hearts and minds of our youth.

The communication system is in direct conflict with nurturing the hearts and minds of the nation's children to enable them to develop their talents to use them in a positive manner and to learn to live peaceably in society with a desire to uplift humanity. The landscape of the nation has changed to embrace immorality with its impact upon the dollar.

Let us review the defined role of the FCC.

> The Federal Communications Commission regulates interstate and foreign communications by radio, television, wire, satellite, and cable. It is responsible for the orderly development and operation of broadcast services and the provision of rapid, efficient nationwide and worldwide telephone and telegraph services at reasonable rates. Its responsibilities also include the use of communications for promoting safety of life and property and for strengthening the national defense.[12]

What act initiated the organization of FCC?

> The Federal Communications Commission (FCC) was created by the Communications Act of 1934 (47 U.S.C. 151 et seq.) to regulate interstate and foreign communications by wire and radio in the public interest. The scope of FCC regulation includes radio and television broadcasting; telephone, telegraph, and cable television operation; two-way radio and radio operators; and satellite communication.[13]

The Federal Communication Commission has neglected its responsibility to the nation's children by yielding to mass media glorification of violence. The moral compass which once guided Americans to embrace the moral standards of living have eroded in favor of big business, corporations, and political leaders who do not know the humble heritage of our nation and more importantly, cares nothing about our humble beginnings—*that is, that the eye of God watched over this nation and brought it into being.* The nation would be wise if it were to acknowledge this and turn around and return the nation back to the American people. Gold, silver, and diamonds are fine, but there is a greater force controlling this universe. In time, we will see the handwriting upon the wall, and it will be too late!

When children are properly nurtured, the wealth of the nation is great. Students will develop a sense of loving themselves and caring for others. They will develop a sense of connectedness with a sense of camaraderie. Students will learn to appreciate their gifts and to internalize the value of encouraging others to succeed. In this type thinking, youth learn the value of working in unity to use their gifts and talents to build a just nation. It is not a philosophy about "me, me, me"; rather, it is a desire to succeed and to encourage others, when possible, to succeed by working hard to develop their gifts and talents. This principle is synonymous to the psychological concept which considers "the whole is greater than its parts"; therefore, we work together in community to shape a great nation. The heart contributes to the maintenance of the human organism.

When we take excellent care of our children, we invest in a guard for our nation. This molding and shaping of the nation's children is bound within the community institutions. The nation can be only as great as its local communities. These communities become the driving force and serve as a thermometer for the nation.

Congressional Concern for Youth Development

During the late 1950s and early 1960s, Congressmen had a great concern for the growth and development of the nation's children. As Congress was involved in a great debate in seeking to pass the Civil Rights Bill of 1964, the mood of some legislators flowed on the college campuses. I recall the summer of 1964, during the debate, while in preparation to perform a dramatic production on the Congressional Civil Rights debate, some students wrote to their legislators to secure literature on this bill. The Congressmen were so obliging to these students they not only sent historical literature on the debate, but also sent monetary value to encourage these students to get the best education possible. These students smiled in delight. They certainly were given a positive image of these legislators. One such legislator was *Senator Hubert Humphrey.*

The unity of this bond overflowed with a sense of caring for our children—providing an educational network to foster educational development and to design programs that would not drain them financially but use creativity in molding great leaders and responsible followers.

Today, we have a different perspective exuding from many minds and hearts of legislators. Prior to the 1970s, members of our government sought to fulfill the precepts of our Constitution, that is, to insure that positive laws were enacted with the strength of caring for the nation's children. They scrutinized bills to insure that no loopholes would be left open to privatizing and corporations to exploit the nation's children by charging high interest-bearing loans. They wrote laws to provide financial assistance to children because they recognized them as being a thread in the flag that represents the United States of America.

Today, there have been too many gaps and abstract legislation that allow big businesses and other financial institutions to take advantage of student loans and student debts. Unfortunately, for our young college graduates, too many of them graduate with a financial noose around their necks to obviate them from being able to purchase a house, start a business, or even to get a job. *Is this the country that made a promise to the children of the nation?* It is inconceivable how America has lost its faith in education and in the children who should be trained as future leaders of the nation. Where does lust and greed end and soul-searching begin to guide one to make a self-assessment to know that the Founding Fathers made it clear that **"We do ordain this U.S. Constitution for ourselves and for our posterity.**" It is, therefore, the responsibility of our legislators to put their minds in a frame of reference to conjure ways and means on how they can provide positive financial programs to teach, train, and nurture the children of the nation. We must not do less than this if we intend to continue to define our nation as a democracy.

Our concern in this chapter is to understand how our nation once cared for its children and designed programs and enacted legislation to make this a reality.

The White House Conferences focused on the Stages of Growth and Development of the nation's children. Professionals from various fields regarding child growth convened at the White House Conference to chart the progress of the nation's children and to design a road map for the future.

One speaker, during the 1952 White House Conference, delivered a message to set the stage for understanding the harmonious concept of child growth and development. During this conference, Erik H. Erikson summarized the eight stages of growth and development for youth in the Midcentury White House Conference.

1. The sense of trust
2. The sense of autonomy
3. The sense of initiative
4. The sense of duty and accomplishment
5. The sense of identity
6. The sense of intimacy (male/female define relationships)
7. The parental sense
8. The sense of integrity

Educators and health practitioners embraced these stages as concepts to guide them in nurturing children.[14]

What was the ethos of the community prior to the 1970s?

The home, church, school, and community were the basic institutions of America. These institutions served as the foundation for our nation. What is the value of each institution that serves as a pillar of strength in the nation? There was a smooth connection between the home, church, school, and community. They formed a cohesive unit, in which each institution assumed its role, responsibility, and accountability for teaching, training, disciplining, and nurturing children to become productive adults and responsible citizens. There was a bond between these institutions. They worked as a unit to reinforce the morals, values, and standards of the community.

The concern for the development of the total child included teaching the soft skills as well as teaching critical thinking skills. Every individual should be grounded in life skills to guide them in realizing their gifts and talents. This process would enable them in exploring three questions. First, "Who am I?" Second, "What is my purpose in life?" Third, "What are my gifts and talents?" Mastering these principles can mold and shape youth in forming their philosophy of life. Young people would learn to explore and learn how they can use their gifts and talents to make a positive difference on a global level. Like John F. Kennedy's Peace Corps, nurturing the youth in our society would equip them with the opportunity to learn to identify, to develop, and to use their talents with a mind and heart to uplift humanity.

Is it our right as a nation to exploit our children to our egotistical financial advantage? Our children are sent out as soldiers to fight wars for which they have neither knowledge nor understanding of the cause of the war. I am reminded of a biblical scripture where God sent his prophet to the children of Israel to remind them the ways of kings and leaders of a nation (Referencing I Samuel 8:11–18, KJV):

> *And he said, This will be the manner of the king that shall reign over you: He will take your sons, and appoint them for himself, for his chariots, and to be his horsemen; and some shall run before his chariots.*
>
> *And he will appoint him captains over thousands, and captains over fifties; and will set them to ear his ground, and to reap his harvest, and to make his instruments of war, and instruments of his chariots.*
>
> *And he will take your daughters to be confectionaries, and to be cooks, and to be bakers.*
>
> *And he will take your fields, and your vineyards, and your olive yards, even the best of them, and give them to his servants.*

> *And he will take the tenth of your seed, and of your vineyards, and give to his officers, and to his servants.*
>
> *And he will take your menservants, and your maidservants, and your goodliest young men, and your asses, and put them to his work.*
>
> *He will take the tenth of your sheep: and ye shall be his servants.*
>
> *And ye shall cry out in that day because of your king which ye shall have chosen you; and the LORD will not hear you in that day.*

The wars have wrought havoc in the lives for many Americans: some did not return, many returned crippled by weapons of war and an inordinate number of diseases that left them handicapped, deranged, and blind. Some were contaminated with other germs derived from contact with agent-orange and other chemical weapons that negatively impact their lives forever. Despite these downfalls, too many soldiers return without adequate health care, lack of housing accommodation, and lack of medicine and counseling services. The saga is an unending story.

To those political pundits who thrive on war, their families inherit millions of dollars to aggrandize their civilian treasury chest to live lavish lives, while that poor soldier had no alternative to decline the war request. Their children and families suffer at the expense of a parent wearing a uniform going off to battle, oftentimes, to fight unnecessary wars—war games to take land and resources that belong to other sovereign nations. No one describes the 21st century American soldier better than John Perkins' *Confessions of an Economic Hit Man.*

In his book *Confessions of an Economic Hit Man*, John Perkins describes the personality and behavior of a soldier prior to and post enrollment. The vast change in the soldier's attitude led him to describe this transformation in 21st century. I suppose the only clear way to describe this transformation is to equate the military work to that of a slave trader who exchanged humanity for a ship full of slaves—cargo to be traded into wealth that will give him money, power, and control. As the Holy Spirit revealed the formula to me, it is: t + c = mpc. In common talk, trade plus commerce equal money, power, and control.

> Today, men and women are going into Thailand, the Philippines, Botswana, Bolivia, and every other country where they hope to find people desperate for work. They go to these places with the express purpose of exploiting wretched people—whose children are severely malnourished, even starving, people who live in shantytowns and have lost all hope of a better life, people who have ceased to even dream of another day. These men and women leave their plush offices in Manhattan or San Francisco or Chicago, streak across continents and oceans in luxurious jetliners, check into first-class hotels, and dine at the finest restaurants the country has to offer. Then they go searching for desperate people.
>
> Today, we still have slave traders. They no longer find it necessary to march into the forests of Africa looking for prime specimens who will bring top dollar on the auction blocks in Charleston, Cartagena, and Havana. They simply recruit desperate people and build a factory to produce the jackets, blue jeans, tennis shoes, automobile parts, computer components, and thousands of other items they can sell in the markets of their choosing. Or they may elect not even to own the factory themselves; instead, they hire a local businessman to do all their dirty work for them.
>
> These men and women think of themselves as upright. They return to their homes with photographs of quaint sites and ancient ruins, to show to their children.

> They attend seminars where they pat each other on the back and exchange tidbits of advice about dealing with the eccentricities of customs in far-off lands. Their bosses hire lawyers who assure them that what they are doing is perfectly legal. They have a cadre of psychotherapists and other human resource experts at their disposal to convince them that they are helping those desperate people.
>
> The old-fashioned slave trader told himself that he was dealing with a species that was not entirely human, and that he was offering them the opportunity to become Christianized. He also understood that slaves were fundamental to the survival of his own society, that they were the foundation of his economy. The modern slave trader assures herself (or himself) that the desperate people are better off earning one dollar a day than of dollars at all, and that they are receiving the opportunity to become integrated into the larger world community. She also understands that these desperate people are fundamental to the survival of her company, that they are the foundation for her own lifestyle. She never stops to think about the larger implications of what she, her lifestyle, and the economic system behind them are doing to the world—or of how they may ultimately impact her children's future.[15]

As a watchman on the tower for the Lord, America, note this day, the Lord is not pleased with this nation! This writing is to apprise you that the country He blessed into being will soon be destroyed by Him if we do not turn around and begin living by His law; doom is our inevitable end—drones and nuclear power are no match against God.

The 21st century has placed the nation in the mode of extreme scientific and technological advancement, but we must remember that we are still members of the human family. Our work should not drive this scientific and technological interest until we lose ourselves as humans, as robots—without loving, caring, sharing, and forgiving. If we ourselves destroy the humanity of our being, we have already prepared ourselves for doomsday. We do not own this world. We are creatures in this world to live peaceably and in harmony with one another. When this ceases to be the global goal, then we, as creatures on God's earth, will come to that common denominator of doomsday—that eschatological prophecy known as the End Times, for all humanity. Our responsibility is to live within the confines of humanity. The dollar may be the force that drives humanity to the nadir, while elevating science and technology to the zenith, but we must remember, God who created this world still holds the reins, forever.

Eisenhower gave a warning to the nation in his Farewell Address, January 17, 1961

> The PROSPECT of domination of the nation's scholars by Federal employment, project allocations, and the power of money is ever present—and is gravely to be regarded. Yet, in holding scientific research and discovery in respect, as we should, **we must also be alert to the equal and opposite danger that public policy could itself become the captive of a scientific-technological elite.**[16]

The World War II Commander of the Allied forces to defeat Adolf Hitler whose military slogan was "Today Germany, tomorrow the world," Eisenhower had foresight in war, military weapons, and a thirst for world power. His farewell address encompassed his experience of the last war fought in this manner. Annie Jacobsen, in *Operation Paper Clip: The Secret Intelligence Program That Brought Nazi Scientists to America,* sounds out the ugly past of how Hitler employed his scientists and doctors to engage their gifts and talents to build and design weapons to destroy a segment of humanity so that he could rule and control the world. Eisenhower's saddest duty in Germany at the close of the war was to visit the extermination camps of Buchenwald and Auschwitz to see the egregious and despicable manner in which human beings had been degraded, less than animals. In fact, Hitler referred to them as *untermenschens*—sub-humans, not human beings at all. Therefore, he reserved the right to assign his doctors to perform various experiments, even while the people were alive, and assigned his scientists to create weapons of the future—weapons, no other people had dreamed of—in order to engineer his control of the universe.

> The production of synthetic rubber required four things: water, flat land, good railway connections, and an abundance of laborers. Auschwitz had all four. Three rivers met in Auschwitz, the Sola, the Vistula, and the Przemsza, with a water flow of 525,000 cubic feet per hour. The land was flat and sixty-five feet above the waterline, making it safe from floodwaters. The railway connections were sound. But most important was the labor issue. The concentration camp next door could provide an endless labor supply because the men were cheap and could be worked to death.[17]

There was just one thing Hitler forgot: "*the earth is the Lord's and the fullness thereof; the world, and they that dwell therein*" (Psalms 24:1).

In essence, Eisenhower would not leave the White House until he had penned this message to humankind about the dangers of war and the megalomaniacal thoughts of ruling the world.

The man, who led the whole allied invasion in Europe to its close in 1945, spoke of ways of keeping peace in his 1961 farewell address.

A VITAL ELEMENT in keeping the peace is our military establishment. Our arms must be mighty, ready for instant action, so that no potential aggressor may be tempted to risk his own destruction.

OUR MILITARY ORGANIZATION today bears little resemblance to that known by any of my predecessors in peace time, or indeed by the fighting men of World War II or Korea.

UNTIL THE LATEST of our world conflicts, the United States had no armaments industry.

AMERICAN MAKERS of plowshares could, with time and as required, make swords as well.

But now we can no longer risk emergency improvisation of national defense; we have been compelled to create a permanent armaments industry of vast proportions.

Added to this, three and a half million men and women are directly engaged in the defense establishment.

WE ANNUALLY spend on military security more than the net income of all United States Corporations.

THIS CONJUNCTION of an immense military establishment and a large arms industry is new in the American experience. The total influence—economic, political, even spiritual—is felt in every city, every state house, every office of the federal government. We recognize the imperative need for this development. *Yet we must not fail to comprehend its grave implications.* Our toil, resources and livelihood are all involved; so is the very structure of our society.

IN THE COUNCILS of government, we must guard against the acquisition of unwarranted

> **influence, whether sought or unsought, by the military-industrial complex.**
>
> *The potential for the disastrous rise of misplaced power exists and will persist.*
>
> **WE MUST NEVER let the weight of this combination endanger our liberties or democratic processes.**

Eisenhower reiterated the American philosophy and her progress.

> WE NOW STAND ten years past the midpoint of a century that has witnessed four major wars among great nations.
>
> Three of those involved our own country.
>
> Despite these holocausts America is today the strongest, the most influential and the most productive nation in the world.
>
> Understandably proud of this pre-eminence, we yet realize that America's leadership and prestige depend, not merely upon our unmatched material progress, riches and military strength, but on *how we use our power in the interests of world peace and human betterment.*
>
> THROUGHOUT AMERICA'S ADVENTURE in free government, our basic purposes have been to keep the peace, to foster progress in human achievement, and to enhance liberty, dignity and integrity among people and among nations.
>
> *To strive for less would be unworthy of a free and religious people.*
>
> Any failure traceable to arrogance, or our lack of comprehension or readiness to sacrifice would inflict upon us grievous hurt both at home and abroad.[18]

Eisenhower urged America to charter the nation's ship "toward permanent peace and human betterment."

> In his farewell address to the nation, President Dwight D. Eisenhower warns the American people to keep a careful eye on what he calls the "military-industrial complex" that has developed in the post-World War II years.[19]

In the current global matrix, humanity has been effaced from the equation of geopolitics—everything is about the dollar, trade and commerce, and the power to control. Technology vs. humanity! Where is the world going? *Where are the preachers and spiritual leaders who would teach the undiluted Word to guide the nation back on track as opposed to making a quick trip to hell, never to rise again?*

What happened to the moral climate where educators participated in the White House Conference for Schools? What happened to the American Psychological Association that was embraced as a watchdog for the nation's children?

What does the Constitution say about our children? What is the cataclysmic shift from community support? Who are these legislators and judges who have failed to nurture the core of America—our children? When we fail to keep watch, our democratic values erode, opening doors for corruption and destruction.

Prior to the 1970s, Congressmen were notable legislators who held the nation's children in great esteem. These legislators embraced the democratic ideas found in the United States Constitution, to provide for the health, education, and welfare of the nation's children. They embraced the fundamental truth of preparing each generation to assume responsibility through good education, whereby, they, too, would develop their gifts and talents to build a just nation.

CHAPTER 3

Reviewing Hypocrisy in a Democracy

Slavery: Dunmore Proclamation and the Declaration of Independence

Prince Henry of Portugal, claiming that he was a missionary bent upon saving the souls of the Africans, took the Africans as 'souls' and sold them as slaves in the ports of Portugal.
Earl Conrad, The Invention of the Negro.

Neglecting children and exploiting another segment of the population as a cheap labor force are the antithesis of a democracy. This book is written to expose the hypocrisy of developing prisons as an economic industry. How did this happen? How did legislators circumvent the "checks and balances" in our democratic government to embrace such a nefarious idea?

What was the true origin of prison expansion?

The sole purpose of this idea was to identify a product that could be converted into an economic industry. The thought process evolved and a solid concept emerged from the minds of the men of a "think tank." The members of this secret think tank conceived a plan for an economic tool to be converted into an industry and controlled by corporate leaders throughout the nation to expand profit and maximize wealth.

The three most important concepts in our world today are trade, money, and power. This power base did not embrace the congressional thought of the 1970s to close some prisons. Instead, their desire was to expand them with profits flowing into the hands of a few individuals who embraced Darwinism—the fittest survive. They were vehemently against closing prisons. The plan was to grow prisons as their 21st century model, and drugs were the bait chosen as the secret means to ignite prison expansion.

The think tank's historical search for a product to grow a prison industry

What would be their product? How could they identify a product? England, the mother country of the thirteen colonies in America, introduced the concept of exploiting people to enhance her economic empire. Slave traders engaged in a flourishing business, pilfering natives from Africa and hurling them on slave ships as a free labor force. The captives were displayed on slave blocks for sale in America.

A large population of Europeans immigrated to America in search of a new way of life. Upon entering America, people who lacked finances were classified as indentured servants. As such, they worked from five to seven years to amortize their voyage. Upon completion of this travel contract, they were free as anyone else to start a new life in the New

World. African Americans had traveled earlier than the 1607 Jamestown group. Some had traveled with Columbus when he landed in America in 1492. One famous accomplice was Estevanico, known as "Little Stephen." There were other blacks who traveled with many Spanish explorers, such as Cabeza de Vaca who explored the southwestern parts of America. There were black men, such as James P. Beckwourth who opened a path through the Sierra Nevada Mountains and made it possible for other pioneers to follow. So, as with others who could not pay for their voyage, there were some black people who were identified as indentured servants. They, too, were free after completing their financial obligation.

The thirteen colonies were spread across the northeastern Atlantic coast of the New World and properly described as the New England, Middle, and Southern colonies. Each section derived its commerce and lifestyles from the geography of the region. The Southern colony had a climate conducive for an agrarian society. Consequently, this section of the country depended upon the slave trade to build its economy.

The land had to be cultivated to grow crops, and it was a monumental task. There were wealthy landowners who oftentimes had been bequeathed land from the throne of England, and they needed a labor force to work the land to realize a profit. The indentured servants were a great labor force, but there was a glitch in this employment plan. The owners were burdened with the task of managing a seven-year rotation labor system. This created an interruption in the work cycle. They needed continuity in their labor force. In their own "think tank," they began to ponder ways to eliminate this constant rotation.

Having a workforce was one concern, *but making the highest profit was the ultimate goal.* Egotistically, they looked for profit with no concern for humanity. They tried to make the natives slaves, but they knew the land better than the owners. They were a people very sensitive to living in nature, free and without constraints. Unable to build a successful permanent labor force with the Indians, they turned their attention to African Americans.

The challenges of maintaining an agricultural economy in the South are clearly explored in *The Political Economy of Slavery* by Eugene D. Genovese. The psychological concept the slave master instilled in the southern white population during slavery was to ignore the economic deprivation the agrarian type lifestyle inflicted upon the general society. The slave master was adept with his cunning language to master mind control of his plantation. It was very interesting how the plantation owner used divisive techniques to control both populations. In the shrewd words of the slave master, he massaged the egos of the poor whites with powerful words, "By the mere fact you are white, makes you superior to all blacks." The manipulative language of the plantation owner further filled the ears of the slaves to keep them from the company of poor whites, "Don't have no dealing with them, they are poor white trash!"

In 1661, the idea of using the African American as a permanent labor force was introduced in the Virginia House of Burgesses. This new legislation became the law of the land. When some missionaries entered into Central and South America, the natives were told they were seeking to evangelize the world. But, for the African American, this mission was not recognized. The Journals of the House of Burgesses of Virginia 1659/60–1693 clarified this point. "*A byll declareing that baptism of Slaves does not Manumit or set them free*" (traditional spelling). The African American would be denied freedom even if he had become a Christian.

What was the fallacy regarding freedom and conquistadors?

We need to unroll the papyrus of history to reveal the role European nations and spiritual conclaves played in sustaining imperial empires and maintaining African American slavery.

The slave trade was initiated by the Portuguese. The recognition of Africans as human beings to be treated as Christians was not a consideration. The value of the African as an economic product secured the blessings of Popes.

> Fifty years before Columbus sailed westward, Catholic Spain and Catholic Portugal were engaged in a rivalry to sack Africa, to seize its inhabitants as slaves and to ship them back to Europe and sell them. Portugal, the first invader, sought and secured the blessing of the Popes and in a series of papal bulls issued from 1443 on there is the spectacle of the Christian Vatican sanctifying the enslavement of Africans on grounds that they were pagans—winking its eye at the profit in the trade.[3]

The economic idea of the African in slave trading as a labor product was approved by Pope Nicholas V and King Alfonso of Spain. Where is the chain that connects humans to God?

> Prince Henry of Portugal, claiming that he was a missionary bent upon saving the souls of the Africans, took the Africans as "souls" and sold them as slaves in the ports of Portugal. He asked absolution for the seamen taking part in the voyages, and Pope Eugenia IV in 1442, for one, granted the request. By 1452 Pope Nicholas V gave to King Alfonso of Spain general powers to enslave "pagans." Pagans meant the Africans who didn't yet know Christ.
>
> So controlling was the power of the Vatican in the conduct of trade into Africa that in 1481 Edward IV of England asked the Pope for permission to trade in Africa.[4]

With no conscience of humanity, there was constant war to control the African slave trade to expand economic empires. Despite pious religious officials, the spiritual concept did not resonate to the concept of recognizing Africans as humans, too—a part of God's creation.

> After a time, and because of the increasing competition from a half dozen countries to secure a foothold in Africa, papal bulls lost their effect—and there was open warfare for control of the slave trade into Africa by a half dozen European countries. By 1600 there was often little pretense about proselytizing. God's work be damned, make the money, said the traders of Portugal, Spain, France, Holland and England.[5]

It is no wonder that Christopher Columbus made a promise to his imperial leaders how he would return with mineral and human wealth.

> Moreover, a hint of the destiny of the African as a slave—and later on as ex-slave rising to second-class citizenship status—was prophesied by the intentions of Christopher Columbus. He beheld the Indians as a slave supply, for he wrote in 1493 to Spain asking for help and promised in return the riches of the New World, 'and slaves, as many as they shall order, who will be idolaters.' Apparently he held it legitimate to enslave the New World natives as long as they weren't Christians. But it did not take long for the emphasis to shift to the African, already a servant in Europe, and later transported annually to New World slavery by the thousands.[6]

The conquistadors of Europe had a primary interest in establishing great economic and political empires, obtaining wealth by raiding the continent of Africa. There was no concern for the freedom of these individuals. Despite their wealth, many Europeans flocked to the New World in search of a new way of life. Georgia, one of the southern colonies, was colonized by debtors who could not amortize their debts. They fled from Europe to avoid prison. Ironically, these same people built an economy that depended on slave labor. Across the Atlantic seacoast, the thirteen colonies were anchored in their way of life to engage in work to enrich the mother country of England. Finally, the colonies united to fight for their own independence.

What was freedom and who made the assessment to qualify individuals for this living status?

This concept of freedom and independence is presented in *Slave Nation: How Slavery United the Colonies and Sparked the American Revolution* by Alfred W. Blumrosen and Ruth G. Blumrosen. How did the subtle question of slavery hang over the nation as an ominous cloud?

> In Slave Nation, the Blumrosens go down seldom explored paths that lead to the pro-slavery compromise that was sewn into the national fabric well before the Revolution. The Revolutionary patriots in the North did not speak openly about maintaining slavery but made it clear to the South that slavery would not be disturbed. There would have been no revolution to create one nation if John Adams, the Massachusetts antislavery stalwart and other northerners had not accepted southern prerogatives on slavery. There would have been no union if both the Northwest Ordinance and the Constitution had not guaranteed the continuation of slavery in the southern territories and the entitlement of owners even to their slaves that escaped to the North. The price of

> freedom from England was bondage for African slaves in America. America would be a slave nation.[7]

The political strategy of England to treat the settlers less than Englishmen abhorred the colonists. They were defiant of the tax laws imposed on them by the crown. When they implored the imperialistic government to rescind one tax, another tax was expediently imposed to remind them they were subjects of the throne of England. The Boston Tea Party was a rebellion that turned into a melee when some men disguised as Indians dumped tea into the harbor to show their anger and to defy the tax imposition.

On March 5, 1770, one black man, Crispus Attucks, a runaway slave, was the first person to shed his blood in the American Revolution.

> Led by Crispus Attucks, a runaway slave, and shouting, 'The way to get rid of these soldiers is to attack the main guard,' they rushed into King Street protest by action. They were fired upon by several men of Captain Preston's company. Attucks was the first to fall; two others were killed instantly; and two others later died from wounds.[8]

Crispus Attucks, too, had dreams of freedom. He believed freedom for the colonies would mean the same for him. The first to shed blood in the American Revolution was this black man.

When the thirteen colonies realized England would never equate them to the status of other Englishmen, they drew up a declaration in 1776 to no longer petition for classification as Englishmen. They would rather fight for their independence.

Hypocrisy in Humanity

The original writing of the Declaration of Independence had to be destroyed because it accused England of forcing slavery upon the colonies. Thomas Jefferson penned that document so elegantly, and it is important for all humanity to view it.

> He has waged cruel war against human nature itself, violating its most sacred rights of life and liberty in the persons of a distant people who never offended him, captivating and carrying them into slavery in another hemisphere, or to incur miserable death in their transportation thither. This piratical warfare, the opprobrium of *infidel* powers, is the warfare of the Christian king of Great Britain. Determined to keep open a market where MEN should be bought and sold, he has prostituted his negative for suppressing every legislative attempt to prohibit or to restrain this execrable commerce; and that this assemblage of horrors might want no fact of distinguished die, he is now exciting these very people to rise in arms among us, and to purchase that liberty of which he deprived them, by murdering the people upon whom he also obtruded them; thus paying off former crimes committed against the *liberties* of one people, with crimes which he urges them to commit against the lives of another.[9]

The reference, "*he is now exciting these very people to rise in arms among us, and to purchase that liberty of which he deprived them…*," is to Lord Dunmore's proclamation penned in 1775 enticing slaves to leave their plantations and to join the British soldiers. All soldiers who joined under the Lord Dunmore Proclamation were promised freedom. In truth, after the American Revolution, some of these slaves were granted freedom and were relocated to Canada.

Lord Dunmore Proclamation and Freedom for some Slaves

> On September 26, 1775, Edward Rutledge of South Carolina made a motion in the Continental Congress that all blacks be discharged from the army. Rutledge was supported by southern delegates, but there were not enough votes to pass the motion.
>
> On November 12, 1775, Washington issued an order prohibiting blacks from enlisting in the Continental Army. Because of poor communication, George Washington had not heard about the Lord Dunmore Proclamation.[10]

England had a great deal to do with luring blacks to fight in the American Revolution. In seeing that George Washington would not use blacks in the war, the English encouraged blacks to fight with their soldiers. On November 7, 1775, Lord Dunmore issued a proclamation allowing blacks to enter the war on the side of the British. Many blacks began to enlist in the British army.

> I do hereby...declare all indentured servants, Negroes, or others (appertaining to rebels) free, that are able and willing to bear arms, they joining his Majesty's troops, as soon as may be, for the more speedily reducing this Colony to a proper dignity.[11]

When George Washington learned about Dunmore's proclamation, he revised his policy about how blacks would participate in the war. The issue was related to prohibiting slaves from participating in the war. John Hope Franklin, in *From Slavery to Freedom*, records Washington's response: "On December 31, he partially reversed his policy regarding the enlistment of Negroes and in a report to the President of the Congress said that he was permitting the enlistment of free Negroes." This act was approved by Congress on January 16, 1776.[12]

It is worth noting that Washington's first move was to enlist only free blacks. Why? Many blacks expected to receive their freedom for fighting in the war. In order to escape this problem, Washington believed it was wise to use free blacks. By doing so, he would not be confronted with a problem of granting freedom to slaves at the end of the war.

While Washington was taking careful steps designing a response on the use of blacks in the American Revolutionary War, Lord Dunmore wasted no time in penning his proclamation with a promise of freedom to slaves who joined the British army. The plantation owners considered Dunmore's proclamation to be a contaminant for their slave supply, and they put stringent measures in place to prevent slaves from running away to join with him. "Edmund Pendleton wrote Richard Henry Lee on November 27, 1775, that slaves were flocking to Dunmore in abundance." 13

The dreams of freedom, for some, were much greater than the threat of death. Some slaves preferred death to bondage. In their perception of abdicating themselves from bondage, they were willing to take the gamble. The general count of runaways reveals shocking numbers.

> Slaves ran away in large numbers even if they had no intention of reaching the British lines. Thomas Jefferson estimated that in 1778 alone more than 30,000 Virginia slaves ran away. Ramsey, the South Carolina historian,

> asserted that between 1775 and 1783 his state lost at least 25,000 slaves. It has been estimated that during the war Georgia lost about 75 percent of her 15,000 slaves.[14]

The desire for freedom took precedence over the fear of death for these slaves.

How did this proclamation affect the American colonies?

The loss of slaves on many plantations instilled fear in plantation owners. They were losing too much of their economic property. Who was the culprit? The motherland who had introduced slaves to the colonies was depreciating the economic supply of many plantations.

> During the remainder of the war large numbers of Negroes escaped to the British lines, seeking the freedom which had eluded them during their stay in the colonies. Wherever the British armies went they attracted many Negroes, and Maryland, Virginia, and South Carolina were especially alarmed over the future of slavery regardless of the outcome of the war. As late as 1781 Richard Henry Lee could write his brother that two neighbors had lost 'every slave they had in the world.'[15]

The slave trade closed in 1808, but other means of fostering the slave supply were used. Yet, the South continued their dependence upon a slave economy. They used various means to circumvent the closing of the African Slave trade.

What was the geography of the South that mandated slave labor?

Robert S. Starobin, author of *Slavery and Industry in the Old South*, addressed this question.

> The Old South was a region of diversity and complexity, contrast and contradiction. The section ranged geographically from the fertile lands of the Tidewater, Black Belt, and deltas to the rugged Appalachian mountain chain of the interior. Piney woods divided the coast from the rolling hills of the Piedmont; a great valley punctuated the mountain range. Rivers provided a natural waterway system for virtually every area, the Ohio, the Mississippi, and the Tennessee rivers defined a fertile interior plateau. Lush forests and swamps complemented rich deposits of minerals and metals. The growing season averaged between six and nine months, while the climate varied from temperate to tropical.[16]

The geography defined a way of life for the South, and to insure survival in this area of the nation, they needed a labor force to develop and maintain an agrarian economy.

> The South's economy was predominantly agricultural and heavily dependent upon the cultivation of several commercial crops. Tobacco and hemp were grown in the upper states, especially in Virginia, Kentucky, and Missouri, while a considerable amount of wheat was raised in Maryland and Virginia. Rice was produced along the eastern coast, especially in South Carolina and Georgia. Sugar was cultivated mainly in Louisiana,

> while corn could be grown almost anywhere. The cotton region, where the South's most important staple grew, extended all the way from the Carolinas to Texas.[17]

The South survived from 1661 to 1865 using free human labor as a way of life. They enhanced their wealth and garnished their lives with pleasures.

> By 1860, there were about four million Negro slaves in the South, and servitude had long since become firmly entrenched in the southern social structure. Slave ownership was so wide-spread that almost 400,000 white families held bondsmen, and as many as two million white persons therefore had direct property interests in slavery. The typical slaveholder was a farmer who owned one or two slave families and a few hundred acres of good land; however, 12 percent of the slave owners—the planter class-owned more than twenty slaves each, monopolized more than half of the slave population, and possessed the best southern lands of all.[18]

The culture of slavery in the South is further presented in *The Peculiar Institution of Slavery* published in 1956 in New York by Kenneth M. Stampp.

> The book describes and analyzes the many different facets of slavery in the South from the 17th through the mid-19th century, including demographics, lives of slaves and slaveholders, the Southern economy and labor systems, the Northern and abolitionist response, slave trading, and political issues of the time.[19]

The 1960s were enriched with black writers who labored to inform as well as to correct misconceptions and the distorted history of the African

American. This liberation era flourished with authors such as Martin L. King Jr., Lerone Bennett, Milton Meltzer, C. Eric Lincoln, Rayford Logan, Vincent Harding, and countless others. However, Kenneth M. Stampp's book played a major role in combating the distortions of a bastion of writers who continued to glorify the institution of slavery.

> An interesting element of the book is how Stampp analyzes the standard view of historians such as Ulrich Phillips that many Southern slave owners were very kind to their slaves and provided well for them. It was sometimes known for slaves to have lives as good as or better than poor Northern workers, however, Stampp exposes this behavior as a selfish strategy, easing the lives of some slaves in order to prevent dissent among the rest, or to prevent possible legal action for mistreatment of slaves, arguing that this treatment did little to convince slaves that their lives were acceptable, and that dissent and opposition were common, making them "a troublesome property.[20]

The erudite African American historian John Hope Franklin's *From Slavery to Freedom* recaptured true tales of how slaves abhorred the American institution. Franklin's anecdotes are a contrast to Ulrich Phillips' portrayal of a "happy life for slaves." This depiction demonstrates how the slaves loathed the life of bondage.

> Self-mutilation and suicide were popular forms of resistance to slavery. Slaves cut off their toes, hands, and mutilated themselves in other ways so as to render themselves ineffective as workers. One Kentucky slave carpenter, for example, cut off one of his hands and the fingers of the other when he learned that he was to be sold down the river. There are several instances of slaves having shot themselves in

> the hand or foot, especially upon being recovered after running away. The number of suicides seems relatively large, and certainly they were widespread. Slaves fresh from Africa committed suicide in great numbers. In 1807 two boatloads of newly arrived Negroes in Charleston starved themselves to death. When his slave woman was found dead by her own hanging 1829, a Georgia planter was amazed since he saw no reason why she should want to take her own life. When two Louisiana slaves were returned to their master after having been stolen in 1858 they unbound themselves and drowned themselves in the bayou. One of the South's wealthiest planters, Charles Manigault, lost a slave by a similar act when the overseer threatened him with punishment. Sometimes slave mothers killed their own children to prevent them from growing up in slavery.[21]

Another greater writer emerged out of Boston, Stanley M. Elkins, an American historian best known for his controversial comparison of slavery in the United States to Nazi concentration camps, collaborated with Eric McKitrick regarding the early American Republic. Elkins' *Slavery: A Problem in American Institutional and intellectual Life* (1959) was the product of his historical dissertation at Columbia University. By comparing slavery to Hitler's concentration camps, Elkins weighed the two environments.

These writers have made a dynamic contribution in archiving books to share the history of a by-gone era. The great comparison of slavery is always that humane statement made by Abigail Adams: "It always appeared a most iniquitous scheme to me to fight ourselves for what we are daily robbing and plundering from those who have as good a right to freedom as we have."[20] The pious heart of Abigail Adams, wife of John Adams, the second president of the United States, was nurtured by the Scriptures of the Holy Book. She internalized the two greatest commands of the universe:

> The first of all the commandments is, Hear, O Israel; The Lord our God is one Lord:
>
> Thou shalt love the Lord thy God with all thy heart, and with all thy soul, and with all thy mind, and with all thy strength: this is the first commandment.
>
> And the second is like, namely this, Thou shalt love thy neighbor as thyself. There is none other commandment greater than these. (Mark 12:28–31, KJV)

Abigail's belief system was shaped in a spirit of love and caring for community. She had worked closely with her mother in the colonial neighborhood where these principles were internalized. "Abigail Smith was born on November 11, 1744, in Weymouth, Mass., the 2nd child of Elizabeth Quincy Smith and the Reverend William Smith. Her father was pastor of Weymouth's North Parish Congregational Church. Abigail's mother, Elizabeth, spent much of her time visiting the sick and distributing food, clothing, and firewood to needy families. Abigail accompanied her mother on these visits putting into practice the lessons taught at her church. Abigail educated herself in her father's library."[22]

Her love letters nurtured a spirit of truth in her husband as she inspired him, despite the arduous journey, to pursue the course of strengthening the direction of the new nation.

The couple, John and Abigail Adams, worked tirelessly to build the nation to set a foundation for future years. It was proper and correct that they were the first couple to reside in the executive mansion—the White House.

At the close of the American Revolution, the thirteen colonies became the United States of America with the signing of *The Treaty of Paris in 1783*. But they had failed to extend the human rights of freedom to

African Americans, who remained slaves until 1865. It took eighty-two more years and a bloody civil war, fought from 1861 to 1865, to grant freedom to the African American. The Thirteenth Amendment abolished slavery in the United States in 1865.

Despite more than two hundred years of free labor, the African American received neither compensation nor reparation for their period of bondage. Therefore, the present think tank is using the same formula for implementing their economic plan for the 21st century—a cheap labor force for a prison–industrial complex.

CHAPTER 4

Rescinding Civil Rights Gains

Part I: Letter from Birmingham Jail

We will have to repent in this generation not merely
for the hateful—words and actions of the bad people,
but for the appalling silence of the good people.
Dr. Martin L. King, Jr.

Part II: Post Civil War, Reconstruction, Election of 1876, and The Compromise of 1877

Part I

The think tank's question regarding bondage became a prime concern. What methods could be used to re-enslave the African American in the 21st century to grow high profits with low financial maintenance? The challenge was to create a pseudo image of him, to portray him as a menace to society unworthy of defense, and to isolate him from mainstream America. Let prisons blossom with him performing the work of a cheap labor force in an economic prison industry.

Planning had to be sound. The think tank conjured a method to promote it, in disguise, as a benefit. It had to catch the attention of the populace and be presented and received as a public good.

There was a problem from the inception. The 1970s was a flourishing time for humanity. It was just two years after the assassination of Dr. Martin L. King Jr., the great Shepherd of the Civil Rights movement. During the struggles and battles from 1955's Montgomery Bus Boycott to the Birmingham jail of 1963, the African American had grown tired of waiting for justice and was now willing to fight the good fight for an equal share in American democracy. A description of the time of waiting was beautifully penned while the peaceful warrior was incarcerated in Birmingham in *Making Null and Void Civil Rights Gains [Rolling the Clock Back to Slavery].*

While we take glimpses of the past in our search to understand our current crisis with the prisons and the secret work to rescind civil rights gains, let us also draw from Dr. King's letter.

LETTER FROM BIRMINGHAM JAIL APRIL 16, 1963.

> My dear fellow clergymen:
>
> While confined here in the Birmingham city jail, I came across your recent statement calling my present activities "unwise and untimely." Seldom do I pause to answer criticism of my work and ideas.... But since I feel that you are men of genuine good will and that your criticisms are sincerely set forth, I want to try to answer your statement in what I hope will be patient and reasonable terms....
>
> I think I should indicate why I am here in Birmingham, since you have been influenced by the view

which argues against "outsiders coming in"...But more basically, I am in Birmingham because injustice is here....

Moreover, I am cognizant of the interrelatedness of all communities and states. I cannot sit idly by in Atlanta and not be concerned about what happens in Birmingham. **Injustice anywhere is a threat to justice everywhere**. We are caught in an inescapable network of mutuality, tied in a single garment of destiny.

Whatever affects one directly, affects all indirectly. Never again can we afford to live with the narrow, provincial "outside agitator" idea. Anyone who lives inside the United States can never be considered an outsider anywhere within its bounds.

You deplore the demonstrations taking place in Birmingham. But your statement, I am sorry to say, fails to express a similar concern for the conditions that brought about the demonstrations.

I am sure that none of you would want to rest content with the superficial kind of social analysis that deals merely with effects and does not grapple with underlying causes. It is unfortunate that demonstrations are taking place in Birmingham, but it is even more unfortunate that the city's white power structure left the Negro community with no alternative.

In any nonviolent campaign there are four basic steps: collection of the facts to determine whether injustices exist; negotiation; self-purification; and direct action. We have gone through all these steps in Birmingham.

There can be no gainsaying the fact that racial injustice engulfs this community. Birmingham is probably the most thoroughly segregated city in the United States.

Its ugly record of brutality is widely known. Negroes have experienced grossly unjust treatment in the courts.

There have been more unresolved bombings of Negro homes and churches in Birmingham than in any other city in the nation. These are the hard, brutal facts of the case....

On the basis of these conditions, Negro leaders sought to negotiate fathers. But the latter consistently refused to engage in good-faith negotiation. Then, last September, came the opportunity to talk with leaders of Birmingham's economic community. In the course of negotiations, certain promises were made by the merchants—for example, to remove stores humiliating racial signs.

On the basis of these promises, the Reverend Fred Shuttlesworth and the leaders of the Alabama Christian Movement for Human Rights agreed to a moratorium on all demonstrations. As the weeks and months went by, we realized that we were the victims of a broken promise. A few signs, briefly removed, returned; the others remained.

As in so many past experiences, our hopes had been blasted, and the shadow of deep disappointment settled upon us. We had no alternative except to prepare for direct action, whereby we would present our very bodies as a means of laying our case before the conscience of the local and the national community.

Mindful of the difficulties involved, we decided to undertake the process of self-purification. We began a series of workshops on nonviolence, and we repeatedly asked ourselves: "Are you able to accept blows without retaliation?" "Are you able to endure the ordeal of jail?"

You may well ask, "Why direct action? Why sit-ins, marches and so forth? Isn't negotiation a better path?" You are quite right in calling for negotiation. Indeed, this is the very purpose of direct action. Nonviolent direct action seeks to create such a crisis and foster such a tension that a community which has constantly refused to negotiate is forced to confront the issue. It seeks so to dramatize the issue that it can no longer be ignored.

My citing the creating of tension as part of the work of the nonviolent resister may sound rather shocking. But I must confess that I am not afraid of the word "tension." I have earnestly opposed violent tension, but there is a type of constructive, nonviolent tension which is necessary for growth.

Just as **Socrates** felt that it was necessary to create a tension in the mind so that individuals could rise from the bondage of myths and half-truths to the unfettered realm of creative analysis and objective appraisal, so must we see the need for nonviolent gadflies to create the kind of tension in society that will help men rise from the dark depths of prejudice and racism to the majestic heights of understanding and brotherhood.

The purpose of our direct-action program is to create a situation so crisis-packed that it will inevitably open the door to negotiation. I therefore concur with you in your call for negotiation. Too long has our beloved Southland been bogged down in a tragic effort to live in monologue rather than dialogue.

One of the basic points in your statement is that the action that I and my associates have taken in Birmingham is untimely. Some have asked: "Why didn't you give the new city administration time to act?" The only answer that I can give to this query is that the new Birmingham administration must be prodded about as much as the outgoing one, before it will act....

We have not made a single gain in civil rights without determined legal and nonviolent pressure.... Lamentably, it is an historical fact that privileged groups seldom give up their privileges voluntarily. Individuals may see the moral light and voluntarily give up their unjust posture; but, as *Reinhold Niebuhr* has reminded us, groups tend to be more immoral than individuals.

We know through painful experience that freedom is never voluntarily given by the oppressor. It must be demanded by the oppressed. Frankly, I have yet to engage in a direct-action campaign that was "well timed" in view of those who have not suffered unduly from the disease of segregation.

For years now I have heard the word "wait." It rings in the ear of every Negro with piercing familiarity. This "Wait!" has almost always meant "Never." We must come to see, with one of our distinguished jurists, that "*justice too long delayed is justice denied.*"

We have waited for more than 340 years for our constitutional and God-given rights. The nations of Asia and Africa are moving with jet-like speed toward gaining political independence, but we still creep at horse-and-buggy pace toward gaining a cup of coffee at a lunch counter. Perhaps it is easy for those who have never felt the stinging darts of segregation to say, "Wait."

But when you have seen vicious mobs lynch your mothers and fathers at will and drown your sisters and brothers at whim; when you have seen hate-filled policemen curse, kick and even kill your black brothers and sisters; when you see the vast majority of your twenty million Negro brothers smothering in an airtight cage of poverty in the midst of an affluent society; when you suddenly find your tongue twisted and your speech stammering as you seek to explain to your six-year-old daughter why she can't go to the public amusement park that has just been advertised on television, and see tears welling up in her eyes when she is told that Funtown is closed to colored children, and see ominous clouds of inferiority beginning to form in her little mental sky, and see her beginning to distort her personality by developing an unconscious bitterness toward white people; when you have to concoct an answer for a five-year-old son who is asking, "Daddy, why do white people treat colored people so mean?"; when you take a cross-country drive and find it necessary to sleep night after night in the uncomfortable corners of your automobile because no motel will accept you; when you are humiliated day in and day out by nagging signs reading, "white" and "colored"; when your first name becomes "nigger," your middle name becomes "boy" (however old you are) and your last name becomes "John," and your wife and mother are never given the respected title "Mrs."; when you are harried by day and haunted by night by the fact that you are a negro, living constantly at tiptoe stance, never quite knowing what to expect next, and are plagued with inner fears and outer resentments; when you are forever fighting a degenerating sense of "nobodiness"—then you will understand why we find it difficult to wait.

There comes a time when the cup of endurance runs over, and men are no longer willing to be plunged into the abyss of despair. I hope, sirs, you can understand our legitimate and unavoidable impatience.

You express a great deal of anxiety over our willingness to break laws. This is certainly a legitimate concern. Since we so diligently urge people to obey the Supreme Court's decision of 1954 outlawing segregation in the public schools, at first glance it may seem rather paradoxical for us consciously to break laws.

One may well ask: "How can you advocate breaking some laws and obeying others?" The answer lies in the fact that there are two types of laws: just and unjust. I would be the first to advocate obeying just laws. One has not only a legal but a moral responsibility to obey just laws. Conversely, one has a *moral responsibility* to disobey unjust laws. I would agree with St. Augustine that "an unjust law is no law at all."

Now, what is the difference between the two? How does one determine whether a law is just or unjust? A just law is a man-made code that squares with the moral law or the law of God. An unjust law is a code that is out of harmony with the moral law.

To put it in the terms of St. Thomas Aquinas: An unjust law is a human law that is not rooted in eternal law and natural law. Any law that uplifts human personality is just. Any law that degrades human personality is unjust.

All segregation statutes are unjust because segregation distorts the soul and damages the personality. It gives the segregator a false sense of superiority and the segregated a false sense of inferiority....

Let us consider a more concrete example of just and unjust laws. An unjust law is a code that a numerical or power majority group compels a minority group to obey but does not make binding on itself. This is difference made legal. By the same token, a just law is a code that a majority compels a minority to follow and that it is willing to follow itself. This is *sameness* made legal.

Let me give another explanation. A law is unjust if it is inflicted on a minority that, as a result of being denied the right to vote, had no part in enacting or devising the law. Who can say that the legislature of Alabama which set up the state's segregation laws was democratically elected?

Throughout Alabama all sorts of devious methods are used to prevent Negroes from becoming registered voters, and here are some counties in which, even though Negroes constitute a majority of the population, not a single Negro is registered. Can any law enacted under such circumstances be considered democratically structured?

Sometimes a law is just on its face and unjust in its application. For instance, I have been arrested on a charge of parading without a permit. Now, there is nothing wrong in having an ordinance which requires a permit for a parade. But such an ordinate becomes unjust when it is used to maintain segregation and to deny citizens the First-Amendment privilege of peaceful assembly and protest.

I hope you are able to see the distinction I am trying to point out. In no sense do I advocate evading or defying the law, as would the rabid segregationist. That would lead to anarchy.

One who breaks an unjust law must do so openly, lovingly and with a willingness to accept the penalty. I submit that an individual who breaks a law that conscience tells him is unjust, and who willingly accepts the penalty of imprisonment in order to arouse the conscience of the community over its injustice, is in reality expressing the highest respect for law.

Of course, there is nothing new about this kind of civil disobedience. It was evidenced sublimely in the refusal of Shadrach, Meshach, and Abednego to obey the laws of Nebuchadnezzar, on the ground that higher moral law was at stake. It was practiced superbly by the early Christians, who were willing to face hungry lions and the excruciating pain of chopping blocks rather than submit to certain unjust laws of the Roman Empire.

To a degree, academic freedom is a reality today because Socrates practiced civil disobedience. In our own nation, the Boston Tea Party represented a massive act of civil disobedience.

We should never forget that everything Adolf Hitler did in Germany was "legal" and everything the Hungarian freedom fighters did in Hungary was "illegal." It was "illegal" to aid and comfort a Jew in Hitler's Germany. Even so, I am sure that, had I lived in Germany at the time, I would have aided and comforted my Jewish brothers. If today I lived in a Communist country where certain principles dear to the Christian faith are suppressed, I would openly advocate disobeying that country's anti-religious laws. I must make two honest confessions to you, my Christian and Jewish brothers. First, I must confess that over the past few years I have been gravely disappointed with the white moderate. I have almost reached the regrettable conclusion that the Negro's great stumbling block in his stride toward freedom is not the White Citizen's Counciler or the

Ku Klux Klanner, but the *white moderate*, who is more devoted to "order" than to justice; who prefers a negative peace which is the absence of tension to a positive peace which is the presence of justice; who constantly says, "I agree with you in the goal you seek, but I cannot agree with your methods of direct action"; who paternalistically believes he can set the timetable for another man's freedom; who lives by a mythical concept of time and who constantly advises the Negro to wait for a "more convenient season."

Shallow understanding from people of good will is more frustrating than absolute misunderstanding from people of ill will. Lukewarm acceptance is much more bewildering than outright rejection.

I had hoped that the white moderate would understand that law and order exist for the purpose of establishing justice and that when they fail in this purpose they become the dangerously structured dams that block the flow of social progress.

Actually, we who engage in nonviolent direct action are not the creators of tension. We merely bring to the surface the hidden tension that is already alive. We bring it out in the open, where it can be seen and dealt with. Like a boil that can never be cured so long as it is covered up but must be opened with all its ugliness to the natural medicines of air and light, injustice must be exposed, with all the tension its exposure creates, to the light of human conscience and the air of national opinion, before it can be cured.

In your statement you assert that our actions, even though peaceful, must be condemned because they precipitate violence. But is this a logical assertion? Isn't this like condemning a robbed man because his possession of money precipitated the evil act of robbery?

We must come to see that, as the federal courts have consistently affirmed, it is wrong to urge an individual to cease his efforts to gain his basic constitutional rights because the quest may precipitate violence. Society must protect the robbed and punish the robber.

I had also hoped that the white moderate would reject the myth concerning time in relation to the struggle for freedom.... Actually, time itself is neutral; it can be used either destructively or constructively. More and more I feel that the people of ill will have used time much more effectively than have the people of good will. We will have to repent in this generation not merely for the hateful words and actions of the bad people, but for the **appalling silence of the good people.**

Human progress never rolls in on wheels of inevitability, *it comes through the tireless efforts of men willing to be co-workers with God*, and without this hard work, time itself becomes an ally of the forces of stagnation. We must use time creatively, in the knowledge that the time is always ripe to do right.

Now is the time to make real the promise of democracy and transform our pending national clergy into a creative psalm of brotherhood. Now is the time to lift our national policy from the quicksand of racial injustice to the solid rock of human dignity.

You speak of our activity in Birmingham as extreme. At first I was rather disappointed that fellow clergymen would see my nonviolent effort as those of an extremist. I began thinking about the fact that I stand in the middle of two opposing forces in the Negro community.

One is the force of complacency, made up in part of Negroes who, as a result of long years of oppression, are so drained of self-respect and a sense of "somebodiness" that they have adjusted to segregation, have become insensitive to the problems of the masses.

The other force is one of bitterness and hatred, and it comes perilously close to advocating violence. It is expressed in the various black nationalist groups that are springing up across the nation, the largest and best-known being Elijah Muhammad's Muslim movement. Nourished by the Negro's frustration over the continued existence of racial discrimination, this movement is made up of people who have lost faith in America, who have absolutely concluded that the white man is an incorrigible "devil."

I have tried to stand between these two forces, saying that we need emulate neither the "donothingism" of the complacent nor the hatred and despair of the black nationalist. For there is the more excellent way of love and nonviolent protest. I am grateful to God that, through the influence of the Negro church, the way of nonviolence became an integral part of our struggle.

If this philosophy had not emerged, by now many streets of the South would, I am convinced, be flowing with blood. And I am further convinced that if our white brothers dismiss as "rabble-rousers" and "outside agitators" those of us who employ nonviolent direct action, and if they refuse to support our nonviolent efforts, millions of Negroes will, out of frustration and despair, seek solace and security in black-nationalist ideologies—a development that would inevitably lead to a frightening racial nightmare.

Oppressed people cannot remain oppressed forever. The yearning for freedom eventually manifests itself, and that is what has happened to the American Negro. Something within has reminded him of his birthright of freedom, and something without has reminded him that it can be gained. Consciously or unconsciously, he has been caught up by the Zeitgeist, and with his black brothers of Africa and his brown and yellow brothers of Asia, South America and the Caribbean, the United States Negro is moving with a sense of great urgency toward the promised land of racial justice.

If one recognizes this vital urge that has engulfed the Negro community, one should readily understand why public demonstrations are taking place. The Negro has many pent-up resentments and latent frustrations, and he must release them. So let him march; let him make prayer pilgrimages to the city hall; let him go on freedom rides—and try to understand why he must do so. If his repressed emotions are not released in nonviolent ways, they will seek expression through violence; this is not a threat but a fact of history. So I have not said to my people, "Get rid of your discontent." Rather, I have tried to say that this normal and healthy discontent can be channeled into the creative outlet of nonviolent direct action. And now this approach is being termed extremist.

But though I was initially disappointed at being categorized as an extremist, as I continued to think about the matter I gradually gained a measure of satisfaction from the label.

Was not Jesus an extremist for love: "Love your enemies, bless them that curse you, do good to them that hate you, and pray for them which despitefully use you, and persecute you."

Was not Amos an extremist for justice: "Let justice roll down like waters and righteousness like an overflowing stream . . ."

And John Bunyan: "I will stay in jail to the end of my days before I make a butchery of my conscience." And Abraham Lincoln: "This nation cannot survive half slave and half free." And Thomas Jefferson: "We hold these truths to be self-evident, that all men are created equal. . . ."

So the question is not whether we will be extremists, but what kind of extremists will we be. Will we be extremists for hate or for love? Will we be extremists for the preservation of injustice or for the extension of justice? . . . Perhaps the South, the nation, and the world are in dire need of creative extremists.

I had hoped that the white moderate would see this need. Perhaps I was too optimistic; perhaps I should have realized that few members of the oppressor race can understand the deep groans and passionate yearnings of the oppressed race, and still fewer have the vision to see that injustice must be rooted out by strong, persistent, and determined action.

I am thankful, however, that some of our white brothers in the South have grasped the meaning of this social revolution and committed themselves to it. They are still all too few in quantity, but they are big in quality. Some—such as Ralph McGill, Lillian Smith, Harry Golden, James McBride Dabbs, Ann Braden, and Sarah Patton Boyle—have written about our struggle in eloquent and prophetic terms.

Others have marched with us down nameless streets of the South. They have languished in filthy, roach-infested jails, suffering the abuse and brutality of policemen who view them as "dirty nigger-lovers." Unlike so many of their moderate brothers and sisters, they have recognized the urgency of the moment and sensed the need for powerful "action" antidotes to combat the disease of segregation.

Let me take note of my other major disappointment with the white church and its leadership.

Of course, there are some notable exceptions. I am not unmindful of the fact that each of you has taken some significant stands on this issue. I commend you, Reverend Stallings, for your Christian stand on this past Sunday, in welcoming Negroes to your worship service on a non-segregated basis. I commend the Catholic leaders of this state for integrating Spring Hill College several years ago.

But despite these notable exceptions, I must honestly reiterate that I have been disappointed with the church. I do not say this as one of those negative critics who can always find something wrong with the church. I say this as a minister of the gospel, who loves the church, who has nurtured in its bosom; who has been sustained by its spiritual blessings and who will remain true to it as long as the cord of life shall lengthen.

When I was suddenly catapulted into the leadership of the bus protest in Montgomery, Alabama, a few years ago, I felt we would be supported by the white church. I felt that the white ministers, priests and rabbis of the South would be among our strongest allies. Instead, some have been outright opponents, refusing to understand the freedom movement and misrepresenting its leaders; all too many others have been more cautious than courageous and have remained silent behind the anesthetizing security of stained-glass windows.

In spite of my shattered dreams, I came to Birmingham with the hope that the white religious leadership of this community would see the justice of our cause and with deep moral concern, would serve as the channel through which our just grievances could reach the power structure. I had hoped that each of you would understand. But again I have been disappointed.

I have heard numerous southern religious leaders admonish their worshipers to comply with a desegregation decision because it is the law, but I have longed to hear white ministers declare: "Follow this decree because integration is morally right and because the Negro is your brother."

In the midst of blatant injustices inflicted upon the Negro, I have watched white churchmen stand on the sideline and mouth pious irrelevancies and sanctimonious trivialities. In the midst of a mighty struggle to rid our nation of racial and economic injustice, I have heard many ministers say: "Those are social issues, with which the gospel has no real concern." And I have watched many churches commit themselves to a completely otherworldly religion which makes a strange, un-Biblical distinction between body and soul; between the sacred and the secular....

I hope the church, as a whole, will meet the challenge of this decisive hour. But even if the church does not come to the aid of justice, I have no despair about the future. I have no fear about the outcome of our struggle in Birmingham, even if our motives are at present misunderstood. We will reach the goal of freedom in Birmingham and all over the nation, because the goal of America is freedom.

Abused and scorned we may be, our destiny is tied up with America's destiny. Before the pilgrims landed at Plymouth, we were here. For more than two centuries our forebears labored in this country, without wages; they made cotton king; they built the homes of their masters while suffering gross injustice and shameful humiliation—and yet out of a bottomless vitality they continued to thrive and develop.

If the inexpressible cruelties of slavery could not stop us, the opposition we now face will surely fail. We will win our freedom because the sacred heritage of our nation and the eternal will of God are embodied in our echoing demands.

Before closing I feel impelled to mention one other point in your statement that has troubled me profoundly. You warmly commended the Birmingham, police force for keeping "order" and "preventing violence."

I doubt that you would have so warmly commended the police force if you had seen its dogs sinking their teeth into unarmed, nonviolent Negroes. I doubt that you would so quickly commend the policemen if you were to observe their ugly and inhumane treatment of Negroes here in the city jail; if you were to watch them push and curse old Negro women and young Negro girls; if you were to see them slap and kick old Negro men and young Negro boys; if you were to observe them, as they did on two occasions, refuse to give us food because we wanted to sing our grace together. *I cannot join you in your praise of the Birmingham police department.*

It is true that the police have exercised a degree of discipline in handling the demonstrators. In this sense they have conducted themselves rather "nonviolently" in public. But for what purpose? To preserve the evil system of segregation?

Over the past few years I have consistently preached that nonviolence demands that the means we use must be as pure as the ends we seek. I have tried to make clear that it is wrong to use immoral means to attain moral ends. But now I must affirm that it is just as wrong, or perhaps even more so, to use moral means to preserve immoral ends.... As T.S. Eliot has said, *"The last temptation is the greatest treason; To do the right deed for the wrong reason."*

I wish you had commended the Negro sit-inners and demonstrators of Birmingham for their sublime courage, their willingness to suffer, and their amazing discipline in the midst of great provocation. One day the South will recognize its real heroes. They will be the James Merediths, with the noble sense of purpose that enables them to face jeering and hostile mobs, and with the agonizing loneliness that characterizes the life of the pioneer. They will be old, oppressed, battered Negro women, symbolized in a seventy-two-year-old woman in Montgomery, Alabama, who rose up with a sense of dignity and with her people decided not to ride segregated buses, and who responded with ungrammatical profundity to one who inquired about her weariness: "My feets is tired, but my soul is at rest."

They will be the young high school and college students, the young ministers of the gospel and a host of their elders, courageously and nonviolently sitting in at

> lunch counters and willingly going to jail for conscience' sake. One day the South will know that when these *disinherited children of God* sat down at lunch counters, they were in reality standing up for what is best in the American dream and for the most sacred values in our Judaeo-Christian heritage, thereby bringing our nation back to those *wells of democracy* which were dug deep by the founding fathers in their formulation of the Constitution and the Declaration of Independence.
>
> Never before have I written so long a letter. I'm afraid it is much too long to take your precious time. I can assure you that it would have been much shorter if I had been writing from a comfortable desk, but what else can one do when he is alone in *a narrow jail cell,* other than write long letters, think long thoughts and pray long prayers? . . .
>
> Yours for the cause of peace and brotherhood,
> Martin Luther King Jr.[1]

Dr. King petitioned his brothers and sisters in the ministry in "*Letter From the Birmingham Jail*" to join him in the struggles of civil disobedience for redress of grievances. His most crucial sentiment in this document is how justice should not have to wait for deliverance. By the mere fact of being a member of the human matrix, justice would be the divine fruit of freedom. He cautioned his brethren in the ministry across the board—black and white. "*Shouldn't you take a stand for right? Aren't you a shepherd of God? If so, why do you stand idle waiting for centuries to bring about the fruits of freedom, justice and equality. There is a Greater Shepherd who will require you to answer for these times on earth and to realize Jesus' birth for all humankind.*"

Well, this think tank disliked the whole idea of the Civil Rights Movement and had a plan to rescind everything and more of what the African American had won. The think tank had drawn upon a greater vision to draw the people into a state of mind where they could see their idea and ultimately accept their insidious plan. The idea was so evil in concept that it would unfurl the documents of history to repeat an ugly phase of American history and present it to the nation in the 21st century as a progressive economic industry. Dr. Martin L. King Jr. would spin over in his grave if he could see the landscape of America today.

If the American government had fulfilled the role of providing justice and equality to all its citizens, the work of Dr. King would not have been necessary. The Civil War had been fought but the 13th, 14th, and 15th Amendments were never enforced by the government.

Part II: Post Civil War And Radical Reconstruction

The Chicanery of Freedom
November 7, 1876, Presidential Election

A deep concern for blacks echoed by two radical white Congressmen, *Thaddeus Stevens* and *Charles Sumner*, spearheaded Radical Reconstruction. The United States Congress, under the leadership of Sumner and Stevens, ratified their plan of Reconstruction and added three amendments to the US Constitution to insure freedom for the newly freed blacks. The Thirteenth Amendment of the Constitution abolished slavery in 1865. The Fourteenth Amendment granted citizenship in 1868, and the Fifteenth Amendment in 1870 granted the freedmen suffrage—the right to vote.

The Radical Republican Reconstruction Plan divided the South into five military districts. These measures were taken to insure the rights of newly freed slaves to be compliant with the 13th, 14th, and 15th Amendments of the United States Constitution. In 1867, each district was under the federal command of a northern general with power superseding authority granted to state governments. The role of each general was to protect the rights of ex-slaves as citizens of the United States. This plan guarded the rights of ex-slaves to enable them to serve in various capacities, to work in all levels of government, and to attend school.

> Reconstruction acts, 1867: The Reconstruction Acts divided the Confederate states except Tennessee into five military districts. Military commanders in the districts were appointed to oversee constitutional conventions in the districts and the creation of state constitutions. This military occupation would last until the states created new constitutions that included black suffrage, the permanent disfranchisement of Confederate leaders, and ratification of the 14th Amendment.[2]

Charles Sumner, U.S. Senator from Massachusetts, was an outspoken abolitionist. Thaddeus Stevens, a U.S. Representative from Pennsylvania, advocated dividing the public land in the south to the newly freed blacks to ensure that each head of the household would get forty acres of land and a hut. Sumner and Stevens defied Abraham Lincoln's and Andrew Johnson's plans of Reconstruction and advocated their plan.

> "Forty acres and a mule: Forty acres and a mule" refers to the desire of Radical Republicans such as Thaddeus Stevens to carry out land redistribution in the South. He wanted to subdivide confiscated land and distribute it among the freedmen. Proposals such as these failed in Congress and state legislatures.[3]

Thaddeus Stevens's heart was nurtured through the spirit of his mother who imbued in him a sense of right and wrong with a desire to uplift humanity.

> As a leader of the radical Republicans' Reconstruction program after the Civil War, Stevens saw the Southern states as "conquered provinces." He sincerely desired the betterment of the lives of African-Americans. He proposed the Fourteenth Amendment, guaranteeing civil rights and was a leader in the impeachment of President Johnson.[4]

Andrew Johnson became president after the assassination of Abraham Lincoln. A man of meager means, growing up in Tennessee, he was at odds with the members of Radical Reconstruction. These Congressmen were very skeptical about leaving the ex-slaves in the South without legislation to protect their newly acquired freedom. Consequently, they passed the Civil War Amendments. To put "teeth" into these laws, they stipulated strict requirements to permit ex-confederates to return to the Union. The new president, Andrew Johnson, was perceived as an impediment to implement strict guidelines for their readmission. The obstinate behavior of President Johnson annoyed the Radical Congressmen who wanted to protect the rights of the newly freed slaves. The disagreement and the boldness of Johnson to carry out his own plan of Reconstruction infuriated these Radical Republicans, and consequently, they began an impeachment proceeding for President Andrew Johnson.

> The Tenure of Office Act was a measure passed by Congress in 1867. It prohibited the president from dismissing any cabinet member or other federal officeholder whose appointment had required the consent of the

> Senate unless the Senate agreed to the dismissal. Johnson's violation of this act caused the impeachment crisis.[5]

The successor of Abraham Lincoln was disliked by the Radical Republicans. They did not like his lenient plan for Reconstruction. They burned the midnight oil to find ways to impeach Andrew Johnson. This opportunity appeared to them when the President tried to flex his muscles by forcing Edwin McMasters Stanton from his position as Secretary of War. The Republicans passed a resolution of impeachment against Johnson for violating the Tenure of Office Act. Salmon Chase of Ohio, sixth Chief Justice of the Supreme Court, presided over the impeachment trial of Andrew Johnson for "High Crimes and misdemeanors" in 1868. Short of one vote to impeach him, Andrew Johnson served out the rest of his term in humility.

This Reconstruction Plan stationed federal troops in the South to prevent ex-confederates from participating fully in Reconstruction, in addition to ensuring blacks the right to exercise their newly acquired rights accorded them by the Constitution. The "Slave Codes" had prohibited education for slaves, but some blacks learned to read and to write through secret means. This period of black participation in politics was often defined as a chaotic time where ignorant, dumb, and incapable men sat in high political offices. Contrary to this view, many blacks who participated in Radical Reconstruction were intelligent men eager to rebuild the South for the benefit of all citizens.

A total of twenty-two blacks were elected to Congress before the 20th century. Two U.S. Senators were elected from the State of Mississippi. Of the twenty blacks serving in the House of Representatives, the largest number, a total of eight, were from South Carolina. There were four from North Carolina and three from Alabama. The States of Georgia, Louisiana, Mississippi, Florida, and Virginia sent one. During Reconstruction, African Americans held important positions as prosecuting attorneys, sheriffs, and recorders of deeds in several states. Blacks in political offices supervised funds to establish some of the first public schools, buildings, and roads.

The election of 1876 cast a dark shadow on the political future of blacks in America. The cloud surrounding the presidential election of 1876 provoked another threat to the union. There was a clash involving the two political parties. Each had different ideologies and economic interests and concerns. The Southerners were interested in regaining power and control of the South, while the Northerners were eager to retain their political power to perpetuate their economic and industrial growth.

> The United States presidential election of 1876 was one of the most disputed presidential elections in American history. Samuel J. Tilden of New York outpolled Ohio's Rutherford B. Hayes in the popular vote, and had 184 electoral votes to Hayes' 165, with 20 votes uncounted. These 20 electoral votes were in dispute in three states (Florida, Louisiana, and South Carolina), each party reported its candidate had won the state, while in Oregon one elector was declared illegal (as an "elected or appointed official") and replaced. The 20 disputed electoral votes were ultimately awarded to Hayes after a bitter legal and political battle, giving him the victory.[6]

On the day of election both parties claimed victory. Samuel Jones Tilden, candidate for the Democratic Party, received 4,288,546 popular votes and Hayes received 4,034,311. Tilden had 184 electoral votes, one less than what he needed to have a majority. Hayes had received only 165 electoral votes. There were 20 votes contested, of which 19 lay in southern states. Tilden needed only one of the 20 votes to claim victory, but Hayes needed all twenty votes. Each candidate claimed the twenty votes. Feelings of animosity were running so high until veteran groups prepared and threatened to march on Washington, D. C., to ensure

Tilden's ascendancy to the office of president. Congressmen were fearful of trusting each other and many began arming themselves for protection.

> Hayes lost the popular vote, but four states had disputed elections which made the outcome in the electoral college unclear. A special commission was created by Congress to decide the matter. And Hayes was ultimately declared the winner in what was widely perceived as a backroom deal.[7]

Finally, a compromise became a popular subject.

> Compromise of 1877: As a result of the electoral vote from the Election of 1876, Congress created a 15-member bipartisan commission, on January 29, 1877, to resolve the dispute concerning the electoral votes between Tilden and Hayes. The committee consisted of five Democrats, five Republicans, and five Supreme Court justices. Hayes was unanimously awarded the electoral votes from Oregon and South Carolina and the ones from Louisiana by a commission vote of 8 to 7.[8]

The North and South agreed on a compromise. The South agreed to yield the Office of President to Rutherford B. Hayes, and the North, under the leadership of Hayes agreed to return control of the South to southern whites.

Rutherford Birchard Hayes, age 54 (1822–1893), was inaugurated as the 19th President of the United States on March 4, 1877.

> The method by which Hayes became president became infamous. When he died in January 1893 the *New York Sun*, on its front page, said: Although his administration was disgraced by no great scandal, the taint of the theft of the presidency clung to it to the last, and Mr. Hayes

> went out of office carrying with him the contempt of the Democrats and the indifference of the Republicans.[9]
>
> There were some scars in the history surrounding the election of 1876. Despite the compromise, ill feelings remained in the hearts of many voters. Amidst accusations of fraud and illicit deal-making, Rutherford B. Hayes triumphed over Samuel J. Tilden, and the result was the most disputed American election until the recounts of 2000.[10]

The similar election confusion of a presidential election took place in the 21st century—the election of 2000 with Al Gore and George W. Bush. In the first count of election returns, Gore was announced the victor. A contested count later yielded the presidency to George W. Bush.

The Reconstruction Period concluded with the Compromise of 1877 which returned the power to southern whites in return for yielding the presidency to Rutherford B. Hayes, the Northern (Republican) candidate. There were two other requests the North yielded to the South. As soon as Rutherford B. Hayes was sworn in for president, he fulfilled the 1877 compromise covenant. The federal troops were withdrawn from the South, David M. Key was placed in the presidential cabinet as Postmaster General, and the South was granted appropriations to rebuild their territory.

The Compromise of 1877: Death Knell for the African American

The period of Radical Reconstruction was short lived, concluding with the Compromise of 1877. This compromise marked the return of white supremacy to the South. Thus, the flowery period of black political experience closed.

In the Compromise of 1877, the North relinquished her responsibility to oversee the rights of Blacks in exchange for the presidency.

The ex-slaves could no longer rely on the North and the Republican Party to oversee and protect their newly acquired rights. The five United States generals were withdrawn from the South. Federal troops adhered to the provisions of the Compromise by departing from southern states as soon as possible. The African Americans were left without any protection to insure their rights as citizens of the United States. They were left at the mercy of ex-slaveholders.

Where were the men of the great Congress Hall whose voices echoed a new way of life for ex-slaves and compensation for their years of servitude in a foreign nation? What happened to the forty acres and a mule to be distributed to each of 4,000,000 slaves? Blacks had contributed free labor in building America from 1661 to 1865. There was land availability. In fact, the United States National Archives and Records Administration reveals that Abraham Lincoln signed the Homestead Act of 1862 on May 20, 1862. A more profound question to ask is why were the ex-slaves sent away empty-handed. There were basically three requirements to obtain the specified western land in the Homestead Act: file an application, improve the land, and file the deed. Surely, the ex-slaves had the work experience to fulfill these requirements. The contemporary writer Randal Robinson addresses this historical concern of reparation in his publication of *The Debt.*[11]

"The South," echoed by these voices, had willingly seceded from the Union; therefore, they were to be considered a conquered province. The "Conquered Province theory" recommended a stringent code to be adhered to readmit ex-Confederate officers in the Union.

> Conquered territory theory: The conquered territory theory was a popular theory held by many Reconstruction policy makers after the Civil War that the southern states which seceded from the Union to form the Confederate

> States of America should be treated as if they were territories conquered from a foreign nation.[12]

America's Two Great Voices against Slavery

Charles Sumner was one the greatest white men who fought for the cause of freedom and justice since the inception of this nation. His driving passion of heart inspired him to pursue the cause of equality for all humankind. He dedicated his political career, twenty-three years, to fighting for this cause. No man suffered as much as he did in pursuit of this journey of faith. The pursuance of this goal became Senator Charles Sumner's life work. He devoted his oratorical skills and talents to make this a reality.

> From the time he first took his oath as senator 23 years earlier, Sumner had eloquently campaigned against racial inequality. His first speech in the Senate attacked the 1850 law that allowed the use of federal resources to capture runaway slaves. In the mid-1850s, he helped to found the Republican Party as a coalition of antislavery political factions. Throughout his Senate career, he repeatedly backed efforts by African Americans and others seeking justice and equality.[13]

Once, Sumner delivered a powerful address speaking against the expansion of slavery in the territory of the United States. The constant fight between the two sections of the country—North and South—was related to the classification of new territories as they applied for admission to statehood. The powerful question was whether the territory would apply for admission as a slave or a free state. This economic and political question was as an apparition threatening the union of the nation. It was just a matter of time before this same question would lead to civil war.

> In his most famous speech—speaking for several hours over two days—Sumner delivered a scathing attack on the supporters of the Kansas–Nebraska Act, which allowed for expansion of slavery into the new territories. "Mr. President," he began, "A crime has been committed.... It is the rape of a virgin territory, compelling it to the hateful embrace of slavery.[14]

What was the Kansas–Nebraska Act?

The immense concern was the need to hold balance between the slave and free states. If Nebraska entered as a free state and Kansas entered as a slave state, the balance of the nation would be maintained.

In United States history, the Kansas–Nebraska Act of 1854 created the territories of Kansas and Nebraska, opened new lands, repealed the Missouri Compromise of 1820, and allowed settlers in those territories to determine if they would allow slavery within their boundaries. The initial purpose of the Kansas–Nebraska Act was to create opportunities for a mid-eastern transcontinental railroad. It was not problematic until popular sovereignty was written into the proposal.

This act was designed by Democratic Senator Stephen A. Douglas of Illinois.

> The act established that settlers could vote to decide whether to allow slavery, in the name of popular sovereignty or rule of the people. Douglas hoped it would ease relations between the North and the South, because the South could expand slavery to new territories but the North still had the right to abolish slavery in their states. Instead, opponents denounced the law as a concession to the slave power of the South. The new Republican

> Party, which was created in opposition to the act, aimed to stop the expansion of slavery, and soon emerged as the dominant force throughout the North.[15]

While presenting his speech, Senator Sumner used literary symbolism to make his delivery. He cloaked slavery in an analogy as to a harlot, with the South being its owner. During this period, the South took pride in their culture, superfluous manners, and quixotic symbols of chivalry with manners indicative of good breeding—a man's character was his honor. The two senators Sumner inferred to, in his address, were Stephen Douglas of Illinois and Andrew Pickens Butler of South Carolina—authors of the Kansas–Nebraska Act.

The vintage question from the inception of the American nation was the human question—should all humanity be free? Would America remain half slave and half free? The constant fight between the two sections of the country—North and South—was related to this classification of new territories as they applied for statehood. The powerful question was whether they would apply for admission as a slave or a free state? The North had an ultimate goal of cleansing the nation of slavery, while the South embraced it as their economical foundation.

> In his speech, Sumner targeted two Democratic senators as principal culprits in this crime. First, there was Stephen Douglas of Illinois. Sumner considered him to be a "noise-some, squat, and nameless animal…not a proper model for an American southern senator's stance as a man of chivalry, and using shockingly explicit and sexually charged language, Sumner accused Butler of taking 'a mistress…the harlot, Slavery.'" Several days later, A House member who was related to Butler entered the Senate Chamber and savagely beat Sumner with a heavy walking stick.[16]

Senator Sumner began his speech on May 20, 1856. On May 22, 1856, two days later, Preston Brooks sought revenge for his cousin, Andrew Pickens Butler.

> Brooks confronted Sumner, who was seated at his desk, writing letters. He said, "Mr. Sumner, I have read your speech twice over carefully." As Sumner began to stand up, Brooks hit Sumner over the head several times with his cane, made of thick gutta-percha with a gold head. Sumner was trapped under the heavy desk (which was bolted to the floor), but Brooks continued to strike Sumner until Sumner wrenched the desk from the floor in an attempt to escape.[17]

The savage attack caught Senator Sumner off guard. He was unprepared to defend himself. Some Congressmen tried to assist him but were restrained by friends of Brooks. It was a brutal caption of American history in our legislative hall. The cane was used in such a forceful manner until it broke.

This surprise beating on May 22, 1856, left its ugly scars. "Sumner suffered head trauma that caused him chronic pain and symptoms consistent with what would now be called traumatic brain injury and post-traumatic stress disorder, and spent three years convalescing before returning to the Senate seat. He suffered chronic pain and debilitation for the rest of his life."[18]

Representative Brooks is remembered in history for the infamous behavior projected on Senator Charles Sumner of Massachusetts. The antislavery speech provoked Senator Brooks to seek a viral revenge for his relative, Senator Andrew Butler of South Carolina. This despicable behavior was applauded in the South but was unacceptable in the North. There was no balm to heal the two divisions. Instead, the cobblestones laid the pathway to the Civil War.

> An attempt to oust him from the House of Representatives failed, and he received only token punishment in his criminal trial.
>
> He resigned his seat in July 1856 to give his Constituents the opportunity to ratify his conduct in a special election, which they did by electing him in August to fill the vacancy created by his resignation. He was reelected to a full term in November 1856 but died five weeks before the term began in March 1857.[19]

Despite a three-year lapse in his political career, Senator Charles Sumner was able to make a comeback to continue his work to uplift humanity.

What was the temperament of Preston Brooks?

A peep into his childhood and growth years sheds some insight. What kind of person was Brooks?

> Born in Roseland, Edgefield County, South Carolina, he was the son of Whitfield and Mary Parsons-Carroll Brooks. Brooks attended South Carolina College (now known as the University of South Carolina) but was expelled just before graduation for threatening local police officers with firearms. In 1840, Brooks fought a duel with future Texas Senator Louis T. Wigfall and was shot in the hip, forcing him to use a walking cane for the rest of his life. He was admitted to the Bar in 1854. Brooks served in the Mexican–American War with the Palmetto Regiment.[20]

Although not severely punished, in less than a year, Preston Brooks died on January 27, 1857. Andrew Pickens Butler, his relative whom he defended, died May 25, 1857. Charles Sumner spent three years in recuperation after the cane beating, but was able to resume his work until his death on March 11, 1874.

> The attack transformed Sumner into a northern hero and assured his place in history books, but his greatest legislative legacy came in the years after the caning. Serving in the Senate until his death, Sumner championed the cause of African Americans, calling for the passage of constitutional amendments to provide civil and political rights to freedmen. In 1870 he introduced what he considered to be his most important piece of legislation, a civil rights bill to guarantee to all citizens, regardless of color, "equal and impartial enjoyment of any accommodation, advantage, facility, or privilege." Sumner predicted it would be the greatest achievement of Reconstruction.[21]

Sumner had worked relentlessly to ascertain the passage of the Civil Rights laws. He worked tirelessly to spearhead legislation to protect the newly freed slaves. His final project was to get the civil rights bill passed.

> Unfortunately, Sumner did not live to see his bill pass, but it occupied his final thoughts. "Don't let the bill fail," the dying Sumner pleaded to Frederick Douglass and others at his bedside. "You must take care of [my] civil-rights bill." Sumner's bill did become law in 1875, but the Supreme Court declared it unconstitutional in 1883. It took another 80 years for Sumner's ideas to

> finally gain legislative endorsement – with the Civil Rights Act of 1964.[22]

Yet, while we review his last words, the heart of the man is revealed.

> The mortally ill senator said that his only regret about dying was that he had not finished preparing his collected writings for publication and that the Senate had not yet passed his civil rights bill. He expired that afternoon. Not since the death of Abraham Lincoln in 1865 had the nation grieved so deeply at the loss of one of its statesmen.[23]

Charles Sumner can be compared to the biblical character of John the Baptist. John entered the world and quickly recognized his purpose for being placed on this earth. He did not seek designer's clothing; rather, he had "his raiment of camel's hair, and a leathern girdle about his loins" (John 3:4). He did not aspire to a diet of caviar and champagne; he consumed a diet of locust and honey. He did not seek the praises of the world; he dedicated himself to fulfilling the mission of his birth. John, on a daily basis, was seen in the Jordan River delivering a message to humanity. "I am the one crying in the wilderness, make straight the path of the Lord" (John 1:23). He engaged his mind, body, and spirit to complete his earthly assignment. Sumner was a man with a great mission, and he embraced his assignment to the last moment of life.

Thaddeus Stevens and Charles Summer were the leaders of Radical Reconstruction. They fought vehemently to disband the slavery institution in America and to write legislation to provide freedom, justice, and equality for the newly freed slaves. Both men lived to see the close of the institution of slavery. Unfortunately, both men died before the election of 1876. Congressman Thaddeus Stevens, who wanted each ex-slave to be compensated with "40 acres and a mule," was born April 4, 1792, and died August 11, 1868. The great fighter Charles Sumner was born January 6, 1811, and died March 11, 1874. He died before the election of 1876. The newly freed slaves lost their best political fighter—March 11, 1874, was a day to be remembered and etched in stone!

How did the Compromise of 1877 affect African Americans?

America neglected its responsibility to enforce the Constitution by failing to uphold the rights of newly freed slaves. Every generation since this period has suffered from the evils of this compromise—the refusal to protect the rights of the African American under the United States Constitution—contributed to all the terrorism, caste system, segregation, discrimination, laws, and policies designed to designate African Americas as second-class citizens.

What happened to the system of *checks and balances* written in the United States Constitution?

When the pillars of righteousness do not stand strong on truth, the scars linger to affect future generations. If the United States Constitution had enforced the rights of the newly freed slaves, there would not have been a need for neither the work of Dr. Martin L. King nor the Civil Rights Movement. The Civil Rights Amendments (13th, 14th, and 15th) added to the U.S. Constitution should have upheld the rights of the African American as citizens.

CHAPTER 5

A Bad Idea Destroys the Principles of a Democracy

Growing Prisons in a Democracy is a Bad Idea

For the tycoons who have invested in the prison industry, it has been like finding a "pot of gold."
Vicky Pelaez.

John F. Kennedy developed a great idea to build our country. American statesmen before the 1970s had an abiding faith in education to develop the children of the nation. This, too, was a good idea. Some ideas are just the opposite of the late president's. The subject of this book is to explore **how negative ideas can contribute to the destruction of our democratic principles** and create ill will in the nation when implementation of such ideas stifle the development of some people, at the expense of satisfying selfish goals and desires of a small group of people. Instead of building the country and improving its reputation globally, these ideas destroy the image of America as a democracy.

The Kennedy Peace Corps was the development of *a good idea*. The President's idea mushroomed into a reality where the foundational structure grew to make real the dreams of democracy. But an *egotistical idea* that precludes the needs of all the people weakens the foundational wall of a democracy. This book explores how a *nefarious idea* can contribute to destroying a democracy rather than building vital structures. This insidious disease is as a cancer, devouring the living cells of a democracy by exploiting human beings to be used as an economic product to grow a prison industry—financed by the tax dollars of Main Street.

There were low prison populations across the nation in America in the 1970s. The mindset of many lawmakers was that prisons were inhumane. Congress had voted decisively to eliminate almost all federal mandatory-minimum sentences for drug offenders. The Federal Bureau of Prisons' plan was to close penitentiaries in Georgia, Kansas, and Washington. Prior to 1973, the majority of inmates were sentenced for crimes related to violence. "From 1963 to 1972, the number of inmates in California declined by more than a fourth, despite the state's growth in population since. The inmate population in New York had dwindled to its lowest level since at least 1950."[1]

The mental health practitioners voiced opinions for more rehabilitative facilities and educational services to address the needs of drug users. They expressed the belief that sentencing policy should not exist solely in the hands of the judicial system.

There were still some advocates reminiscent of Florence Nightingale, Elizabeth C. Stanton (born November 12, 1815, Johnstown, NY), Susan B. Anthony (born February 15, 1820, Rochester, NY), and Dorothea Dix (1802–1887, Cambridge, MA)—great social activists who worked tirelessly in the 19th century to pursue the cause of health, fairness, and meaningful work to uplift humanity. Dix walked through the prisons and learned "the plight of the mentally ill—some were housed in dungeon cells, the insane chained to walls, filthy, underfed, and without heat." She saw, "insane persons confined in cages, closets, cellars, stalls, pens, chained, naked, beaten with rods, and lashed into obedience."[2]

Miss Dix also found insane persons crowded together in cold rooms as if they were animals. They were often chained, kept naked in cages, and whipped into obedience. Miss Dix went from state to state reporting what she saw. In time, the states provided better care for the insane, keeping them apart from criminals. She dedicated her life to better the conditions of prisoners and the insane. When she died on July 17, 1887, she was beheld as a great humanitarian and inscribed in American history as a reformer with a love for uplifting humanity.

The question today is this: Where are the Dorothea Dixes', Susan B. Anthonys', and other reformers who care about uplifting humanity? In our times, too many suffering people are turned loose from mental institutions to allow for alternative use of land to build housing developments for the dollar and not for the care of the ill, less fortunate, the abused, and the uneducated.

The next question to ask: What happened in society to induce this rapid change? A more appalling observation was with ethnicity. The African American prison population was low in 1970. The Correctional Association of New York statistics of March 2003 reveals, "African Americans make up 50.3% of the prison population." How did this happen? They represent only 12.4% of the State's population, so why is their prison rate so high? Another important fact to examine is this: "About 49% of the inmates are serving time for first time felony convictions and 57% of the offenders sent to State prison in 2002 were convicted of nonviolent crimes." What is the factor that is causing an increase in the nonviolent crime rate?

A Nefarious Idea Simmered in a Democracy: Dialectic Principle in a Democracy

A secret think tank was opposed to the legislative action of closing some prisons. This group sat behind closed doors and conjured an idea to increase the number of prisons. This think tank's idea was to create secret means to keep prisons opened as well as to design a plan to grow them into an industry. The plan is not complicated. It is simple thinking using the dialectic principle to manipulate the dynamics in people to accept the think tank's plan without realization.

The steps to achieve the goal of growing prisons will demonstrate this dialectic principle. The secret prison think tank moved their idea through these various stages to attain their economic empire. This list will open new lenses to reveal how psychology is applied to motivate an individual to respond in kind to the will of a think tank.

Study each step carefully to understand the methodology activated to control the mindset of the American populace.

I will discuss some of the stages in detail in chapter six and as you study these steps, you will become aware of the logic to turn your mind to the think tank's vision.

The think tank conceived an idea of an economic tool (human product) and conjured a method to promote it in disguise. The planning had to be sound. It had to be a theme to catch the eye of the populace and to be presented as a common good. There was a problem from the inception of this plan. The 1970s was a flourishing climate for humanity. The idea was so evil in concept until it would unfold the documents of history to repeat an ugly phase of American chronicles and present it to the nation in the 21st century as a progressive economic industry.

Vicky Pelaez asked a profound question in her article, "The Prison Industry in the United States: Big Business or a New Form of Slavery?" She presents her observation to mirror the current crisis when she frames the most pertinent question, is it "Big Business or a New Form of Slavery?" Pelaez's description provides ammunition for writing a response: *"For the tycoons who have invested in the prison industry, it has been like finding a pot of gold."* Our mission in this book is to understand the simile of wealth as being 21st century's "pot of gold" for prison pirateers.[3]

What *Pot of Gold* does this writer reference?

She, historically, alludes to the original slave ships (from the 1600s to 1808) that hurdled myriad ships by the thousands, bearing wares of black gold, to be sold in the market place of America on slave trade blocks. From these blocks, stolen Africans—black gold—were distributed in the South where the agrarian society depended upon a free labor force to accrue economic profits. Who will answer the question or make the comparative analysis of the colonial slave trade to the prison industrial economy? Ms. Pelaez has masterminded the slave-prison concept to expose the furtive design of modern-day slavery: "They don't have to worry about strikes or paying unemployment insurance, vacations or comp time. All of their workers are full-time, and never arrive late or are absent because of family problems; moreover, if they don't like the pay of 25 cents an hour and refuse to work, they are locked up in isolation cells."[4]

How did such a nefarious idea get such a strong hold of the populace to choreograph a cruel repeat of a bygone history in America?

The stronghold is so intense until the voices from various organizations in the nation fall upon death ears. "Human rights organizations, as well as political and social ones, are condemning what they are calling a new form of inhumane exploitation in the United States, where they say a prison population of up to 2 million—mostly Black and Hispanic—are working for various industries for a pittance."[5]

How lucrative is the prison economy?

Pelaez gives a bird's eye view into the prosperity of the prison industry.

> There are approximately 2 million inmates in state, federal and private prisons throughout the country. According to California Prison Focus, "no other society in human history has imprisoned so many of its own citizens." The figures show that the United States has locked up more people than any other country: a half million more than China, which has a population five times greater than the U.S. Statistics reveal that the United States holds 25% of the world's prison population, but only 5% of the world's people. From less than 300,000 inmates in 1972, the jail population grew to million by the year 2000. In 1990 it was one million. Ten years ago there were only five private prisons in the country, with a population of 2,000 inmates, now, there are 100, with 62,000 inmates. It is expected that by the coming decade the number will hit 360,000, according to reports.[6]

The southern economy at one time flourished with textile mills and other industries. During the 1980s and 1990s, these industries were confronted with downsizing and closings. To sustain and build their economic base, many local communities turned their attention to corroborating with a prison economy. Ms. Pelaez has identified some communities and economies that invest in prison contractual work.

> Who is investing? At least 37 states have legalized the contracting of prison labor by private corporations that mount their operations inside state prisons. The list of such companies contains the cream of U.S. corporate society:

> IBM, Microsoft, AT&T, Wireless, Texas Instrument, Dell, Compaq, Honeywell, Hewlett-Packard, Nortel, Lucent Technologies, 3Com, Intel, Northern Telecom, TWA, Nordstrom's Revlon, Macy's Pierre Cardin, Target Stores, and many more.[7]

These companies have truly found a "pot of gold" in a flourishing prison industry. The only factor of interest for these businesses and corporations is their main goal. They devoted their attention to how they could perpetuate a prison industry to supply their economic system with a cheap labor force where they could pay the least for the most.

> All of these businesses are excited about the economic boom generation by prison labor. Just between 1980 and 1994, profits went up from $392 million to $1.31 billion. Inmates in state penitentiaries generally receive the minimum wage for their work, but not all; in Colorado, they get about $2 per hour, well under the minimum. And in privately-run prisons, they receive as little as 17 cents per hour for a maximum of six hours a day, the equivalent of $20 per month. The highest private prison is CCA [Correctional Corporation of America] in Tennessee, where prisoners receive 50 cents per hour for what they call "highly skilled positions." At those rates, it is no surprise that inmates find the pay in federal prisons to be generous.[8]

Pelaez does not waste any time highlighting the salient features of a profiteering America at the expense of exploiting prison labor. She cites examples of businesses and companies who truly embrace prison labor as a "pot of gold." In a brief summary, she lists a few companies who value prison labor to fulfill their profit motive.

> A company that operated maquiladora (assembly plant in Mexico near the border) closed down its operations there and relocated to San Quentin State Prison in California. In Texas, a factory fired its 150 workers and contracted the services of prisoner-workers from the private Lockhart Texas prison, where circuit boards are assembled for Companies like IBM Compaq.
>
> [Former] ***Oregon State Representative Kevin Manniz*** recently urged Nike to cut its production in Indonesia and bring it to his state, telling the shoe manufacturer that "there won't be any transportation costs; we're offering you competitive prison labor."[9]

What hidden doors opened to prepare the way for extensive prison expansion?

Drugs fulfilled a vital role in luring many subjects into prisons, but some legislation and changes in laws contributed to growing the prison industry. As we explore these avenues, you will need to put on your thinking cap. Eric Schlosser addresses the prison growth issue. He describes it, in part, as a state of mind. "The lure of big money is corrupting the nation's criminal-justice system, replacing notions of public service with a drive for higher profits."[10]

Ross Sandler, founding director of New York Law School's Center for New York City Law, responded in humanity, "*Judges were not in the business of protecting constitutional rights, they were in the business of running prisons.*" Ross Sandler's *Democracy by Decree: What Happens When Courts Run Government* was published in 2003 with co-author David Schoenbrod.

Eric Schlosser, in *The Prison-Industrial Complex*, gives a vivid description of the 21st century prison economic industry.

> It is a confluence of special interests that has given prison construction in the United States a seemingly unstoppable momentum. It is composed of politicians, both liberal and conservative, who have used fear of crime to gain votes; impoverished rural area where prisons have become a cornerstone of economic development, private companies that regard the roughly $35 billion spent each year on corrections not as a burden on American taxpayers but as a lucrative market; and government officials whose fiefdoms have expanded along with the inmate population. Since 1991, the rate of violent crime in the United States has fallen by about 20 percent, while the number of people in prison or jail has risen by 50 percent.[11]

The steps and stages of this corrupt idea are presented in chapter **six**. The selection of the product (human beings) to grow prisons is a replica of American slavery.

What spiraled the prison growth in America—in a democracy?

We commend Ms. Pelaez for her writing and research in a quest to challenge the populace to look beyond trade, wealth, power, and control to realize the need to make a contribution to uplift humanity.

I smile to myself, as a historian, to note how the patriotic fighters of the American Revolution dedicated themselves to their work to uproot truth, define justice, and stay the course until the work culminated into the United States of America. Thomas Paine wrote *Common Sense*, to motivate the colonists to fight for their independence from England. Patrick Henry also stimulated the populace with his resounding voice,

Give me liberty or give me death! Now since that time, our nation is at the crossroads. Despite our status as being the superpower of the world, we are stumbling in the malaise of destroying our destiny as a future nation. Our state of immorality has tainted our souls and prevents the spiritual breath of life to lift us from our morass of depravity. We are unable to teach, train, discipline or nurture our children because we are under the spell of flexing our muscles. We fail to realize, in our "pseudo greatness," that we have lost our place with God. We have corrupted ourselves to the state where Rome and the Babylonian empires were during their decline. The saddest tale to be told is that either we do not recognize our state of existence or we do not care.

Who has contributed to this surge and rise in growing prisons into an economic industry is the subject of this book. Remember our three questions: What is the problem? What caused the problem? What must be done to rectify this problem? Growing prisons is the problem. A think tank with an idea to grow prisons as an economy caused the problem. African Americans must develop and design a cooperative strategy to detour their children from the door of the prison–industrial complex.

In our times, slavery has raised its ugly head again, in a new form and in a new century. Where are the caretakers who were knitted under a system called *checks and balances* to insure the rights of all its citizens? Did greed, somewhere along the democratic road, cause a breach in the system to allow Satan to raise his ugly head? What happened to love and brotherhood? What happened to "This land was made for you and me"? Did greed promote acquisition and purchase at any price? Did we think about our nation's reputation across the world? Did we think about God who blessed this nation into being?

Alexis de Tocqueville visited America in 1830 and was astonished at the morals and principles that held the nation together after winning their independence from England. He was puzzled at the glue that held fast the home, church, school, and community—the basic foundation of the nation—held it tightly with unity. He was most impressed with the spirituality of the nation depicted in the schools, media, and community. In his conclusion, he reasoned that faith was the true component of the nation's strength. It was a nation that propounded God throughout its territory.[12]

My question today is this: Have we lost our faith in America? Do we know the same God who blessed this nation into being can call it into accountability and wipe it from the face of this earth? Are there any voices left to speak truth, justice, and equality? ***Did someone remove the blindfold from the statue of the lady of justice?***

If so America, we are in the saddest state we have known since the inception of this nation. But there is a moral lesson, if we were to take it. Recall, I implore you, the lesson of Nineveh. Because of wickedness and sin, God sent Jonah to minister to this nation. I wonder if one can find a Jonah in America? Why are the *sacred voices so silent*, void of sounding truth to the nation? Jeremiah 23:1 says, "*Woe be unto the pastors that destroy and scatter the sheep of my pasture! Said the LORD.*"

I wonder how do they compare trade, commerce, wealth, power, and control to the mighty power of God. I wonder why their tongues cleave to their palates without mumbling a word of truth to beseech the nation to turn around. I wonder why servants of God will not minister unto a nation that was once built by God. But in all the wondering, the Spirit of God promises a cleansing upon this nation, soon and very soon, if she does not turn around.

CHAPTER 6

The Developmental Stages: How to Grow a Prison Industry

An Evil Plan Becomes a Reality in a Democracy!

Almost fifteen years ago the Correction Association of New York documented how New York's governors and politicians had rapidly increased prison funding while cutting funding to higher education.

What is the problem? The problem is that in the 1970s there was a low prison population nationally, but the 1980s emerged with a burgeoning growth of prisons to spiral a prison industry. To understand this social phenomenon, we must take it step by step to comprehend the furtive development of the undemocratic idea. President John F. Kennedy had a good idea when he developed the Peace Corps, but this prison growth idea is a nefarious plan in defiance of humanity.

Developmental Stages

STAGE 1 Conjuring the idea

Members come together as a think tank for a particular purpose. The particular purpose is usually gelled around an issue, a social problem, a means on how to improve or to create an economic system. This think tank can be as few as one or as many as twelve people. The particular focus in the 1970s was a social problem. Congress had studied the national statistics on prisons and decided to make changes by enacting legislation to make some closings. The think tank viewed this as an opportunity. Instead of closing prisons, they thought to develop an idea with a need factor. Let us take a wide spectrum of society to see how we can transform these prisons into an economic concept with financial benefits to our think tank. What if we were able to establish a need to keep the prisons opened? The process becomes a workable concept—increase the inmates, grow the prisons, and create an industry.

STAGE 2 What to do to increase prison growth

The think tank had a concept, and the second stage was to brainstorm to develop means and ways to grow the prison population, shrewdly, without the populace recognizing the plan. The members of the group were given assignments to study data related to the concept. The general consensus extended beyond the natural prison growth. There was a need to identify a creative method to grow the prison population. Studies across the nation revealed a substance that could be used to cause the increase in prison population. "An illegal substance" that would be a quick method to swell the prison population—better than baking powder to cause bread to rise in an oven! The think tank selected drugs as the bait to lure people into the prisons.

What must we do to increase the crime statistics to make this a reality? We can create a pool of cartels to make drugs highly accessible in specified communities. We will saturate this population for purchase, sale, and distribution.

STAGE 3 Provide legal services to increase the prison population

The think tank selected its method to increase the prison inmate population. Drugs would not stand alone. The think tank realized the need to coordinate the drug methodology to maximize the purpose by using the drug bait. Each stage required careful planning. There was a need for drug cartels to work in specified neighborhoods and communities. There was a need to increase the police force in defined geographical areas. To do this job with all deliberate speed, there was the need to motivate law enforcement officers by providing them with incentives to do a great job. A daily assignment was given to force officers to fulfill a quota to insure an increased prison population in a very brief time. Now, in summary, we have the drug cartels for distribution. We have an increase in law enforcement, and we have made provisions to provide incentives to fulfill daily quotas.

We will have to increase the law enforcement in these communities to carry out this work. Now, we have to apply psychology to our security system. We have to increase the police force and make them *"bull dogs"* in these communities. Our plan will be executed with an assigned daily quota. The work to increase jails would become a reality in a concise span of time. The daily quotas will overwhelm the present prison system and mandate a construction force to build more prisons.

To build more prisons we will need to increase our labor supply. This will provide employment for the construction industry and the prison compounds. We can build a prison in a 10-month period. We will not only have a force of workers to construct prisons, but a labor force to operate these prisons—perpetual employment for our people. In order to manifest our idea, we need everyone in this figment of imagination to play his role well.

Let us summarize the vital area transitions we must undergo to complete this economic model. First, we have to create a climate to verify the need for prison expansion. Secondly, we have to get top people to give credence to our theme, "Get Tough on Crime." We have to get the right people to give a voice to the theme to give it "life." We need leaders in high-power administrative capacity to resound this voice before the people—leaders, politicians, legislators. These voices must resonate with the people to cause them to rally against crime. The media would play a vital role to recoil the theme and use perpetual criminal graphics to accentuate the message, "Get Tough on Crime!" The same message would exacerbate the media, tabloids, and action centers.

STAGE 4 Create a theme to elicit populace support

The think tank must have the support of the populace. In their brainstorming sessions, various issues are reviewed. The theme has been selected, "Get Tough on Crime." The cry reverberates through the media. Crime must be stopped. It is a cancer gnawing at the core of our society. What work must we do to increase the crime statistics to promote this goal?

STAGE 5 Use professional and political voices to resound the theme

A small group speaking in a low voice, saying, "Get Tough on Crime," would not mesmerize the nation. The think tank uses their political and media connections to accentuate the message and to give credence to the theme. They get presidential candidates to integrate the theme in their campaign speeches.

STAGE 6 Get media to promote the theme

To really catalyze the theme, get media to use television coverage of some horrific crimes that occur in neighborhoods across the nation. Use the psychological concepts of fear and intimidation and get the populace on the "hype."

STAGE 7 Use psychological focus to move the populace into an action mode

Showcase brutal murders, crime, and theft occurring on a frequent basis to quickly place people in an emotional state. The intimidation, the hype, and the fear will move the populace into a state of abhorrence, and this is where the think tank would like them to be. This behavioral mode will move the people into a state where they will become active and demand something be done. The think tank is happy about the progress of this idea because this stage will mandate legislators and government officials to respond to this created social problem.

The populace will communicate with their representatives to demand action be taken to ameliorate this social issue. Some will mail letters to their state legislators to demand enactment of laws to get this crime under control. The think tank is happy to see the progress of their idea. Their hands are clean and free. The people are sending smoke signals to the lawmaking body demanding something be done and it must be done immediately! The hands that work behind the scene are invisible to the public. The visual presented to the populace is the scenario surfacing, repetitively, in the media, *Get Tough on Crime*—whether real or prepaid scenarios.

STAGE 8 Get the populace to give legitimacy to the idea

When the people rise up with fear, get on the hype, and call their legislators to task, they have fulfilled the think tank's goal. Now the populace has given legitimacy to realize their idea. Our theme, "Get Tough on Crime," has motivated the citizens into action where they demand their legislators to enact laws. The lawmakers have the support to legitimatize them to do something to eradicate this social ill. The think tank is almost ready to toast stem glasses but there are still more hoops to overcome.

Get legislators to write prescriptive laws to designate populations to be used in the scheme of modern-day slavery. The legislative response, implementation, lobbying, and bargaining would pave the path for prison expansion. Who are the stakeholders? Corporate investment in prisons, privatizing prisons, states, and governors!

STAGE 9 Get officials to respond to their constituents

Nationally, the state legislators gather in their halls to study problems and to write laws respectively, on what can be done to rectify the lawless climate across the nation.

The most important decision being made by these legislators is to work closely with the governors of various states to review their budgets on what can be done to put crime under control. The legislators flex the financial pocket streams of the states. What is the budget like? How much can we spend? What are our priorities? There is also the psychological question. If I fail to act or fail to address this social issue, will this affect my opportunity for re-election? The think tank is very much aware of persons whom they can count on to write new laws to address social issues as well as to provide appropriations. Questions appear and reverberate. What programs should I cut and what programs should I support? There is always the question of the consequences or what can

I get in exchange for supporting a particular bill? Will the governor support me in this area or block my legislation in another area?

STAGE 10 How to keep the prisons full to grow an industry

During this stage, the think tank is looking at two great factors. How to grow the prison industry and how to perpetuate a prison industry? What agencies must we corroborate with to achieve these objectives? We have the drug bait. We have an increased law-making population in specified communities. We have drafted a plan to fulfill daily quotas. Since our ultimate goal for prison growth is to create an economic industry, we have to devise means and ways to keep prisons full.

We are not concerned about screening individuals to become inmates. We do not have time to cull the population for the mentally ill, the illiterate, or the addicted. All we want is to identify a body guilty of the specified crime. Just like we needed the populace to legitimatize prison expansion, we need an agency to screen them without any concern for their state of being. The voices of Elizabeth Stanton, Dorothea Dix, and Susan B. Anthony are no longer present in our society. Therefore, we do not have to concern ourselves with involving other agency services to screen for alternative programs. We can do a one solitary screening—put them all in prison.

STAGE 11 Get the criminal justice system to do the "screening"

The New York state criminal justice system was revised in the 1980s. Governor Mario Cuomo had the opportunity to replace the seven judges. The criminal justice system will administer sentencing and determine length of prison stay. The criminal justice system will be the sole agency to sentence nonviolent criminals. With this concept, we can envision an industry where the laws will be designed to perpetuate long sentences in prisons. These long sentences will provide a workforce for long periods of time without interruptions.

STAGE 12 Design laws for the specified population

Our laws must be so designed that only the specified population will be affected. There will be double standards in disguise. Prison sentences will vary from use of white powder cocaine to rock-cocaine. We will have sentencing laws with definite term stays regardless of the crime—first time or several times will all get the assigned time or life (3-strikes law.) Our laws will ensure that blacks will carry the heaviest sentence in prison to ensure a cheap labor force for our prison industry.

Funding Prisons vs. Funding College Education

STAGE 13 Increasing prison inmates is our priority, not increasing college students

In our 21st century, we have embarked on a great prison economy, furtively, and we will perpetuate this industry as slavery was perpetuated in America from 1661 to 1865. During the period of slavery, the South depended on slaves to grow their agrarian society. Education, during institutionalized American slavery, was prohibited. The concern was for physical labor. Today, we will grow the prisons as an economy for corporate America, in a democracy. Our idea has been realized. We have replicated this prison model across the nation.

In *Education and Incarceration in NYS, Recalculating the fate of New York's Youth, from Cuomo to Cuomo*, William Martin and Andrew Pragacz reveal the serious status of Black and Hispanic students' college financial opportunities being truncated by ***New York state's drive to maintain a prison industry.***

> Almost fifteen years ago the Correction Association of New York documented how New York's governors and politicians had rapidly increased prison funding while cutting funding to higher education. Charting that gap revealed a stark outcome: as **state funding for SUNY/CUNY fell throughout the 1990s, prison spending rapidly advanced to overtake spending on higher education.** The recommendation was clear: irrational prison spending should be cut and higher education funding restored. This did not happen: in the following ten years stated expenditures on prisons continued to grow.
>
> Current political announcement and media coverage suggest that these long-term trends may be faltering and that a brighter future may await New York's youth. In this report we examine this larger landscape for the present. Looking at long-term trends, we highlight hopes for the future—and worries about growing disparity, despite changes in mass imprisonment and higher education, in the life chances of poor, Black and Latino youth across the state.[1]

Despite how Black and Hispanic minorities encounter financial challenges to complete undergraduate college degrees, they are confronted with a more critical challenge to obtain graduate education.

> *In the wake of declining support, New York State's elite schools and universities have become less and less representative of the state's population.* Even when disadvantaged students make into higher education they are likely to encounter poorly funded community colleges, which have seen their share of state appropriations shrink faster, and cuts deeper than elite SUNY institutions. Coupled with

> rising tuition rates, the Tuition Assistance Program (TAP) has been slashed over the past several years, pushing up levels of debt for poor, Black, and Latino students. In short, while every student in New York State is getting less and paying more, this conclusion stands out: Poor, Black, and Latino students are getting even less and paying even more for higher education, producing yet another reinforcement to the barrier to equality.[2]

Is maintaining a prison industry at the expense of denying full educational opportunity to the nation's children the right course for our nation?

In *"New York State of Mind?: Higher Education vs. Prison Funding in the Empire State,"* Robert Gangi, Vincent Schiraldi, and Jason Ziedenberg illustrate how funds for prisons have a higher priority than funds for higher education. Below is a summary, and the entire report may be retrieved from ERIC (eric.ed.gov).

> This paper examines trends in the support of public higher education versus that for prisons in New York State over the last decade and concludes that the dramatic rise in funding for prison expansion has come at the expense of higher education. This paper notes that since fiscal year 1988, operating budgets at New York's public universities have plummeted by 29 percent, a nearly equal trade-off in actual dollars; in 1995 New York ranked forty-fifth among states in per capita state appropriations for higher education, even though the state has the fourth highest per capita income in the nation.

> Also noted is that the Rockefeller drug laws and the second offender law have resulted in fully 62.5 percent of the people sent to prison in 1997 being committed for nonviolent offenses at a cost to the state of $680 million yearly; during the same period substantial tuition hikes at the State University of New York and City University of New York were imposed to compensate for the $615 million reduction in state higher education funding. The paper urges that these laws be repealed and replaced with cheaper, more effective drug treatment programs.[3]

Should the children of the nation suffer neglect of achieving a college education in lieu of giving the political reins to a few individuals who thirst for power, money, and control? This is the moral question to ask if we are to uphold a democracy—**"ordain this Constitution for ourselves and our posterity.**"

How to Grow a Prison Industry

DRUGS

POLICE

DESIGN LAWS

SENTENCING

The Idea Development

IDEA
(The thought)

Concept
(Develop the idea)

The Plan
(Goal, strategy, itemized steps for execution)

Model
(Design, guidelines for implementation)

Theme: "Get crime under control"

Political Voices
(Credible political leaders)

Hype
(Instill fear in the populace)

Hysteria
(Graphic scenarios/fear)

Legitimacy
(Populace on a hype to motivate legislators for action laws)

Media
(Repetitive scenes and dramatic graphics of crime on TV and tabloids)

Criminal Justice
(Design sentences and long-term incarceration, independent of any screening for other services)

State Legislature
(Design laws and appropriate funds)

Ignore the Screening Process for Sentencing
(Lump the mentally ill, illiterate, and the drug-addicted—ignore psychological services for this population)

The United States is one of the world's leading jailers.

"More than 2.2 million people are currently incarcerated in US jails and prisons, a 500 percent increase over the past forty years."

Jed S. Rakoff,
Mass Incarceration: The Silence of the Judges,
The New York Review of Books,
May 21, 2015/ Volume LXII, Number 9, pp.14–17

A War on African Americans

- Destroy schools in minority communities
- Drug Arrests Triple
- Jail Sentences Quadruple
- Skip college—Go Directly To Jail

What Is The Problem?

The 21St Century Design

- Resembles Nazi Concentration Labor Camps Copy of the Nazis before them . . .
- Strange Math in the Census: USA has only 5% of the world's population, but has 25% of the prison population
- Mandatory Minimum sentencing for prison growth

America Leads The World In Prisons (10th Edition)

Roy Walmsley
World Prison Brief (images.derstandard.at)

- Prison population total (number in penal institutions incl. pre-trial detainees)
- Country with largest prison population in each table

Table 1 AFRICA

Northern Africa	
Morocco	72,000
Western Africa	
Nigeria	54,144
Central Africa	
Cameroon	24,000
Eastern Africa	
Ethiopia	112,361
Southern Africa	
South Africa	156,370

Table 2 AMERICAS

North America	
USA	2,239,751
Central America	
Mexico	246,226
Caribbean	
Cuba	57,337
South America	
Brazil	548,003

Table 3 **ASIA**

Region / Country	Figure
Western Asia	
Saudi Arabia	47,000
Central Asia	
Kazakhstan	48,684
South Central Asia	
India	385,135
South Eastern Asia	
Thailand	279,854
Eastern Asia	
Taiwan	65,288

Figures not available Eastern Asia:
North Korea (Democratic People's Republic of Korea)

Table 4 **EUROPE**

Region / Country	Figure
Northern Europe	
United Kingdom	
England and Wales	84,430
Southern Europe	
Spain	68,220
Western Europe	
Germany	64,379
Europe/Asia	
Russian Federation	681,600
Central and Eastern Europe	
Ukraine	137,965

Table 5	**OCEANIA**	
	Australia	29,383

WorldPrisonBrief;prisonstudies.orgl Institute for Criminal Policy Research. World Prison Population csdp.org.

[Roy Walmsley, International Centre for Prison Studies was established in 1997. It was decided from the outset that the Centre should be independent of government .42 Store St,LondonWC1E7DB,UnitedKingdom.] Heuni (ISBN: 1236-8245. Paper No. 15, World Prison Population: Facts, Trends and Solutions by Brian Ikachuk and Roy Walmsley, 25-page-paper. HEUNI, The European Institute for Crime Prevention and Control, affiliated with the United Nations, P.O. Box 157, FIN-00121 Helsinki, Finland. Tel: +358-9-18257880.e-mail:heuni@om.fi. http://www.fn.fi/heuni/

Voices to Promote the Prison Industrial Complex Theme

President Richard Nixon

"[President Nixon] emphasized that you have to face the fact that ***the whole problem is really the blacks.*** The key is to devise a system that recognizes this while not appearing to."

—H.R. Haldeman, Nixon's Chief of Staff.

(Haldeman Diaries. G. P. Putnam's Dons).

Governor Nelson Rockefeller

Due in part to Rockefeller-style laws, the nation's prison population exploded from 330,000 in 1973 to a peak of 2.3 million. That meant building hundreds of new state and federal prisons.

Mario M. Cuomo

Starting in 1983, the Cuomo Administration built over 33,000 prison spaces, more than the number built by all previous administrations combined. Construction costs alone for these more than 33,000 spaces, counting debt service, will come to nearly $6 million. Operating costs for these spaces comes to $990 million each year.

—The Correctional Association of New York, 1995.

Barry Goldwater (Arizona)

Voted against the Civil Rights Bill. As a 1964 Republican presidential candidate, used the fear of crime tactic to attract the white middle-class voter.

—(en.m.wikipedia.org).

Ronald Reagan

Declared war on drugs, but left the borders open.

CHAPTER 7

"Get Tough on Crime": The First New York Prison Builders

Nelson A. Rockefeller

> ***But Rosenblatt says prosecutors in New York realized that the laws were doing unexpected and troubling things. White people were using a lot of drugs in the 1970s and committing a lot of crimes, yet the people being arrested and sent to prison under the Rockefeller laws came almost entirely from poor black and Hispanic neighborhoods.***
>
> Judge Albert M. Rosenblatt.

Drug Laws Set the Foundation for a Prison Industry in New York

Nelson A. Rockefeller was elected four terms as governor of New York. He baffled his administration when he made a political conversion to introduce his drug laws to design harsh sentences for drug users and abusers. Was this new political cataclysm a natural response to the social issue of the times, or was it a furtive plan to create an economic industry with political advantages?

What was the truth behind "Get tough on crime"? What factors influenced Governor Rockefeller to take such a harsh stand against crime related to drugs?

> The Rockefeller Drug Laws are the statutes dealing with the sale and possession of "narcotic" drugs in the New York State Penal Law. The laws are named after Nelson Rockefeller, who was the state's governor at the time the laws were adopted. Rockefeller, a staunch supporter of the bill containing the laws, had Presidential ambitions and so wanted to raise his national posture by being "tough on crime." If this strategy worked, he would no longer be seen as too liberal to be elected. He signed it on May 8, 1973.[1]

What role did politics play in motivating the governor to push through such veracious laws?

If there were presidential ambitions or political posturing, the laws were firmly planted in New York.

> Under the Rockefeller drug laws, the penalty for selling two ounces (57 g) or more of heroin, morphine, "raw or prepared opium," cocaine, or cannabis or possessing four ounces (113 g) or more of the same substances, was a minimum of 15 years to life in prison, and a maximum of 25 years to life in prison. The original legislation also mandated the same penalty for committing a violent crime while under the influence of the same drugs, but this provision was subsequently omitted from the bill and was not part of the legislation Rockefeller ultimately signed. The section of the laws applying to marijuana

> was repealed in 1979, under the Democratic Governor Hugh Carey.[2]

Rockefeller's stroke of the pen introduced the "Rockefeller Drug Laws." New York became the model for other states.

> The adoption of the Rockefeller drug laws gave New York State the distinction of having the toughest laws of its kind in the entire United States—an approach soon imitated by the state of Michigan, which, in 1978, enacted a "650-Life Law," which called for life imprisonment, without the possibility of parole for the sale, manufacture, or possession of at least 650 grams (1.43 lb) of cocaine or any Schedule or Schedule II opiate.[3]

"The Jan. 4, 1973, edition of the New York Daily News reports that Gov. Rockefeller's State-of-the State Speech called for a life sentence for drug pushers."

> The Rockefeller drug laws sailed through New York's Legislature. And pretty quickly this idea of getting tough, even on petty criminals, went viral, spreading across the U.S. Other states started adopting mandatory minimum and three-strikes laws—and so did the federal government—and so did the federal government.[4]

Despite this new legislative approach, some members of Rockefeller's administration were not convinced of the radical change. "From the start, Rockefeller's policy drew sharp criticism from drug treatment experts, and some politicians, who called the sentences draconian." Joseph Persico, a close aide to Rockefeller, heard the words of this early plan in 1972. He listened to the governor's new approach on addressing the drug social issue with an about-face from his traditional views and policies. He could not believe his ears. As he listened, Rockefeller revealed his thoughts. *"For drug pushing, life sentence, no parole, no probation."* As his aid for many years, Persico was witnessing a drastic change in the governor's thoughts and views on drugs.

> Rockefeller launched his campaign to toughen New York's laws at a press conference in January 1973—almost exactly 40 years ago. He called for something unheard of: mandatory prison sentences of 15 years to life for drug dealers and addicts—even those caught with small amounts of marijuana, cocaine or heroin.[5]

The cataclysmic change in the governor's thoughts caught many New Yorkers by surprise. "There were harsh criticisms from health practitioners who specialized in drug treatment, but no one really understood what the laws would mean or how many millions of people they would touch." **Albert Rosenblatt** was astonished at the new demeanor disclosed with the new drug proposals. He watched the unfolding of this new policy of drugs with apprehension.

> But Rosenblatt says prosecutors in New York realized that the laws were doing unexpected and troubling things. White people were using a lot of drugs in the 1970s and committing a lot of crimes, yet the people being arrested and sent to prison under the Rockefeller laws came almost entirely from poor black and Hispanic neighborhoods.[6]

Rosenblatt made an observation of the population inundating the courtrooms. This was a strange phenomenon. The Rockefeller call was to bring drug criminals under control, but there were obvious double standards in subjecting people to these new drug laws.

> We were aware of it. I mean, it's hard not to be aware of it when you see a courtroom and when you see a cadre of defendants—many of whom or most of whom were people of color.[7]

The inequity under the laws was visible and real. The New York prison population quickly spiraled around the nation.

> Due in part to Rockefeller-style laws, the nation's prison population exploded from 330,000 in 1973 to a peak of 2.3 million. That meant building hundreds of new state and federal prisons. By 2010, more than 490,000 people were working as prison guards.[8]

The Rockefeller drugs laws appeared to flow from nowhere, and began to do damage to human life everywhere, in the nation. How has this ever-growing force moved from a drug law to rectify a drug crime to convert itself into a prison–industrial complex? Did Rockefeller have a sincere interest in combating crime, or was it the line "Get tough on Crime" an introductory model to permeate the nation, in a democracy? "Studies put the price tag of America's vast prison system between $63 billion and $75 billion a year."[9]

Nelson Aldrich Rockefeller (July 8, 1908–January 26, 1979) was born at the beginning of the 20th century. He was the 49th Governor of New York (1959–1973). The governor had presidential ambitions. In the preparatory climb up the political ladder, Rockefeller held several positions. He was the 41st vice president in the Gerald R. Ford administration (1974–1977). He was politically classified as a liberal. Rockefeller commenced work in FDR's administration on December 20, 1944. He worked with FDR on Latin American affairs. After Roosevelt's death in April of 1945, Rockefeller remained in President Harry S. Truman's administration until August 17, 1945. He worked in Eisenhower's administration on welfare programs. Rockefeller's ultimate goal was to become president of the United States.[10]

Rockefeller was a presidential candidate in 1960, 1964, and 1968. In August 1974, Richard Milhous Nixon resigned to avoid impeachment, his successor, Gerald R. Ford, became president. Finally, Rockefeller joined him as the 41st vice president. Despite having served as vice president, he was not placed on President Ford's 1976 Republican national ticket as a running mate. The year 1976 marked the close of his political ambitions and he returned to New York. As governor of New York, he expanded the State University of New York into the largest public education system in the world, expanded the state parks and highway systems, created the Council on the Arts, proposed the first statewide minimum wage law in the country, and appointed an unprecedented number of women to head state agencies. He oversaw massive building projects, including the Empire State Plaza, Lincoln Center, and the World Trade Center.

"In December 1973, however, Nelson Rockefeller resigned as governor and his deputy Malcolm Wilson took over to serve the year remaining on his term."[11]

But the roots from the prison seed extended to children in the public school system. They, too, are affected by the Rockefeller prison germ. Many schools have begun to resemble pre-prison camps. I remember the joyous years of teaching without searches, guards, and gates. Beginning in the 1980s, many schools began using school security gates. I could never fathom why our government would not secure the borders to prevent the spillover of drugs into black neighborhoods and communities across the nation. An article written by William Lynch III, addresses an age-old question, "I Am My Brother's Keeper: Why We Must Change the Code."

> In America, young men of color have been in a crisis for decades, if not centuries. As my father's dear friend Marian Wright Edelman says, our country suffers from a "cradle-to-prison pipeline": entrenched institutions and

> policies that predispose disadvantaged children, especially children of color, to a life of crime and poverty, instead of one that fosters an ability to reach their full potential in life. A child's school years are such a critical juncture in the timeline that other activists use the term "school-to-prison pipeline" to discuss all the hurdles children face in schools. A cornerstone of the school-to-prison pipeline has been overly punitive school discipline codes, with disciplinary action applied disproportionately to people of color.[12]

Throughout the prison system, even in public schools, the prison bait has set a mold for future prison entrapment.

Madison Gray presents clear insight in his article "A Brief History of New York's Rockefeller Drug Laws" in *TIME* magazine.

> In the late 1960s and early 1970s, New York legislators faced the drug problem they feared was growing out of control. Federal statistics showed as many as 559,000 users nationwide and state police saw a 31 percent increase in drug arrests by 1972. In response Gov. Nelson Rockefeller, a liberal-leaning Republican who was said to have had presidential aspirations, created the Narcotic Addiction and Control Commission in 1967, aimed at helping addicts get clean. After the program proved too costly and ineffective, New York launched the Methadone Maintenance Program, which similarly caused little reduction in drug use. But by 1973, calls for stricter penalties had grown too loud to ignore prompting Albany to enact legislation that created mandatory minimum sentences of 15 years to life for possession of four ounces of narcotics—about the same as a sentence

> for second-degree murder. The statues became known as the Rockefeller Drug Laws—a milestone in America's war on drugs and the subject of one of the most abrasive legal tug-of-wars in the nation. The laws almost immediately led to an increase in drug convictions, but no measurable decrease in overall crime.[13]

There is important logic in Gray's article which addresses a severe neglect in the sentencing process. The furtive plan of growing prisons began in the 1970s and grew into an industry in the 1980s. The original role of sentencing excluded health practitioners and other services to screen individuals who would become inmates to the prisons. The criminal justice department concerned itself with the crime, and there were no provisions for screening the individual for optional placements. Consequently, prisons swelled, including the victims who were health challenged and educationally deficient.

> Meanwhile, critics argued that they criminalized what was primarily a public health problem, incarcerated non-violent felons who were better off in treatment, caused a jump in recidivism rates, and prevented judges from using discretion in sentencing. In January, during his State of the State address, New York Gov. David Paterson told his audience: "*I can't think of a criminal justice strategy that has been more unsuccessful than the Rockefeller Drug Laws.*"[14]

When emotions override reasoning, justice is, as a culprit, in denial. The underlying problem of boldness in the drug industry is the invasiveness of humanity being reduced to a commodity, worthy only of some economic value. These are synonymous to basic threats to American principles of democracy.

What is the history of the Urban Development Corporation?

The Urban Development Corporation was founded in 1968—a year challenging for both the state and the nation and had as its goal to be a special tribute to acknowledge the death of Dr. Martin L. King, Jr. This year also marked the assassination of Attorney General Robert F. Kennedy. These foremost leaders had committed their lives to the work of making a difference in uplifting humanity across the nation. What greater tribute it would be to acknowledge the work of these social warriors to use the UDC as a design to build low income housing for the people.

When Hugh L. Carey became the 51st governor of New York, he initiated a redesign of the UDC. Somewhere in the reorganization, the original purpose was lost. Instead of constructing low income housing for the people, this corporation has been used in various ways for multi-purposes unrelated to the original plan. *In 1970, Business Week claimed that the UDC was "emerging as the most powerful state agency in the country for coping with urban growth."*[15]

> In 1975, the Corporation was reorganized and its mission expanded from developing housing to economic development. The finances were reorganized and the corporation assumed a less aggressive development stance, and its mission was refocused to finance other ambitious state projects and has been used frequently by governors to implement projects that circumvent formal legislative or voter scrutiny.[16]

Hugh Carey served two terms as governor of New York from January 1, 1975, to December 31, 1982. He inherited the financial decline from the profligate years of Nelson A. Rockefeller.

> The four terms as governor, Mr. Rockefeller had built a legacy for state universities and highways but also of much higher taxes and enormous debt. The pattern was repeated at the local level under Mayor John V. Lindsay, a Republican turned Democrat, New York City had to borrow money for day-to-day operations. The 1974–75 recession opened yarning deficits and exposed years of unsound practices.
>
> On Jan. 1, 1975, Mr. Carey declared in his inaugural address, "*This government will begin today the painful, difficult, imperative process of learning to live within its means.*"[17]

It was Carey's responsibility to re-establish New York on a sound financial pathway. The political task was so demanding until the state was short of filing for bankruptcy. His two terms were dedicated to the financial rebirth of the state.

However, after the financial redirection of the UDC, the state of New York did not return to its original purpose to fulfill its mission—"*to facilitate large-scale low-income housing developments in urban neighborhoods that had traditionally been white and middle-class.*"[18]

Nelson Rockefeller, Hugh Carey and Mario Cuomo set the New York Prison Model

Rockefeller was the 49th governor of New York from January 1, 1959, to December 18, 1973. He introduced drug laws that carved the pathway to prison expansion. Being elected four terms, he resigned his last year, and Malcolm Wilson, his lieutenant governor, completed his last year to enable him to pursue his higher political ambitions. Some writers have viewed Rockefeller's cataclysmic change from a liberal serving humanity to designing the harshest drug laws ever passed in the nation was a reflection of his political ambitions.

What role did Hugh Carey's play in building the prison pathway in New York? Carey's redesign of the UDC realized the financial means to support an ever-growing prison population. The final actor, Mario Cuomo, solidified the work of the two governors by establishing a national prison model.

> Former Gov. Hugh Carey, conscious of the surge in inmates, proposed $500 million in new bonds to finance prison construction two years ago, only to have voters turn him down (a similar proposal was approved in neighboring New Jersey).[19]

Executive Intelligence Review critiqued the work of Carey and the Urban Development Corporation.

> Even before the UDC was redesigned by Governor Carey to foster large-scale-developments to benefit real-estate developers well suited to the laundering of illegal drug money, it had the aroma of being a key payoff mechanism for the Democratic Party. Through control of the UDC, Cuomo, and Carey before him, were perfectly situated to receive millions of dollars in kickbacks from contractors.[20]

This corporation never found its way back to the pathway of building housing for the poor. The people's mission was absorbed in political and economic harangue. We can ask a question: Who is watching the pot that freedom, justice, and equality may prevail? Are our times so polluted with the driving force of personal motives that the desire to do the right thing is suffocated into silence?

The Dialogue on the New York $500 Million Bond Issue for Prisons

Members of the New York State Legislature failed to take heed to the statistics before them, outlining drugs as the force, driving the prison population to the heights of mandating a continuous prison construction program. From the 1970s to the 1980s, New York's prison population soared. There was one grave question put before the legislature: Would the legislature and correction officials address the issue related to overcrowded prisons? The New York State Legislature passed a $500 million bond-issue bill to address prison congestion, but would the people of New York vote in favor of this bill to authorize prison construction?

The dialogue below takes place prior to the populace vote. Note the questions, the comments, and the issues some voice as a contributing cause to the rising prison population.

"A New $500 Million Prison Bond Issue, but Why and for What?"

> "Even before they had restored order, officials knew what had triggered last week's uprising at the Westchester County Jail: overcrowding. And with 23,595 prisoners in custody last week and a capacity for only 22,749, New York State authorities were worried, too. But the problem isn't new; during the last decade, the inmate population has doubled, more than matching the growth in state facilities.
>
> "The Legislature responded this month by passing a $500 million bond issue to build new cells and renovate old ones. But it **still needs the voters' approval** and several groups, arguing that more prisons will only breed more prisoners, are campaigning against it."
>
> *The Week in Review* asked Thomas A. Coughlin 3d, Commissioner of the State Department of Correctional

Services, State Senator Ralph J. Marino, chairman of the Crime and Corrections Committee, and Donald J. Newman, Dean of the School of Criminal Justice at the State University of New York at Albany, to discuss prisons and prisoners with Richard J. Meislin, Albany Bureau Chief of *The New York Times*, and Richard Levine, an editor of *The Review*. Excerpts from their conversation follow.

Question: "If we build more prisons, won't we just fill them with more prisoners?"

Mr. Coughlin: "The statement that prisons breed more prisoners has no basis in fact. Seventy percent of the people that left the system in 1974 have not come back. As for whether or not we need more prisons, I think the answer is clearly yes. More people are going to jail for longer periods of time and that's what's raising the prison population."

Mr. Marino: "I agree. I sponsored the bond issue to build more than 4,000 cells and add capacity at the local level. These jails are bulging because the Legislature has passed some tough laws on gun control and on putting away violent felons with mandatory sentences."

Mr. Newman: "I admit that right now we have a very crucial problem of housing, but I think it's a short-range problem. Prisoners and college students are age-cohorts. (As people are predicting a decline in college students) everybody is projecting a decline in the prison-aged group. If we could hold out for a few years, we shouldn't need these prisons. And if we build them, there's a Parkinson's law that we'll have to keep filling them."

Mr. Coughlin: "I have to take issue with that. All of our projections indicate that the prison population will not continue to rise at its current rate. But we have Ossining, which was built in the mid-1800s. We have Attica. Ten years ago the McKay Commission said it shouldn't have more than 1,200 people. Now we've got 1,700 in it.

"We have to make up for this very drastic bulge in population, and we have to look down the road and say we're not going to run a prison system in the 1990's that was started in the mid-1800's. You know, our cells don't have hot and cold running water. The cells at Ossining are 45 feet square. The system needs a renovation."

Mr. Newman: "I have no quarrel with renovation, and if you're going to build new prisons to replace the old ones, I have no problem with that. The problem is that very few prisons have closed."

Mr. Coughlin: "We're on record to close Ossining. It was supposed to (happen) when we were to buy Rikers Island, but it didn't. (State and city officials have been unable to agree on a plan to transfer some facilities on that island) But in the bill to fund the renovations is a cutoff date—1987—when we're going to close Ossining."

*Mr. Marino: "***The problem also is that, whereas we spend $350 million a year to run our prison system, we don't spend one dime to prevent crime.*** Until we start focusing on our youngsters, the spiral will continue.

We are finding out children are committing very serious crimes at very early ages. **If we can interrupt this kind of behavior by giving these children the support services they need, it would go a long way to prevent crime.** Once that child is in a secure institution, the pattern of criminal behavior has been established and it's very difficult to reverse."

Mr. Newman: "We seem to be attacking the crime problem by fiddling with sentencing or building more institutions. I think we're working at the wrong end of the stick. If you look at the chances of children in Harlem or the South Bronx, where they have as much as 50 percent unemployment, fiddling with *sentencing is not going to do anything*."

Mr. Coughlin: "From a philosophical and maybe even naïve perspective, I believe this bond issue will settle this discussion. *If the people want tougher sentencing, better prosecution and jail to go along with that, they're going to vote this bond issue in.* **If this bond issue goes down, then that's a clear indication from the people that they want to start looking at social programs to reduce crime**."

Mr. Newman: "We have two problems—one is the crime rate, the second is the proportion of offenders sent to prison. The crime rate could be steady and you could get more people going into prison. One of the things that's happening is that there is no *monetary incentive for judges in this state to keep the offender in the community.* It's cheaper for the county or the city to send them to the state rather than try to develop community *alternatives which the county would have to pay for.*"

Question: "Why don't you avail yourself of the Supreme Court's recent decision and put two inmates in each cell?"

Mr. Coughlin: "The Supreme Court, in its wisdom, has put a very dangerous thought into some people's minds. This state hasn't double-celled in 50 years. Double-celling is an onerous process. Our average cell is about 48 square feet. The cell size they were talking about in the Supreme Court case was 63 square feet.

"If we were to go to double-celling in the state—which we're not going to do, as far as I'm concerned—we had better be prepared for *a major uprising in the institutions.* It's the type of abrupt policy change that tips institutions over. People have to have space" [nytimes.com].

Mr. Newman: "I think the Supreme Court's decision was a goofy one. It was talking about a new prison. It would be havoc right now in Attica to double-bunk. On the other hand, in the long run it was probably right for the wrong reasons. *If we continue to build prisons, we're going to continue to fill them.*"

Mr. Coughlin: "***In 1971, New York had about 17,000 cells and 12,000 prisoners. For years, there was excess capacity.*** Then *Rockefeller came along and passed the drug laws.* Believe me, those drug laws would have been passed whether or not there was prison space."

Mr. Marino: "*We're sentencing for much too long and we ought to have alternatives, picking out certain crimes and saying,* 'Well, for these crimes you're not going to go to jail. What you will do is work in the community.'

"First-time burglary, robbery that doesn't involve use of a gun, purse-snatching and certainly, the so-called white-collar crimes, which don't involve a violent personality, lend themselves to that type of sentencing. I think if the *Legislature and the Governor started to define those crimes,* perhaps we could take some of the pressure off 'Corruption on a Large Scale.'"

Question: "It's been a decade since Attica. Has enough been done to prevent another uprising?"

Mr. Coughlin: "I don't know. The system has changed markedly since Attica. Some of the changes were good changes; some were too far. There are two events in recent correctional history you have to look at. Attica and the (guards) strike. The correction officers of 1979 were fed up, just the way the inmates in 1971 were fed up. We made changes for the inmates; I think we have to make changes for officers. We have to get a system that is balanced."

Mr. Newman: "The thing that is baffling and miserable is the terrible overcrowding. And the long sentences!"

Mr. Marino: "I think generally we treat our prisoners very humanely in New York State. But you're never going to satisfy inmates because they've lost their freedom. Basically they're very unhappy people. I am scared that,

> despite all we can do in the Legislature and despite all the Commissioner has done and is trying to do, the ingredients are always there for an explosion. I just hope we can get through the summer."[21]

The dialogue outlined many issues and concerns with the New York prison system. To summarize a few: sentencing, lack of screening system to make proper placement, long sentences, and the psychological impact of "*empty jails invite more criminals.*"

WHAT WAS THE RESPONSE OF THE PEOPLE TO THE BOND ISSUE?

Mr. Coughlin was correct. He said there was one of two ways the bond issue could be settled. "If the people want tougher sentencing, better prosecution and jails to go along with that, they're going to vote this bond issue in. If this bond issue goes down, then that's a clear indication from the people that they want to start looking at social programs to reduce crime." In 1981, the people of New York made known their feelings about prisons. The voters defeated the $500 million bond issue for new prison construction.

This message, alone, was a voice from the people resisting prison construction. This $500 million bond issue was defeated during the Hugh Carey administration. He was the governor from January 1, 1975, to December 31, 1982. In 1983, Cuomo became the governor.

> The state comptroller, Edward V. Regan, a Republican, said that Cuomo was defying the wishes of the electorate, which had voted not to spend money on prisons, and that his financing scheme was costly and improper. Bonds

> issued by the Urban Development Corporation carried a higher rate of interest than the state's general-issue bond.[22]

So, the voice of the people was ignored and Mario Cuomo continued his prison building program. Over twelve years as governor, he spent $7 billion on prison expansion. *This dollar sign is greater than what is spent for our children's college education.* Cuomo went on to set a prison model for the nation.

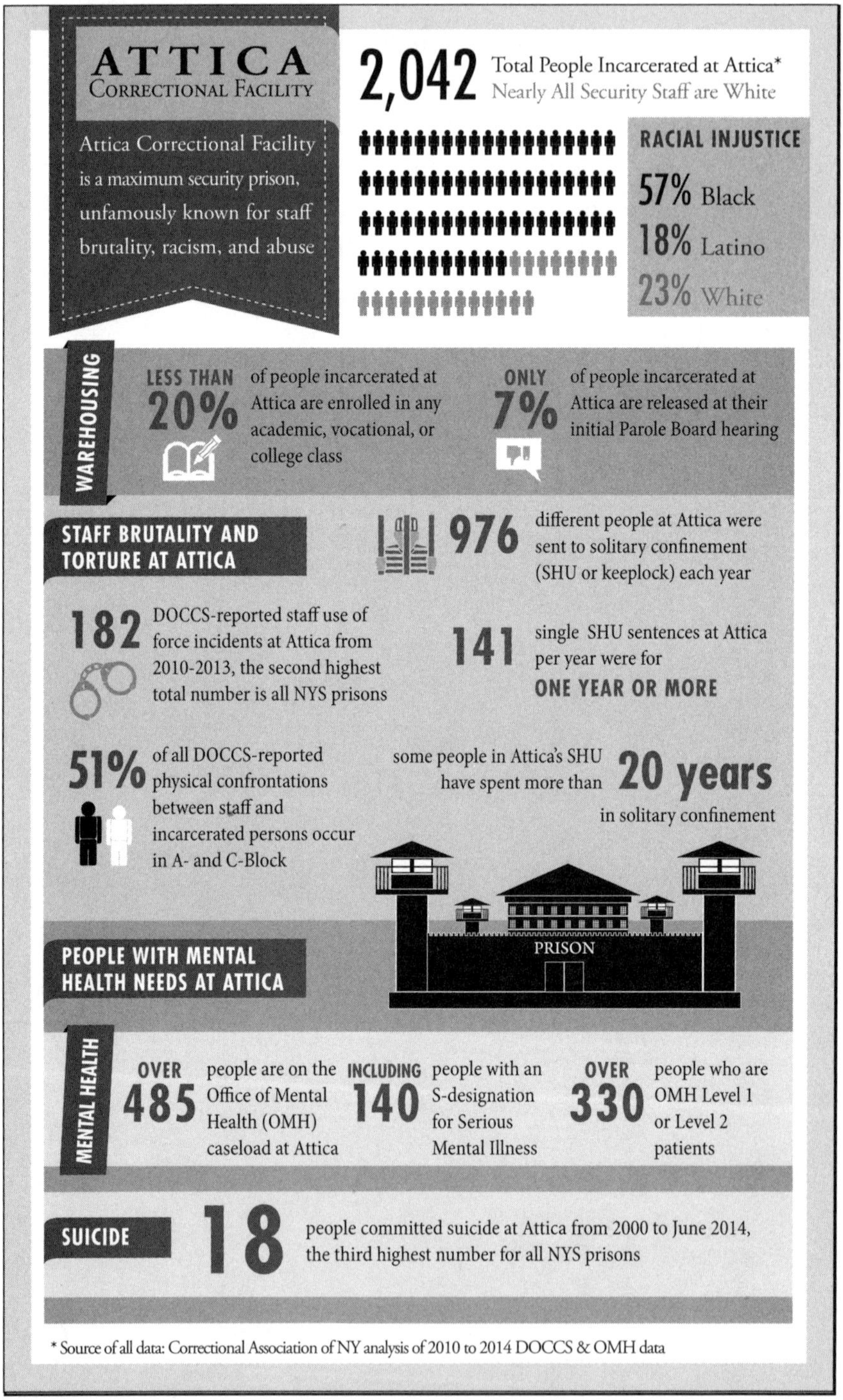
ATTICA
Correctional Facility
Attica Correctional Facility is a maximum security prison, unfamously known for staff brutality, racism, and abuse
2,042 Total People Incarcerated at Attica*
Nearly All Security Staff are White
RACIAL INJUSTICE
57% Black
18% Latino
23% White
WAREHOUSING
LESS THAN 20% of people incarcerated at Attica are enrolled in any academic, vocational, or college class
ONLY 7% of people incarcerated at Attica are released at their initial Parole Board hearing
STAFF BRUTALITY AND TORTURE AT ATTICA
976 different people at Attica were sent to solitary confinement (SHU or keeplock) each year
182 DOCCS-reported staff use of force incidents at Attica from 2010-2013, the second highest total number is all NYS prisons
141 single SHU sentences at Attica per year were for ONE YEAR OR MORE
51% of all DOCCS-reported physical confrontations between staff and incarcerated persons occur in A- and C-Block
some people in Attica's SHU have spent more than 20 years in solitary confinement
PRISON
PEOPLE WITH MENTAL HEALTH NEEDS AT ATTICA
MENTAL HEALTH
OVER 485 people are on the Office of Mental Health (OMH) caseload at Attica
INCLUDING 140 people with an S-designation for Serious Mental Illness
OVER 330 people who are OMH Level 1 or Level 2 patients
SUICIDE
18 people committed suicide at Attica from 2000 to June 2014, the third highest number for all NYS prisons
* Source of all data: Correctional Association of NY analysis of 2010 to 2014 DOCCS & OMH data

SOLITARY CONFINEMENT

New York State Prisons

More than **4,500** People Are in Solitary in NYS Prisons Today

95% of disciplinary hearings result in guilty findings

DOCCS imposes over **14,000** SHU sentences each year

8,000 sentences of 3 or more months

3,900 sentences of 6 or more months

MENTAL HEALTH CRISIS IN NEW YORK STATE PRISONS

24% of suicides occurred in the SHU.

NYS prison suicide rate is **59%** higher than national average for incarcerated persons.

From 2010-2013 in the 220-bed therapeutic alternative to solitary units for people with serious mental illness:

300 people received **6** months SHU time

148 people received **35** months SHU time

35 people received **5** months SHU time

8 people received **10** months SHU time

Over **700** people on the OMH caseload are still in Special Housing Units each day. That's **19%** of all people in SHU.

RACIAL DISPARITIES IN NEW YORK STATE PRISONS

New York State Population by Race

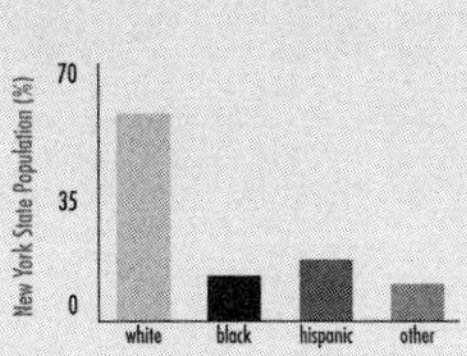

New York State Prison Population by Race

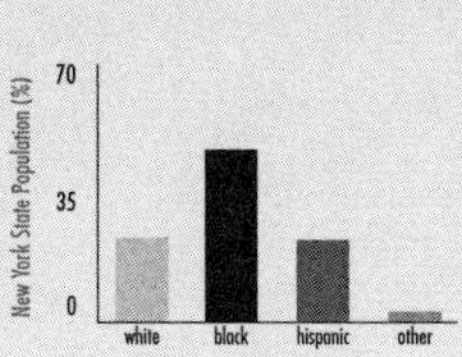

New York State Long Term Solitary Confinement Population by Race

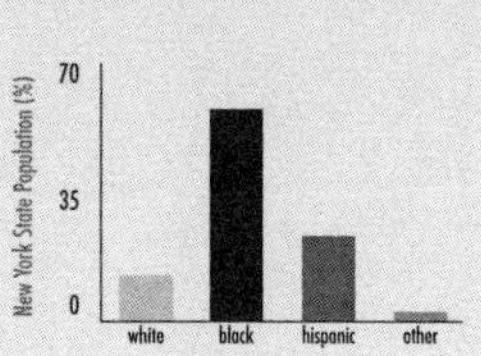

Source: DOCCS and OMH Data

CHAPTER 8

Mario M. Cuomo: A Prison Model for the Nation

Starting in 1983, the Cuomo Administration built over 33,000 prison spaces, more than the number built by all previous administrations combined.

The Correctional Association of New York, February 1995.

Mario M. Cuomo was installed the 52nd governor of New York on January 1, 1983. He gave his state address where he was installed as governor. His response to the Rockefeller's drug legislation was simple. Rockefeller laid the foundation with his drug laws. What were the results of Rockefeller's drug legislation? His drug laws had doubled the inmate population in New York prisons.

A week after Cuomo's installation as governor, the Sing Sing prison riot erupted. Sing Sing was an aging prison site located upstate in Ossining, New York. This facility was founded in 1828, known as Ossining Correctional Facility. "It is a maximum security prison operated by the New York State Department of Corrections and Community Supervision in the village of Ossining. It is located about 30 miles (50 km) north of New York on the east bank of the Hudson River." The name was derived from the name of a Native American nation, "Sinck Sinck," from whom the land was purchased in 1685.[1]

Cuomo was governor of New York from 1983 to 1994. He constructed more prisons than any of his predecessors. The people sent a message to the governor not to build prisons, but Mario Cuomo circumvented the voice of the people by finding alternative means to continue his prison building program. In one such example, Cuomo diverted the state's Urban Development Corporation designated for building housing for the poor to construct his prison program.

Cuomo graduated from St. Johns University in Queens, New York, and earned his law degree from St. John's School of Law in 1956. Earning a law degree is one thing, but having someone to open a door to provide growth and experience can nurture the career of an individual to fruition. Hugh Carey and the former governor were friends. In fact, "Governor Carey was the first one to bring Cuomo into government." Both men were graduates of St. John's University.

After completing law school, Cuomo began his work as a "confidential legal assistant to Judge Adrian P. Burke of the New York State Court of Appeals, the highest court in New York. After gaining some legal experience, he entered private law practice in 1958.[2]

In 1972, Cuomo was called upon by Mayor John Lindsay to resolve the Forest Hills housing controversy. He engaged in community work assigned to him by Mayor John Lindsay.

> Cuomo first became widely known in New York City in the late 1960s when he represented "The Corona Fighting 69," a group of 69 home-owners from the Queens neighborhood of Corona, who were threatened with displacement by the city's plan to build a new high school. He later represented another Queens residents group, the Kew Gardens-Forest Hills Committee on Urban Scale, who opposed Samuel J. LeFrak's housing proposal adjacent to Willow Lake in Queens. In 1972, Cuomo became known beyond New York City

> when Mayor John Lindsay appointed him to conduct an inquiry and mediate a dispute over low-income public housing slated for the upper-middle-class neighborhood of Forest Hills.[3]

During the 1974 New York election, Rep. Hugh Carey and State Senator Mary Anne Krupsak became governor and lieutenant governor. Krupsak highlighted her career as becoming the first woman to be lieutenant governor of New York. Hugh Carey was installed as the 51st governor of New York on January 1, 1975. Cuomo failed to win the seat to be lieutenant governor, but Carey remembered his protégée and appointed him secretary of state in 1975.[4]

Cuomo wasted no time laying the cobblestones to advance his career. In 1977, he unsuccessfully sought the office as mayor of New York City.

> The New York City mayoral election of 1977 occurred Tuesday, November 8, 1977. Incumbent mayor Abraham Beame, a Democrat, was challenged by five other Democrats, including Representative Ed Koch, New York Secretary of State Mario Cuomo, and feminist activist and former Representative Bella Abzug for the Democratic nomination. Koch won the initial vote in the Democratic primary as well as a runoff vote held between him and Cuomo. In the general election, Koch beat Cuomo, who ran on the Liberal Party ticket, and Roy M. Goodman, who ran on the Republican ticket.[5]

What was the political relationship between Mary Anne Krupsack, Lieutenant Governor of New York, and Governor Hugh Carey? Krupsack served a full term as lieutenant governor but decided not to run with Carey in his bid for a second term. Instead, she ran as an independent candidate for governor.

> Elected with Governor Hugh Carey, Krupsak became upset with how Carey treated her in office and felt she was not given enough to do. After committing to run for a second term with Carey in 1978, Krupsak decided to withdraw from the ticket and instead challenge Carey for the Democratic nomination for governor.[6]

Krupsak was unsuccessful in her bid for governor, but she had set a historical record as being the first female to serve as lieutenant governor of New York.

Cuomo was elected lieutenant governor during Carey's second term as governor of New York, serving from January 1, 1979, to December 31, 1982. Carey paved the political pathway for his rising star. Cuomo benefitted from this political mentorship from Hugh Carey.

Cuomo's Call for Prison Construction, not Border Security

New York

There was a reorganization of the court system prior to Cuomo's administration. Upon taking office, Cuomo inherited the responsibility of making court appointments. He had the opportunity to make seven or more appointments during his administration.[7]

1. Richard D. Simons, 1983–1997
2. Fritz W. Alexander, 1985–1992
3. Vito J. Titone, 1985–1998
4. Steward F. Hancock Jr., 1986–1993
5. Joseph W. Bellacosa, 1987–2000
6. George Bundy Smith, 1992–2006

7. Howard A. Levine, 1993–2002
8. Carmen Beauchamp, 1994–2012

The New York Court of Appeals is the highest court in the State of New York. The Court of Appeals consists of seven judges: the Chief Judge and six associate judges who are appointed by the Governor to 14-year terms. The Chief Judge of the Court of Appeals also heads administration of the state's court system and, thus, is also known as the Chief Judge of the State of New York.

The Criminal justice system consists of three main parts: 1) *Legislative* (create laws), 2) *adjudication* (courts), and 3) *corrections* (jails, prisons, probation and parole, criminal penalties and rehabilitation efforts—means of maintaining the rule of law within society—to effect public and social order).

The criminal justice system had the sole responsibility of sentencing inmates to prisons. The mentally ill were assigned without regard to their state of being. The illiterate were lumped in the same category. The addicted population was rarely referred to alternative programs for services to address their needs. Governor Cuomo expanded the prison population three times as much as all governors combined. Was this a need, or was this a farce to introduce a prison industry using humans as a product to saturate the wealth of a few to engender a new economic industry, in a democracy?

In his 1987 New York State of the State Address, "Cuomo boasted of putting 10,000 'dangerous felons' behind bars." Governor Cuomo's foremost plan was to expand prison construction. He wasted no time applying psychology to initiate this plan. *The New York Times* painted a frightening scene to emphasize the need for prison expansion.

Elizabeth Kolbert's article, "As Inmates Pour In, Cuomo Plans 3,000 Beds in Prison Gymnasiums," on June 3, 1989 dramatizes the need for prison expansion. Inmates were crowded in a gymnasium because there were no cells to accommodate them. The scene sent a message to the New York State Legislature that, to avoid unsafe conditions, they needed to get busy writing legislation to alleviate this dangerous situation. Soon the voices rang out, debating the need for building more prisons.

> To cope with an influx of almost 3,000 inmates over the summer, New York State will begin housing prisoners in gymnasiums starting next week, Gov. Mario M. Cuomo said today.
>
> State officials said the surge in the prison population, which is expected to grow to almost 50,000 over the next few months, was a result of record numbers of arrests for drug-related crimes.[8]

The true scenario made the point real. To deprive a population in this situation could cause a prison provocation, that is, to deprive regular inmates from having access to recreational activities, which would normally take place in the gymnasium. Of course, lawmakers viewed this as a serious threat that could ignite some prison unrest. This could also serve as a psychological ploy to send the message to the New York State Legislature to emphasize the need for prison expansion and to enable the think tank's idea to come to fruition. Building one facility would set the economic mode into a continuous drive for a steady construction building plan

The economic prison design for cheap labor in some counties is so real until they depend upon New York courts to provide assignment and sentences within a definite time frame.

> The prison system is also under strain because New York's highest court ruled last fall that the state was legally obligated to take custody within ten days after they are sentenced. Counties work with jury system to expedite sentencing. Westchester and Suffolk, and the

> state's Sheriff Association have sued the state for failing to transfer prisoners quickly enough.[9]

The sentencing process operates as a business to fulfill a labor schedule. The inmates are hurdled in and lined up to fulfill the economic demand. *There were more than 1,600 so called "state ready" prisoners—900 of them in New York City—who are awaiting transfer from local jails to state penitentiaries.*[10] Specified communities were designated to benefit from the prison labor force. Ironically, these inmates were lured into prisons by drugs to serve as a cheap labor force. While these inmates served time, their families were left behind, to fight anyway they could for survival in urban communities.

New York State Legislative Debate

The voices of the New York State Legislature opened the prison debate. Is there truly a need to expand prisons? Are there other methods to pursue without turning the wheel for prison expansion? The lawmakers were divided. Some Republicans were in favor of expansion, while some Democrats searched means and ways to use alternatives to prevent growth and expansion of prisons. The partisan debate was filled with disagreement and varying ideology.[11]

A curious question to ask is what is the primary factor contributing to the rapid prison growth? There were some responses. "State officials said the surge in the prison population, which is expected to grow to almost 50,000 over the next few months, was a result of record numbers of arrests for drug-related crimes."[12]

What was the inferred meaning of the above statement? Was there a belief that the rising prison population was drug related? If so, why?

Finance

How would New York finance prison expansion? Voices in the legislative chamber reverberated. The dialogue covered the gamut of the plan before them. "The plan is expected to cost $60 million, and administration officials said they did not know where the money would come from. Since the state is financially strapped, they said they would probably have to delay other projects to finance the plan."[13]

Need Factor/Cost Factor

"The Governor stressed that the move was temporary, and said legislative leaders had agreed to 'authorize sufficient expansion in state prison cells to allow replacement of the temporary housing with permanent beds.' Four new prisons would be needed to house 3,000 inmates."[14]

Legislative Response

But legislative officials said, while they had agreed to try to provide permanent housing for all inmates, they had not agreed on a specific number of new cells. Privately, however, several officials said they expected at least four new prisons to be built at a total cost of more than $250 million. Sites have not been chosen. The announcement came amid intense negotiations between the Cuomo administration and the State Legislature over the state's acute prison overcrowding. State prisons are now at 114 percent of capacity.[15]

Did any one make an assessment of the factors that swelled the prisons?

The prison growth had remained in a natural mode until 1973. From this time to the 1980s, the prison system spiraled out of control. The problem fit within the boundaries of statistical analysis. The birth year of prison expansion in 1970s revealed a contrast of prison growth in the 1980s. In 1982, *Warden Wilson J. Walters* made a true comparison of the prison growth pattern.

> I came here in July 1980 when the population was 1,400. January 1982, A and B Blocks were full and we were running over 2,100 inmates. I have no control over intake, outtake, or how long they stay once they come here.
>
> We replaced a new lieutenant every one and a half weeks for all of 1982. Sergeants turned over at about the same rate, and sometimes we had 60 to 100 new officers every two weeks.[16]

How could such a drastic population growth thrive within the nation without accessing the true cause for public taxes to guide the state into a prison building industry?

The 1980s signaled the decade where prisons began their incorporation. The process was masterminded in this decade to have prisons placed on the stock market—corporations using human products as a cheap labor force.

Governor Rockefeller called a press conference in January 1973 to introduce his new political stance, "Get tough on crime." As referenced earlier, he set the foundation for prison growth with his Rockefeller Drug Laws. His political ambitions were his driving passion. With Rockefeller's groundwork securely laid, Governor Cuomo commenced his prison construction industry in 1983. There were varying degrees of political thought about whether the Empire State should partake in prison expansion as in the June 3, 1989, scenario penned by Elizabeth Kolbert, special to *The New York Times*. Some legislators discussed alternative plans.

Alternative Programs

What alternatives did New York legislators discuss? Several democratic members of the legislature preferred prison options. They discussed alternative means to obviate prison expansion. They wanted to end the prison-building program.

Some legislators voiced a need for alternatives. The "*shock incarceration*" program was highlighted. This program was designed for the nonviolent inmate. With this particular tactic, the individual would be under electronic monitoring while engaged in a work-release program. This monitoring situation allowed the inmate to wear a battery-powered bracelet with transmittal signals to a telephone-connected box. This box is equipped to alert police or probation officers if the inmate moves too far away.[17]

Another system, known as *the automatic-dialing machine calls the prisoner's home at random times and matches the voice that answers to the prisoner's recorded voiceprint.*[18] These and other alternatives to prison expansion were voiced by some Democrats. The Democratic-controlled Assembly leaders *argued that putting more people in state prisons has done little to reduce crime. They wanted to see fewer prisons and more alternative programs, including one that would let addicted prisoners have reduced sentences if they accept drug treatment.*[19]

The New York Republican-controlled senate had a different perspective on how offenders should be punished. In their perception, those alternative programs mentioned were just not substantial. They wanted criminals to be housed behind the prison wall. They were reluctant to alternative methods. There was no need to handle prisoners with a gentle hand. They were solidified in their approach and demanded prison expansion to accommodate violators of the law. Christopher Mega, Brooklyn Republican, chairman of the Senate Crime and Correction Committee, said, "People who want to expand 'shock' are looking at pie in the sky."[20]

It is quite interesting that despite the voices, the New York State Legislature did not order stats to make a comparative analysis of why the prison population was soaring out of control in one decade—from 1973 to 1983.

> **Charles Booth**, a spokesman for the corrections officers union, said, *Naturally, we're not pleased, but there's nothing we can do. What we need is new officers darned fast as we can get them.* State criminal justice officials have raised alarms about overcrowding for months. It is the inevitable consequence, they said, of the increasing number of drug-related arrests and convictions from stepped-up law enforcement efforts like New York City's Tactical Narcotics Teams program.[21]

The Hit Twice Tactical Narcotics Teams (TNT) was a visible demonstrable response to the problem.

> **Hit Twice by T.N.T.** program, in which undercover officers saturate an area and try to arrest every drug buyer and seller they can, has put a particular strain on the state prison system, said James Flateau, a spokesman for the state's Corrections Department. The program has led to scores of repeat felony convictions, and a state prison sentence—a sentence of one year or more—is mandatory after a second conviction.[22]

However, there existed a greater need to go beyond Band-Aid treatments to explore ways to discover and solve the derivation of the problem related to prison congestion.

The idea of the 1970s think tank manifested itself and packaged an economic plan into a model to be shared across the nation. Prisons were being anchored and accelerated to operate as an economic industry.

Upstate growth counties supported by criminal justice system

Two counties have benefited from prison labor in New York State, namely, Suffolk and Westchester counties. These two counties have had access to prison construction programs as well as creating jobs for their communities. "The plan announced today calls for up to 3,000 inmates to live in gyms at 14 medium-security prisons. Each prisoner would have his own cubicle. Up to 900 guards would be hired."[23] The June 3, 1989, scenario had a two-fold objective: to grow prisons and to provide jobs.

The eco-political prison plan works hand in hand to provide economic growth for upstate counties at the expense of using prison labor. The plan is so solidified until the counties received legislative support to ensure prison construction without delay. "Flateau said today that there were more than 1,600 so-called 'state-ready' prisoners—900 of them in New York City—who are awaiting transfer from local jails to state penitentiaries." Who is building downstate urban communities to prevent another population of youth to be lost to the prison industry?[24]

Destroying one community to build another

The prison-building program developed rural communities in upstate New York. Communities that were affected by the financial downswing of the economy in the 1980s looked to innovative means to restore their economy. The prison-construction program was an answer to some of these problems. Prison construction brought employment to many in these communities. The staffing of these prisons provided additional jobs for these communities. Ironically, these upstate communities were being restored at the expense of destroying urban communities. The Correctional Association of New York says, "About 75% have children. About 70% are nonviolent offenders." *Since the 1970s, the ratio of women in prison has increased twelvefold.* The 1980s crack academic played havoc with the black family. Who would account for the lives destroyed, the children left without parents, and the devastation thrust upon them with the drug–arrest–prison scenario?

Mario M.Cuomo's Model for the Nation

The Correctional Association of New York statistics describes Mario M. Cuomo and his work with building prisons. "Starting in 1983, the Cuomo Administration built over 33,000 prison spaces, more than the number built by all previous administrations combined (February 1995)." In a very brief time, Mario Cuomo had established a model to permeate the nation. Ann Richardson, the 45th and second female governor of Texas (January 17, 1995, defeated by George W. Bush in 1994) was so influenced by Cuomo's prison model that she wasted no time building a prison model for her state. California emulated the model and has become the largest prison state in the nation. Cuomo was governor for four years, but his prison model continue to rise across the nation—in a democracy.

The scenario is plain and clear. Drop drugs in the black community, use drugs as a bait to incarcerate, and use inmates to resemble old-time slavery in America (1661–1865) to operate a cheap labor force for corporations on the backs of blacks. The *modus operandi* is simple—devise and design laws to perpetuate a prison–industrial complex.

CHAPTER 9

Nonviolent Offenders Responsible for Prison Growth

Do we rehabilitate or do we incarcerate—that is the question?

> *California now has the biggest prison system in the –Western industrialized world, a system 40 percent bigger than the Federal Bureau of Prisons. The state holds more inmates in its jails and prisons than do France, Great Britain, Germany, Japan, Singapore, and the Netherlands combined.*
>
> Eric Schlosser

What is the real problem related to prison expansion? Eric Schlosser does not hesitate to explore the factors contributing to prison expansion across the nation. He is baffled at the growth in nonviolent population. While the violent population remains in a natural growth mode, the nonviolent population spirals out of control to necessitate a continuous prison-building enterprise.[1]

The New York model has spread to Texas and other parts of the nation. Eric Schlosser accentuates how the nonviolent prison model has gone viral while the violent prisoner population remains at a normal growth pattern. What two questions should we ask? First, do prisons rehabilitate, or do they incarcerate for profit? Second, why is the nonviolent population spiraling out of control?

The prison-construction building plan

Schlosser has studied the trends of prison expansion in California which serves as a scoreboard to understand the national prison-construction plan. Schlosser sheds insight on the growth pattern in California.

> Inmates were placed in New Folsom, while it was still under construction. The prison was badly overcrowded even before it was finished, in 1987. It has at times housed more than 300 inmates in its gymnasiums. New Folsom—like old Folsom, and like the rest of the California prison system—now operates a roughly double its intended capacity. *Over the past twenty years* the State of California has built twenty-one new prisons, added thousands of cells to existing facilities, and increased its inmate population eightfold.[2]

The evidence in statistics identifies "drug bait" as the leading factor contributing to the increase in the prison population.

> Nonviolent offenders have been responsible for most of that increase. The number of drug offenders imprisoned in the state today is more than twice the number of inmates who were imprisoned for all crimes in 1978. California now has the biggest prison system in the Western industrialized world, a system 40 percent bigger than the Federal Bureau of Prisons. **The state holds more inmates in its jails and prisons than do France,**

> **Great Britain, Germany, Japan, Singapore, and the Netherlands combined.** The California Department of Corrections predicts that at the current rate of expansion, barring a court order that forces a release of prisoners, it will run out of room eighteen months from now. Simply to remain at double capacity the state will need to open at least one new prison a year, every year, for the foreseeable future.[3]

How can the nation categorize the expanse of its incarceration?

As we observe the statistics, there are varying layers of prison growth.

> Today the United States has approximately 1.8 million people behind bars; about 100,000 in federal custody, million in state custody, and 600,000 in local jails. Prisons hold inmates convinced of federal or state crimes; jails hold people awaiting trial or serving short sentences. The United States now imprisons more people other country in the world—perhaps half a million more than Communist China. The American inmate population has grown so large that it is difficult to comprehend: imagine the combined populations of Atlanta, St. Louis, Pittsburgh, Des Moines, and Miami behind bars.[4]

We, the people in a democracy, must ask the resounding question: What caused the increase in the prison population?

> State officials said the surge in the prison population, which is expected to grow to almost 50,000 over the

> next few months, was a result of record numbers of the Drug Enforcement Agency (DEA) within the Justice Department.[5]

If drugs were the issue for the increase in the prison population, it would have been more reasonable for officials to focus on what could be done with drugs in understanding the growth in the prison population.

DEMOCRACY: SECURING THE BORDERS OR LEAVING THE NATION'S CHILDREN VULNERABLE TO DRUGS!

The age-old question is resounded: Will we protect the nation's children in a democracy, or will we increase the cash in our wallets? What is most important in the 21st century?

Charles Rangel of New York voiced his concern about the impact drugs would have upon the nation's children.

> May 17, 1988, Rep Charles Rangel (D-NY) Op-ed in the New York Times titled "Legalize Drugs? Not on your life." He chastises President Reagan for not doing enough to battle illegal narcotics and calls crack "the worst drug epidemic in our history."[6]

The crack epidemic of the 1980s wrought havoc with the African American community because this drug affected the female population. This designed drug played a major role in destroying black children and families across the nation. While incarceration increased, family life decreased and mandated a need to conjure ways to address the various issues of displaced children—children with no one to care for them and no positive role models. The repercussion from drugs and incarceration destroyed the ladder for many black children. Drug signs were plastered in black communities near schools designated as a "Drug Free Zone." The restriction limit was 25 feet. How ironic? A city in the nation of the free, the most powerful nation in the world, and drug marketeering cannot be stopped!

Instead of voicing an opinion for prison construction, there was a visible need to devise methods and plans to secure the borders to protect schools and communities across the nation.

July 1988. Jessie Jackson, presidential candidate

> Rev. Jesse Jackson gives speech at Democratic National Convention in Atlanta, GA, and calls for real war on drugs, demanding reforms to interdiction efforts. "You can't just 'say no,'" Jackson tells Democrats. He suggests that "bankers" and other high-placed individuals are enabling the drug trade and blames the drug epidemic on poverty. Jackson suggests that the federal government hasn't made a sincere effort to stop the drug trade. "We must end the scourge on the American culture."[7]

To further understand the sudden rise in the prison population, there is a need to look at the various tactics used to grow the inmate population.

The increased number of drug-related arrests shows a direct correlation to the increased police servicing particular areas. In New York, there was the TNT, known as the Tactical Narcotics Teams program. Members of this team went undercover to saturate specified areas. James Flateau, a spokesman for the New York Corrections Department, registered his opinion of the New York TNT.

> The program has led to scores of repeat felony convictions, and a state prison sentence—a sentence of one year or more—mandatory after a second conviction.[8]

An important question to ask would be, has there been a cooperative effort with all government forces to secure borders to reduce the flow of drugs into the country? Where is the snowball? Drugs are used to increase the inmate population, yet only the criminal justice system has a monopoly for sentencing! Why not a joint effort with other services to participate in screening inmates prior to sentencing? This process would eliminate the misplacement of inmates, consequently lower the prison rate, and provide adequate services to this population.

CHAPTER 10

Prisons on the Stock Market

The Big Question: Who Benefits from the Prison Industry?

They don't have to worry about strikes or paying unemployment insurance, vacations or comp time. All of their workers are full-time, and never arrive late or are absent because of family problems; moreover, if they don't like the pay of 25 cents an hour and refuse to work, they are locked up in isolation cells.

VICKY PELAEZ

The idea conjured in the 1970s was realized in the 1980s and is flourishing in the 21st century. It was conceived by a think tank seeking to grow prisons into an industrial economy, using inmates as the commodity. This section of this book will focus on how these inmates are used as an economic product.

During the period of American slavery (1661–1865), the plantation owners devised a system to fulfill their economic plan. The slaves were divided into domestic and field servants. The domestic workers of a lighter hue worked in the slave master's "big house." The darker complexion slaves worked in the fields from "kin to can't," from the time they could see to the time they could not see.

The field servants performed the hardest work for the longest length of time. The maintenance of slaves was kept at minimum. The men received two pair of pants, shirt, jacket, and a pair of shoes. The women were given a few yards of calico cloth. The children wore shirt gowns and did not receive shoes until they had reached working age. The food diet consisted of fat back, corn mush, and molasses. There were rules to govern the lives of slaves. These rules were compiled as the Slave Codes. These laws prohibited the slaves from acquiring an education. Anyone caught trying to teach a slave to read or write was severely punished and set forth to be an example for other slaves who may have been contemplating modeling that behavior. The "Codes" were a set of mean and cruel laws written to instill fear in the hearts and minds of the slaves as well as to denigrate their character as human beings. This caption of slavery was more than a century ago.

How do the prison–industrial magnates compare to old American slavery?

The motive of low maintenance and high profits in 21st century prison industry *mimics the plantation system in America*. The goal of these prison giants is one thing—the highest profit for the lowest cost, is another. Vicky Pelaez makes a true economic comparison of American slavery in "The Prison Industry in the United States: Big Business or a New Form of Slavery?" "For the tycoons who have invested in the prison industry, it has been like finding **a pot of gold**. They don't have to worry about strikes or paying unemployment insurance, vacations or comp time. All of their workers are full-time, and never arrive late or are absent because of family problems; moreover, if they don't like the pay of 25 cents an hour and refuse to work, they are locked up in isolation cells."[1]

The *drug bait* and the magnetized police force have successfully filled the prison cells to realize a cheap labor force. The daily quotas of these officers maintain the cells to fulfill the goal of the prison industry. "Corporate stockholders who make money off prisoners' lobby for longer sentences, in order to expand their workforce."[2]

The system is so cruel and inhumane; this prison industry is like a replication of Hitler's model wherein human beings were housed in forced slave labor and concentration camps. Since we have alluded to the misuse of humans in Germany, let me use the correct terminology for this labor. The people who were economically exploited during World War II were not considered humans; they were classified as *untermenschen*. In *Operation Paperclip*, Annie Jacobsen applied the terminology to describe how people were treated as subhuman. "In the case of the handicapped and the mentally ill, the *Untermenschen* theory was used by German doctors and technicians to justify genocide." In our context of prison industry analysis, the inmates were treated as a commodity to insure a cheap labor force.[3]

The United States—A Prison Nation

We reviewed the concepts of freedom and independence in chapter three with Alfred W. and Ruth G. Blumrosen referencing their book, *Slave Nation: How Slavery United the Colonies and Sparked the American Revolution.* **These authors, prophetically, defines the character of the nation when they write, "The price of freedom from England was bondage for African slaves in America. America would be a slave nation." From the 17th century to the 21st century, the African American has been an economic slave—from plantation to prisons. Ms. Pelaez shares the portfolio of modern day slavery that drives the prison economic market in America. The cheap labor force of inmates wields the wheels on Wall Street.**

Pelaez shares statistics on how prisons in America have been growing exponentially.

The United States Prism on Prisons

The United States:

- Has 25% of the world's prison population, but only 5% of the world's people, a half million more than China
- From less than 300,000 inmates in **1972**, the jail population grew to two million by 2000
- In **1990** it was one million
- Ten years ago there were only five private prisons in the nation with a population of 2000 inmates
- Now there are 100, with 62,000 inmates
- The coming decade is expected to rise to 360,000[4]

There are basic and frightening questions to ask and, more importantly, to which we must receive answers. Where was the *Woman of Blind Justice* when the prison industry was being incorporated in a democracy? Where are the *checks and balances of our United States Constitution* which supposedly oversees the balance of justice in the nation? Why was the prison industry permitted to move so aggressively, without being stopped by the hands of justice? Within one decade, the prison population increased by one million. Where are the Congressmen who have constituency across the nation to represent the scales of justice? Is our system of democracy on a holiday, or is it dead and buried?

Why are there so many prisons?

Vicky Pelaez sheds some insight.

- The private contracting of prisoners for work provide incentives to lock people up
    - Corporate stockholders make money off prisoners
        - Lobby for longer sentences [inflate laws for their advantage]
        - Longer sentences expand their workforce [Driving-force]

- Progressive Labor Party: "The system feeds itself"
    - "The prison industry of being an imitation of Nazi Germany with respect to ***forced slave labor*** and concentration camps."
    - The prisons are the fastest growing complex in USA[5]

Let us continue to examine the **gold mine** of the prison–industrial complex to understand how the prison inmates are used as a cheap labor force. There are no brakes to stop this industrial machinery, so it seems. It has been defined as being "one of the fastest-growing industries in the United States with its investors located on Wall Street." The industry is well organized and connected.[6]

> This multimillion-dollar industry has its own trade exhibitions, conventions, websites, and mail-order/Internet catalogs. It also has direct advertising campaigns, architecture companies, construction companies, investment houses on Wall Street, plumbing, supply companies, food supply companies, armed security, padded cells in a large variety of colors.[7]

From the 1970s to the 21st century, the prison industry has been permitted to thrive in a democracy.

Where is Ms. Lady Justice? Where is the US Congress?

The prison industry has a continuous supply of inmates to feed the wheels of corporations. How are these inmates used to make a profit for the prison economy? There are no limits. The inmates are assigned various jobs to fulfill contracts for multiple businesses and corporations.

"The federal prison industry produces 100% of all military helmets, ammunition belts, bullet-proof vests, ID tags, shirts, pants, tents, bags, and canteens." Besides providing for the military, these prison workers "supply 98% of the entire market for equipment assembly services; 93% of paints and paintbrushes; 92% of stove assembly; 46% of office furniture." Believe it or not, but the prison inmates "are even raising seeing-eye dogs for blind people."[8]

Pelaez and La Prensa are so thorough in their research that one may need a pair of 3-D glasses to believe their statistical reports.

Its investors are on Wall Street.

Jailing persons of nonviolent crimes perpetuate labor supply for Wall Street corporations

- The multimillion-dollar industry has its own trade exhibitions, conventions, websites, and mail-order/Internet catalogs
    - Direct advertising campaigns
    - Architecture companies ON WALL STREET
    - Construction companies
    - Investment houses
    - Plumbing, supply companies, food supply companies, armed security, and padded cells in a large variety of colors[9]
- The federal prison industry produces:
    - 100% military helmets
    - Ammunition belts
    - Bullet-proof vests
    - ID tags
    - Shirts
    - Pants
    - Tents, bags and canteens
- Prison workers supply:

- 98% of the entire market for equipment assembly services
- 93% of paints and paintbrushes
- 92% of stove assembly
- 46% of body armor
- 36% of home appliances
- 30% of headphones/microphones/speakers
- 21% of office furniture
- Airplane parts
- Medical supplies
- Prisoners are even raising seeing-eye dogs for blind people[10]

WHO IS INVESTING IN THE PRISON–INDUSTRIAL COMPLEX?

- 37 states have legalized the contracting of prison labor by private corporations—mounting their operations inside state prisons
  - The cream of US corporate society
    - IBM
    - Boeing
    - Motorola
    - Microsoft
    - AT&T
    - Wireless
    - Texas Instruments
    - Dell
    - Compaq
    - Honeywell
    - Hewlett-Packard
    - Nortel
    - Lucent Technologies
    - 3Com
    - Intel
    - Northern Telecom
    - TWA
    - Nordstrom's
    - Revlon
    - Macy's
    - Pierre Cardin
    - Target Stores[11]

Business and corporate profits

- These businesses are excited about this economic boom generated by prison labor
    - Between 1980 and 1994, profits increased from $392 million to $1.31 billion
        - Inmates in states penitentiaries generally receive minimum wage
            - In Colorado, they get about $2.00 per hour and will work under the minimum stature
            - In privately run prisons, they receive as little as 17 cents per hour for a maximum of 6 hours a day, the equivalent of $20 per month
            - The highest paying private prison is CCA (Correctional Corporate America)
            - In Tennessee inmates receive .50 cents per hour for what is classified as skilled positions. They can earn $1.25 an hour for eight hours, sometimes overtime, and can send from $200–$300 a month home.
- "Work designed for third world labor markets flourishes in USA prisons"
        - "[Former] Oregon State Representative Kevin Manniz recently urged Nike to cut its production in Indonesia and bring it to his state, telling the shoe manufacturer that 'there won't be any transportation costs; we're offering you competitive prison labor (here).'"[12]

Privatizing prisons paved the way for corporations by Pelaez and LaPrenza

- Privatizing boomed under the government of Ronald Reagan and Bush Sr., but reached its height in 1990 under William Clinton, when Wall Street stocks were selling like hotcakes.
    - "Clinton's program for cutting the federal workforce resulted in the Justice Departments contracting of private prison corporations for the incarceration of undocumented workers and high security inmates."
- Private prisons are the biggest business in the prison–industry complex
    - 18 corporations guard 10,000 prisoners in 27 states
- Private prisons receive a guaranteed amount of money for each prisoner, independent of what it costs to maintain each one
    - Russell Boraas, private prison administrator in Virginia, says, *"the secret to low operating costs is having a minimal number of guards for the maximum number of prisoners."*
    - The CCA (Correctional Corporate of America) has an ultra-modern prison in Lawrenceville, Virginia, where
        - 5 guards on dayshift
        - 2 at night watch over 750 prisoners
        - Reduction of time for good behavior [an incentive][13]

As you continue to do reading and research, use the articles below to commend these dedicated writers and historians for critiquing our democracy to make real the promise for all citizens.

References

Albany Times Union, Prisons? Rural towns want in: Lots of competition upstate for 8,650-bed jail expansion proposal, undated.

Bob Bergland, Rural Mental Health – *Report of the National Action Commission on the Mental Health of Rural Americans*, Journal of Cultural Community Psychology, vol. 9, no.2, 1988.

Bureau of Justice Statistics, "Lifetime Likelihood of Going to a State or Federal Prison, 1997.

Elizabeth Kolbert, Special to the New York Times, June 3, 1989, *As Inmates Pour In, Cuomo Plans 3,000 Beds in Prison Gymnasiums.*

Eric Schlosser, *The Prison-Industrial Complex*, The Atlantic

Fox Butterfield, *Number of Inmates Reaches Record 1.8 million*, The New York Times, Mar. 15, 1999.

Rose and Clear Report (1998), Dina Rose and Todd Clear of the University of Florida, "Incarceration, Social Capital, and Crime: Implications for Social Disorganization Theory." Criminology, Vol. 36, no. 3, 1998.

Tracy Huling, Washington, C.C., *Prisons as a Growth Industry* in

Rural America: An Exploratory Discussion of the Effects on Young African American Men in the Inner Cities. April 15–16, 1999.

Vicky Pelaez and El Diano-La Prensa, "The Prison Industry in the United States: Big Business or a New

Form of Slavery?" New York and Global Research 10 March 2008

CHAPTER 11

States Use Bond Issues to Support Prisons in the 21st Century

Traditional revenue bonds find construction of a facility that actually generates revenue for use in debt repayment. Since prisons don't generate any revenue, the crafty state treasurers had to figure out a way to create some.
FORBES.

How do states support and maintain prisons? Review New York, New Jersey, California, and Texas. In this section, you will have the opportunity to read through bond issues proposed and/or acted upon in three other states. You have read about the bond-issue discussion that took place in New York in Chapter 7.

Bond Issues: Prison Financial Support Systems

(New York, New Jersey, Texas, and California – Examples)

New Jersey

Oct. 20, 1987. "As Prison Opens in Jersey, Officials Support a Bond Issue," by Alfonso A. Narvaez, Special to The New York Times, Published October 21, 1987 (nytimes.com)

> Newark, Oct. 20—A new $83 million medium-security prison was officially opened here today by city county and state officials, who used the occasion to urge voters to approve a $198 million prison bond issue on the Nov. 3 ballot.
>
> The new 1,000-bed prison, the Northern State Prisons, was built with funds from a 1982 prison construction bond issue and its already more than half occupied.
>
> Governor Kean said that despite the additional beds at the new prison and the construction of a 324-bed addition at the Rahway State Prison, New Jersey was facing a critical shortage of cells.
>
> "We don't want to see New Jersey prisons run by judges," the Governor said. "There are a good many states where the elected officials neglected to prepare for new prisoners and the judges have ordered prisoners released or are running the prisons themselves."
>
> The need for prison cells for sentenced inmates is so great that prisoners were being sent to the new prison even before it was completed. Today, there are 545 inmates here, land officials expect that it will be at capacity within a few months.

According to correction officials, there are about 17,000 state-sentenced inmates in New Jersey, with about 2,000 of them in county jails awaiting placement. Prisoners sent to Northern State will be from counties in the region. About 125 more inmates come into the state correction system than are released each month.

Officials said that the state's prison system average about 6,500 inmates during the 1970s but that a new criminal code, changes in the parole system, requirements for speedy trials and mandatory minimum prison sentences for people convicted of crime involving a gun or the sale of narcotics near a school have resulted in the prison population more than doubling. State Senator Frank X. Graves, a Democrat who is the Mayor of Paterson and the author legislation providing tough, mandatory minimum prison sentences for certain crimes, said that in 1981, 11,700 people were convicted of committing a crime with a gun but that in 1985 there were only 7,700 cases in that category.

"Mandated sentencing does work," the Senator said as he called for approval of the bond issue.

Other state legislators who have actively supported prison construction said that they would rather be dedicating a school or a hospital but that the public had a right to be protected and have criminals put away.

"We cannot allow the lawless element to run wild," said Mayor Sharpe James of Newark, but he added that more jobs and education programs were needed so that potential criminals would have a socially acceptable way of obtaining the things they needed.

Residents of Newark were given first preference in being hired as guards and as civilian personnel at the

> prison. Of the 371 people employed, 217 are Newark residents and 26 live in other parts of Essex County.
>
> The prison now has 163 correction officers, as well as a support staff that includes doctors, nurse, teachers, social workers, psychologists and chaplains.
>
> The new prisons will eventually have a staff of about 560, with an annual payroll of $13.5 million.
>
> The prison, near Newark International Airport, is made up of six two-story buildings, each with 160 cells, a disciplinary unit with 24 cells and a hospital unit. The one-person cells, which are about 8 feet by 10 feet, contain a built-in pallet, a desk attached to the wall, a toilet and a sink.

"This is very comfortable space," said Guillermo Estevez, a member of the board of trustees of the state prison system, who said he had been held for about 19 years as a political prisoner in his native country. "In Cuba, we have five people in half the space. What happened to creative thinking?

You may wish to write some annotations to the New Jersey bond issue to illustrate how state legislatures engage in dialogue to seek ways and means to support their prisons. Put your creative mind to work by critiquing how California and Texas view bond issues as a means to provide financial support for their prisons. As you write your annotations, consider four questions:

1. What is the main factor contributing to the cause of prison growth?
2. What is being done to rectify this cause? At the state level? Nationally?
3. What is the source of the factor that has an enormous negative impact upon family, children, home, schools, and communities?
4. Why is this nonviolent crime permitted to thrive in a democracy?

Sacramento, California
Bond Issue Dialogue

["Presley Plans to Push $500 million Prison Bond Issue February 27, 1987 Leo C. Wolinsky, Los Angeles Times Staff Writer, February 27, 1987]

> SACRAMENTO – Senator Robert Presley (D-Riverside), a key player in the Los Angeles prison dispute, said Thursday that he intends to propose a $500-million bond issue to finance expansion of the state's overcrowded prison system, including a new penitentiary in a rural part of Los Angeles County.
>
> Presley, the Senate's chief negotiator on prison matters, said the state does not have enough money to build the penitentiaries needed to house the more than 700 felons who enter California's already strained correctional system each month.
>
> The most immediate need, he added, is money for 2,200-cell rural facility, which has become a key bargaining chip in efforts to break a deadlock over the building of a prison in Los Angeles County. Gov. Deukmejian has indicated support for building two prisons in the county, so long as one of them is on his preferred site on Los Angeles' Eastside.
>
> During a breakfast session with The Times Sacramento Bureau, Presley also said the rural prison probably will not be built in Castaic, as some Democratic lawmakers have urged. Instead, he indicated that Senate negotiators plan to select a site from among several previously studied locations near the Antelope Valley desert towns of Palmdale and Lancaster or in Gorman, a

sparsely populated community in the mountains between Castaic and Bakersfield.[3]

Texas Bond Issue

"PRIVATE PRISONS ARE ROTTEN TO THE CORE": 2/25/2010

Texas: Private prison fraud plays major role in campaign [http://www.dallasnews.com/sharedcontent/dws/newstexassouthwest/stories/DN-Trailmix_24TEX.aart.State Edition 1.4c2a01f.html 12:00 AM CST on Wednesday, February 24, 2010 The Associated Press Perry blasts Hutchison law firm on prison deal]

> AUSTIN – Hit with accusations of spreading "cronyism" throughout state government, Gov. Rick Perry is hitting back, arguing that the law firm where Kay Bailey Hutchison used to work with her husband, Ray, was found by a federal civil jury to have defrauded investors in a 1990s-era private prison deal.
>
> Hutchison campaign called the move an 11th-hour dirty trick, saying the court has already absolved Ray Hutchison and his firm and that the civil jury was acting without proper authority.
>
> At issue are private prisons built in six Texas counties, financed by bonds that the Hutchison law firm helped put together. The project was a financial disaster and the state wound up buying them at a fire sale price.
>
> The records show Ray Hutchison was the lawyer who affirmed that the developers' debt-financing plan met legal requirements. Kay Bailey Hutchison listed her husband's law firm, Hutchison, Boyle, Brook and Fisher, as her employer in 1989, and she reported $25,000 income

from the firm that year. Hutchison's campaign says she did no work on the prison bonds.

"Keep Local Control of Our County Jail."

[The Associated Press]

Grayson County jail bond issue still headed for a vote by Jerrie Whiteley Herald Democratnews.heerladdemocrat.com; Monday, February 22, 2010; 9:23 PM

SHERMAN – Voices of experience, passion, frustration and exasperation mingled Monday in the grand East Courtroom at the Grayson County Courthouse as county leaders wrestled one more time with issues surrounding the county jail.

Should commissioners put off the $20 million bond election tentative set for May or should they proceed as planned? If they proceed as planned, who is or should be in charge of getting information out to the people about the need for the bond? Does anyone, anywhere think the bond election has a hope of succeeding?

Those questions and more were hurled at commissioners from their colleagues and audience members. By the time the dust settled, commissioners had rejected a plan calling for a citizen's committee to do further study on the jail issue. They also refused to even second the motion for a plan to put the jail bond election off until November.

Before the name calling could get started in earnest, a voice from the Court's past took the floor. Former County Judge Horace Groff steered the county's governing body for more than 20 years and suggested their problems might have started way back then.

There are those in the community who feel if I had done a better job, you wouldn't be dealing with this issue today." Groff said, and then waited as the laughter erupted around him. All joking aside, Groff told commissioners he would suggest that they designate a citizen's committee to study the need for the bond and to present their findings to the public. He said the best bond issue presentations come from that type of support.

Groff urged commissioners to step back from their plan to hold a vote on the bond issue in May and give the idea a chance.

I think most bonds are dead on the arrival and then it is up to the governing body to try to develop the necessary public support to demonstrate the need and get as much community support for it," Groff urged.

Commissioner Johnny Waldrip said he would go along with Groff's desire to have the matter slow down, but asked how long that would take. Groff said it could probably be done in six months if the people selected to serve on the committee were willing to work at it several nights a week.

Waldrip proposed a plan to allow each commissioner and Grayson County Judge Drue Bynum to pick two residents for a committee to work on the jail issue. Saying he thought the idea of moving the jail bond election back from May to November smacked of politics to him. Waldrip said he would like to see those 10 people be picked out of the masses of Grayson County residents who are not elected officials and who are not connected to elected officials.

His remarks seemed aimed at those made by Commissioner Gene Short, who said the public doesn't have enough information to make a decision about a jail bond at this point. Short said the county should back away from the bond election right now and put the idea up for a vote in November. He also pointed out roughly $1 million worth of payments for various services or bonds that are about to end. He said that money could, in the future, be put towards the price of the jail and that increased in the county rate. Short said that could make a bond election more acceptable to the public.

Reducing the increase in the tax rate, however, wasn't enough for Bynum. After several blunt but civil exchanges with Short about the subject, Bynum laid out his opinion.

"Let me make it perfectly clear, I don't want to raise the tax rate to build a jail," he said. "I will allow the people to vote on that because for six months they have been saying that 'I wanted the opportunity to vote.' And I will do everything I can be done in 62 days or less" (within the May election time frame).

He added, however, that when election day comes, he doesn't see himself supporting the bond issue.

Short then asked each commissioner individually if he planned to vote in favor of the bond.

Commissioner David Whitlock quickly answered in the negative. Waldrip said he hasn't made up his mind on the issue. **Commissioner Jackie Crisp said he didn't see himself supporting the bond issue either because people are already saddled with too much tax.** Crisp's frustration with the whole matter seemed to boil over a bit.

He said all anyone ever tells him is to listen to the people and he agrees with that principle. What, he wondered aloud, does one do, however, when the people don't agree?

"Which one do you listen to?" Crisp asked.

Grayson County Sheriff Keith Gary said he wants to do what is expected of him, but he feels that he doesn't have the information he needs to put the issue out for voters in a way that has any hope getting the bond passed.

(THE public) wants the same thing that they have seen in school bond elections. They want architectural drawing inside and out," he said, nothing he doesn't have those to present. Additionally, he said, he doesn't even know how many parking places to request from the city of Sherman to replace the ones that will be taken up by the expansion.

Sherman Mayor Bill Magers said he couldn't provide Gary with any answers because no one has told him, or the city, the number of spaces needed. Magers promised that the city wants to help, but then took issue with some of the information the county could be using to make decisions. He said previous reports on the jail have overestimated both the county's population and the number of offenders. Without better information, Magers said help from the city will be hard to come by.

Short questioned why anyone would want to go forward with the bond election when there were so many questions still left up in the air and when further research seemed to be needed.

His answer came in the final vote of the day. With two commissioner's voting for the idea of designating a citizen group and of putting the election off and two voting against it, the tie breaker came down to Bynum.

The words he spoke weren't new to him. He has said in the past that he believes that the people of the county don't need to make a decision about the jail because they voted for representatives who are perfectly capable of making the decisions. He left no mystery about his retention of that ideal and voted against putting off the vote.

"Some of you haven't liked any decisions we have made thus far," Bynum said, "That's okay, too. There is an opportunity in November to change it. Therefore I am going to vote 'no' on the citizen's committee and the motion fails."

"Whoa." Short said loudly.

Then Short moved to rescind the bond election set for May and call one for November and to bring an architect on board and get a more refined plan. His motion failed to draw a second.

Though the commissioners talked a great deal amongst themselves of the dilemmas they faced, they also heard from several audience members. Some like Tony Beaverson expressed his disapproval of the idea of not allowing a larger citizen's group to study the idea and accused commissioners of cherry picking people to go on the committee would share their point of view.

Thomas Nuckles said he thinks there are several other options that commissioners could try to reduce the number of beds needed before they start building a new jail. He stressed the need for 'good quality information' on which people can base their decision to either support or reject the bond issue.

Roger Eppler first congratulated and then chastised the Court for its actions with regard to the jail. At first he said he was proud of the fact that the Court was planning

> on moving forward and not spending more money on further study. Then, when Waldrip moved to slow down, Eppler returned to the podium and said he disagreed and thought that was a move in the wrong direction.[4]

You have had the opportunity to read through the discussion of bond issues as a means for many states to finance and maintain a prison system. The New York prison-building model established by Cuomo set a model for a national prison industry, using nonviolent crime stats to swell the prison population. In 1981, the people voted against a bond issue to grow prisons. However, Governor Cuomo ignored the people's response and circumvented their voice by misusing the Urban Development Corporation to fulfill his goal of growing a prison industry in New York to mirror the nation.

> In his 1987 State of the State address, having just been re-elected by a landslide, Cuomo boasted of having put nearly 10,000 "dangerous felons" behind bars. The inmate population of New York's prisons had indeed grown by roughly that number during his first term in office. But the proportion of offenders being incarcerated for violent crimes had fallen from 63 percent to 52 percent during those four years. In 1987 New York State sent almost a thousand fewer violent offenders to prison than it had in 1983. Despite having the "toughest anti-drug program" and one of the fastest-growing inmate populations in the nation, New York was hit hard by the crack epidemic of the 1980s and the violent crime that accompanied it.
>
> From 1983 to 1990 the state's inmate population almost doubled—and yet during that same period the violent-crime rate rose 24 percent. Between the passage of the Rockefeller drug laws and the time Cuomo left

office, in January of 1995, New York's inmate population increased almost fivefold. And the state's prison system was more overcrowded than it had been when the prison boom began.[5]

How do Bond Issues support the Prison Industry? bond issue work as a means to support prisons?

FORBES ON BOND PROCESS

The difference between traditional revenue bonds and lease revenue bonds is one of mechanics. Traditional revenue bonds fund construction of a facility that actually generates revenue for use in debt repayment. Since prisons don't generate any revenue, the crafty state treasurers had to figure out a way to create some.

Here's what they came up with: The state creates an entity or agency to build the prison. The agency floats bonds to the public to cover construction of the facility. The agency then leases the right to use the completed prison to the state. The state pays the entity lease payments. The entity uses the lease payments to service the bond debt. Essentially, the state takes money from one pocket (the general fund appropriations to the prison system) and puts it into another pocket (the agency created for the facility), and then the agency distributes the money to the bondholders.

"The state dips into the general fund for payment as if this were a regular lease. Title to the facility cedes to the state once the bonds are repaid and retired. You may ask if this is a state-sponsored debt? Technically, no, it does not appear on the state's balance sheet because the state doesn't own an asset on which it is obligated to pay. Instead, the state can stop making the lease payments if it so chooses. However, if the state did that, there would likely be a downgrade of its credit rating. Further, the resulting cost in higher interest on future bond issues would likely far exceed any savings.

These bonds are tax exempt at the state level if issued by the holder's state of residence. Lease-revenue bonds pay interest at tax-exempt rates. Yields are slightly higher than yields on general obligation bonds.

Where can your money feel safe? Not many places lately. For the municipal bond market, it seems that all the usual suspects for bond repayment-property tax, sales tax and income tax-are declining fast. This can place the revenue stream in jeopardy, which could also place your coupon payments in jeopardy. Not so for prison bonds. Since these are state lease obligations, the state has the authority to raise taxes if necessary to pay its obligations.

One caution: Prison bonds of the lease revenue variety pay a higher interest rate for a reason-they're more risky than regular general obligation bonds. The state's general fund does not back repayment as it does general obligation bonds. Instead, continued repayment of prison bonds is subject to lease payments from the states, which are themselves subject to legislative appropriations. Should appropriations cease, the bonds will default.[6]

Prison systems incarcerate offenders.

Any state that would stop making lease payments on its correctional facility bonds and set incarcerated offenders out on the streets would have some explaining to do. The stakes are too high for society to permit such default. We think the risk is minimal for prison bonds.[7]

Do the Research: The Flourishing Drug Market

From the 1940s to 21st Century

Beaty, Jonathan & Gwynne, *The Outlaw Bank: A Wild Ride into the Secret Heart of BCCI* [Bank of Credit and Commerce/, Random House, 1993

Bevilaqua, John, *"Harry Anslinger: Head of the Bureau of Narcotics since 1930,"* Education Forum,

Block and Weaver, *All is Clouded by Desire*. Burt Kanter, the co-founder of Castle Bank.

December 4, 2009, http://educationforum.ipbhost.com/index.php?showtopic=15084 (accessed May 20, 2014).

Cockburn, Alexander and Jeffrey St. Clair, *Whiteout: The CIA, Drugs and the Press.* Verso, 2014.

Cressey, Donald R., Theft of a Nation (New York: Harper and Row, 1969).

Declassified OSS [Office of Strategic Services] documents show that Donovan's [General William "Wild Bill"] plans for the creation of a Special Intelligence Service to gather intelligence from countries throughout the world dates back to September 25, 1941. See "Memo Col. Donovan from Wallace B. Stevens," WN #24299.

Graham, Jamie Cameron, *"The Secret History of the CIA's Involvement in the Narcotics Trade"* (doctoral dissertation, School of Politics and International Relations, University of Nottingham, 2009), http://www.scribd.com/doc/113413267/CIA-and-the-Narcotics-Trade.

Iran-Contra Affair, *Report of the Congressional Committees Investigating the Iran-Contra Affair,* 100th Congress. 1st Session, H. Rept No100-433, S. Rept No. 100-216, pp. 164, 166, 228, etc.

Kwitny, Jonathan, *The Crime of Patriots,* (New York: Norton, 1987).

Kruger, Henrik, *The Great Heroin Coup: Drugs, Intelligence and International Finance* (Boston: South End, 1980).

Lernoux, Penny, In Banks We Trust (New York: Penguin Books, 1986).

Marshall, Jonathan,, *The Iran-Contra-Connection: Secret Teams and Covert Operations in the Reagan-Era* (Boston: Sound End Press, 1987).

McCoy, Alfred, *Testimony before the Special Seminar focusing on allegations linking CIA secret operations and drug trafficking*, convened February 13, 1997, *by Rep. John Conyers*, Dean of the Congressional Black Caucus. See Alfred McCoy, "CIA Involvement in Drug Trafficking," The New Renaissance, 1997, www.voxfux.com/features/cia_drug_trafficking2.html.

McCoy, Alfred, *The Politics of Heroin in Southeast Asia* (New York: Harper and Row, 1972), p. 7.

Nathan, James A., *Dateline Australia: America's Foreign Watergate?'*

Newark, Tim, "*Pact with the Devil?*" History Today 54, no. 4 (2007), http://www.historytoday.com/tim-newark/pact-devill) accessed May 20, 2014)

Parry, Robert, *Secrecy & Privilege: Rise of the Bush Dynasty from Watergate to Iraq* (Arlington, VA: Medium Consortium, 2004), 112-38, etc.: Scott, Road to 9/11, 99-107.

Scott, Peter Dale, *"Deep Events and the CIA's Global Drug Connection,"* Global Research, September 8, 2008, http://www.globalresearch.ca/deep-events-and-the-cia-s-globaldrugconnection/10095(accessed May 20, 2014).

Scott, Peter Dale, *American War Machine: Deep Politics, the CIA Global Drug Connection, and the Road to Afghanistan* (Washington, DC: Rowman and Littlefield, 2010).

Scott, Peter Dale, *Drugs, Oil, and War: The United States in Afghanistan, Colombia, and Indochina*, Rowman & Littlefield Publishers, 2003.

Seagrove, *The Marcos Dynasty* (New York: Harper and Row, 1988), p. 361.

Trento, Joseph, Prelude to Terror: *The Rogue CIA, the Legacy of America's Private Intelligence Network* (New York: Carroll and Graf, 2005).

Sterling, Claire, *Octopus: How the Long Reach of the Sicilian Mafia Controls the Global Narcotics Trade* (New York: Simon and Schuster, 1990).

Valentine, Douglas, *The Strength of the Wolf: The Secret History of America's War on* Drugs (New York: Verso, 2006).

Weiner, Tim, *Legacy of Ashes: The History of the CIA* (New York: Doubleday, and Row, 1972), p. 7

Williams, Paul L. *Operation Gladio,* (New York: Prometheus Books), 2015.

CHAPTER 12

Sentencing to Perpetuate a Prison Industry

For too long, too many judges have been too quiet about an evil of which we are apart: the mass incarceration of people in the United States today. It is time that more of us spoke out.

Jed S. Rakoff, "Mass Incarceration: The Silence of the Judges. May 21, 2015, The New York Book Review. Borders open, drugs flourish, and prisons remain at maximum capacity.

Black Man: Target for Destruction

4. (Black Males in Prison)

> "Between 6.6% and 7.5% of all black males ages 25 to 39 were imprisoned in 2011, which were the highest imprisonment rates among the measured sex, race, Hispanic origin, and age groups."[1]
>
> [Source: Carson, E. Ann, and Sabol, William J., "Prisoners in 2011" (Washington, DC: US Dept. of Justice Bureau

of Justice Statistics, Dec. 2012), NC1239808, p. 8. http://www.bjs.gov/content/pub/pdf/p11.pdf

Drugs: The Incarcerating Bait

The think tank behind the secret wall who designed the plan for prisons as an economic industry had neither care for the structural composition of the geographical nature of America nor its principles as a democracy. The blight of drugs upon our institutions—homes, schools, churches, and communities—were no concern to this nefarious group. For the black community, drugs became the primary source for increasing the prison rate. Despite the decrease in violent crime, drugs are the overwhelming factor used to spiral the prison growth across the nation. In the 21st century analysis, if it were not for the drugs, the prisons would be at an all-time low. The Correctional Association of New York reveals the drug as the one factor responsible for prison growth.

> Over 90% of the inmates locked up in NYS prisons today for drug offenses are there because of two mandatory sentencing laws that were passed over 20 years ago, in 1973. Rockefeller Drug Laws require harsh prison terms for the session or sale of relatively small amounts of drugs. For example, a person convicted of selling two ounces of a narcotic or of possessing four ounces of same must receive a minimum prison term of 15 years to life. The Second Felony Offender Law requires a prison term for all repeat felons regardless of the nature of the offense or the background or motivation of the offender (New York Correctional Association of New York, February, 1995).

Drugs alone have destroyed many schools, homes, and communities across the nation. Just observe the impact this insidious germ, which has been permitted to run rampant, has on our society. The Correctional Association of New York shares the reality through statistics:

> As of December 31, 1994, there were 8,433 drug offenders locked up in NYS prisons under the Rockefeller Drug Laws. It cost nearly $253 million per year to keep these offenders imprisoned ((New York Correctional Association of New York, February, 1995).
>
> As of December 31, 1994, there were 12,838 drug offenders locked up in NYS prisons under the Second Felony Offender Law. It cost over $385 million per year to confine these people in prison (New York Correctional Association of New York, February, 1995). As of December 31, 1994, there were 6,340 people locked up in NYS prisons for drug possession, as opposed to drug selling. Some of these offenders were confined under the Rockefeller Drug Laws, some under the Second Felony Offender Law. It costs over $190 million per year to keep these people in prison (New York Correctional Association of New York, February, 1995).
>
> Of the 23,140 commitments to the NYS prison system in 1994, 10,508 or 45% were for drug offenses. In 1980, 886 drug offenders were sent to State prison, 11% of the total commitments for that year (New York Correctional Association of New York, February, 1995).

The billion-dollar drug industry is that **"pot of gold"** described earlier by Vicky Pelaez for the prison–industrial complex in America, thriving in a democracy and subsidized by mainstream taxation.

The gross picture of viewing racial disparities in enforcement and incarceration is a testimony to the desire to send the black man back into the period of slavery in America, identified as 1661 to 1865. This topic is greatly researched by the Sentencing Project with Marc Mauer and other social science vanguards for humanity as The Justice Policy Institute office, replete with resources, related to this subject. I will leave them to continue with their immense work.

Who does the sentencing?

When Mario Cuomo was inaugurated governor of New York in 1983, the state criminal justice system was under revision. As governor, he had the opportunity to assign judges to the New York State Court of Appeals, New York's highest court. During this pioneering history under the Cuomo administration, New York commenced growing a prison industry. Our concern in this chapter is the screening of prisoners by the criminal justice system.

The great desire to increase prisons thrust upon the criminal justice system an immense responsibility—the sole body for sentencing. The assignment was not shared with other health practitioners to address alternative placements. The idea was to grow the prison industry with people regardless of their health status or need component. Inmates were screened for neither mental health nor literacy. It was a general assignment based on the criminal justice system. Consequently, many inmates who were in dire need of other services were deprived. The criminal justice system had a monopoly of this authority to insure a rising prison rate. This increasing inmate rate contributed to the building of a prison–economic industry.

The goal of sentencing during the Cuomo administration was to grow prisons with deliberate speed. Communities in upstate New York, such as Suffolk and Westchester, depended upon prison labor to grow their economies. In many cases, legislation was designed to fulfill this purpose with deliberate speed. While inmates were used to build these communities, who cared for the children, families, and communities that were left behind because of this incarceration? This legislation was simply concerned with building upstate communities with prison labor.

Who are these people locked behind the prison wall?

Eric Schlosser answers this question: "The raw-material of the prison industrial complex is its inmates: the poor, the homeless, and the mentally ill; drug dealers, drug addicts, alcoholics, and a wide assortment of violent sociopaths." Have state legislatures neglected their responsibility to these people? What happened to the funds that should have been designated to provide services for these people? A look at the categorization of this population will reveal a neglected population without proper services to enable them to better their lives.

- About 70 percent of the prison inmates in the United States are illiterate. Perhaps 200,000 of the country's inmates suffer from a serious mental illness, not the criminal justice system.
- Sixty to 80 percent of the American inmate population has a history of substance abuse. Meanwhile, the number of drug treatment slots in American prisons has declined by more than half since 1993.

What is the true story?

Is this health challenged population used to inflate the prison rate, or has the state neglected its responsibility for servicing these prison inmates? What failures in society contributed to placing this populace on the prison pathway, hidden behind a dark wall from the presence of mainstream society?

Drugs, nonviolent crimes, and long prison sentences Sentencing Designed to Fulfill an Economic Demand

Another facet of the sentencing process was the act of carefully modifying criminal behavior to assign time frames in the sentencing process. The significance of this careful design is to determine an inmate's length of stay in prison. These laws and the definition of sentencing were designed to fulfill the concept of prison growth. How could a prison industry blossom with short-term sentences? The drug laws coincided with fulfilling this economic principle.

The drug factor played a vital role to inflate prison growth. The prison population had decreased in the 1970s, and today one can make a vital comparison. The growth in prison is a result of nonviolent crime as opposed to violent crime. The nonviolent arrests, in large, are drug related. "Since 1991, the rate of violent crime in the United States has fallen by about 20 percent, while the number of people in prison or jail has risen by 50 percent." This criminal exposure factor reveals an un-natural prison growth indicative of a contrived plan to swell the population to validate its existence as an economic prison industry. Eric Schlosser says, "Prisons have become a cornerstone of economic development, private companies that regard the roughly $35 billion spent each year on corrections not as a burden on American taxpayers but as a lucrative market: and government officials whose fiefdoms have expanded along with the inmate population." There is a great need to design long sentences to perpetuate the inmate population as a cheap labor force on the stock market of America.

The legislation has defined and designed sentences based on drug arrests to strengthen the prison industry. A quick look at a few of these laws will reveal this purpose.

Correctional Association Of New York Statistics

Mandatory Sentencing February 1995

Laws, Women, and the Rockefeller Drug Law

- "The harshest provisions of the Rockefeller Drug Laws require a judge to impose a present term of no less than 15 years to life for anyone convicted of selling 2 ounces or possessing 4 ounces of a narcotic."
- "The judge cannot take into consideration—the individual's character or whether she is a first-time offender has a minor role in the drug transaction, has a substance abuse problem, or is a parent."

Laws and Drug Offenders in New York State

- "Over 90% of the inmates locked up in New York State prisons today for drug offenses are there because of two mandatory sentencing laws that were passed over 20 years ago, in 1973. The Rockefeller Drug laws require harsh prison terms for the possession or sale of relatively small amounts of drugs. For example, a person convicted of selling two ounces of a narcotic or possessing four ounces of the same must receive a minimum prison term of 14 years to life."
- "The second felony law requires a prison term for all repeat felons regardless of the nature of the offense or the background or motivation of the offender."

Double Standards In Prisons: Drugs

The prisons are inundated with a set policy of double standards—differential treatment for different populations. Understanding this important legal concept is to understand the heart of the interest in perpetuating a prison economy. We will focus on these various unjust laws.

There is a need to view drug litigation, ethnicity of the prison population, and especially the inflated population of black and Hispanic men locked behind the prison wall.

Legislation for drug use and sale varies in sentencing the inmate population.

- Possession of 2 ounces or less of rock-cocaine is 10 years [rock-cocaine is used primarily by non-white population].
- Possession for cocaine powder of 5 ounces of powder-cocaine is 5 years ["white-powder is used by white, middle-class or rich people"].
- "The 1973 Rockefeller anti-drug laws mandate 15 years to life for possession of 4 ounces of any illegal drug."

The "three strikes" law played a vital role in growing prisons. This law alone necessitated the building of twenty new federal prisons. The statistics are very clear on verifying the ethnicity of the growing prison population.

What sentencing fails to do in a democracy

"Studies and experience have shown that the majority of people who use and sell drugs in New York State and the nation are white."

Despite these stats, "African Americans and Latinos comprise 93.8% of the drug offenders in New York State prisons. African Americans comprise 47.4%; Latinos, 46.4%; whereas whites make up 5.7%."

Albert Rosenblatt, retired judge from New York, was astonished at the new demeanor disclosed with the new drug proposals. He watched the unfolding of this new policy of drugs with apprehension. "But Rosenblatt says prosecutors in New York realized that the laws were doing unexpected and troubling things. White people were using a lot of drugs in the 1970s and committing a lot of crimes, yet the people being arrested and sent to prison under the Rockefeller laws came almost entirely from poor black and Hispanic neighborhoods." [Recoil, chapter 7].

Read John Chisholm's "The Milwaukee Report," [2010] in the latter part of this chapter, where double standards holds the rein. "According to the Vera Institute of Justice, prosecutors in Milwaukee declined to prosecute forty-one percent of whites arrested for possession of drug paraphernalia, compared with twenty-seven percent of blacks." This statistical analysis lines up with Judge Albert Rosenblatt's observation.

The Correctional Association of New York reveals double standards

This fact makes it clear that laws are designed to create a specified population to be the product of an economic prison industry. This is a contrived and unnatural growth of the prisons. The system resembles the social structure in American slavery where the overseer supervised the plantation.

In upstate New York, prisons create jobs in these communities. **"Eighty-two percent of the Correction Officers in New York State prisons are white**; the largest concentration of white corrections staff serves in upstate localities where the inmate population is primarily black."

How do these double standards and contrived inflated prison populations affect the non-white population? The Correctional Association of New York, March 1991:

> Although the prevalence of illegal drug use among white men is approximately the same as that among black men, black men are five times as likely to be arrested for a drug offense. As a result, about half the inmates in the United States are African Americans. One out of every fourteen black men is now in prison or jail. One out of every four black men is likely to be imprisoned at some point during his life time. *The number of women sentenced to a year or more of prison has grown twelvefold since 1970.* Of the 80,000 women now imprisoned about 70 percent are nonviolent offenders. About 75 percent have children.

Felony Probation March 1991

"There are three times as many young white men on felony probation in New York as in the prison system; young black male offenders are more likely to be in prison than on felony probation."

Employment

"82 percent of the correction officers in New York State prisons are white; the largest concentration of white corrections staff serves in upstate localities where the inmate population is primarily **black**."

Social Culture

"There is a direct correlation between the size of the black population of a state and the incarceration rate of that state."

Frequency of Arrest by State

"In New York, young black men are over twenty three times more likely to be locked up than young white men."

"On any given day, one in four young black men is under the control of the criminal justice system in New York—more than twice the number of all black men enrolled full time in college in New York." "Blacks in the United States are incarcerated at a rate four times that of blacks in South Africa, 3109 per 100,000, compared to 729 per 100,000."

The Surreptitious Plan For Prison Construction

The Inception Years
STATE PRISONS

Prison Expansion
"In January 1973 there were 12,500 persons in the State prison system. Today there are over 58,000."

The Mario Cuomo National Model
"The [Mario] Cuomo Administration has built or authorized nearly 30,000 prison spaces since 1983. In the past 9 years, the State has opened 27 new prisons."

Prison Cost
"The current average cost of State prison construction is about $180,000 per space when complete debt charges are included. So the total construction costs of the approximately 30,000 beds added or about to be added to the State system will come to about $5.4 billion. The State pays $670 per call, per month in debt service alone."

Prison Operating Cost
"In fiscal year 1982/83 the State spent about $840 million to cover prison operating and construction costs. In the current fiscal year, the State

has allocated nearly $3 billion for total expenditure—that is about $8 million a day."

Violent offenders and Nonviolent offenders

"In recent years the State has used more and more prison space for drugs and other nonviolent offenders and less for violent offenders."

"In 1980, 886 drug offenders were sent to State prison, 11 % of the total court commitments for that year."

"By 1990 the number of drug offenders sent to State prison had grown to 10,785, 46 % of the total. By contrast, the number of violent offenders sent to State prison in 1983 was 7,926, 63 % of total count commitments; in 1990 the number of violent offenders sent to State prison was 7,435, 32 % of the total."

CITY JAILS 1980/81

"It costs about $58,000 to keep an inmate in a New York City Jail for one year."

"In 1980 there were about 7,000 inmates in City jails. Today there are about 21,000."

"The City's jail operations budget grew from $120 million to 1981 to about $770 million for the current year."

Question: Can a difference be made in reducing prison construction?

THE WORK OF MAYOR DAVID DINKINS VS. PREVIOUS GOVERNORS

The Correctional Association of New York, February 1995

Are prisons for real or contrived?

> After 2 years of expanding the jails, New York's ***Mayor David*** *Dinkins' Administration* moved to "downsize"

the system. The City shut down at least 4 jails, and reduced its jail population to 17,600 and its annual jail operations budget to about $680 million. Given the Giuliani Administration's new law enforcement policies emphasizing an increase in "quality of life" arrests, the jail population has begun to rise again, now exceeding 19,000.[29]

What is the question? Is prison construction synonymous to the physiognomy of the official occupying the power office? If so, why does prison construction increases under non-black leadership? The true question is, how can just laws benefit all the people to prepare and to train them to live in a true democracy?

PRISONER PROFILE IN NEW YORK
The Correctional Association of New York
150th Year Anniversary

STATE PRISONS [February 1995]
There are over 66,000 people in New York State Prisons, up from 12,500 to 1973 and 28,500 in 1983.

Black and Hispanic Composition
African Americans make up about 50% of the prison population. They represent 12.4% of the State's population.

Latinos make up about 33% of the State's inmate population and 10.8% of the overall population.

Women Growing Population
There are about 3,600 women in State prison. They make up 5 ½ % of the total inmate population.

Addicted Population
60-70 % of inmates—38,400 to 44,800—have a history of drug abuse.

Illiterate Population
75 % of prisoners have no high school diploma.

2015 REEL ON PRISONS IN 21st CENTURY

The New Yorker, May 11, 2015,
"The Milwaukee Experiment" by Jeffrey Toobin.

JOHN CHISHOLM, District Attorney in Milwaukee County, Wisconsin: Racial imbalance in American prisons takes a stand to make a difference: Racial inequality in Criminal Justice.

We, first acknowledge, *The New Yorker* magazine with its writer, Jeffrey Toobin, for publishing this article. We give kudos to the profound work of John Chisholm, District Attorney, for embracing and supporting this crucial project. Blessings are extended to this team for their courage, endurance, fortitude, and, most of all, faith in humanity.

> Like many people in the criminal-justice system, John Chisholm, the District Attorney in Milwaukee County, has been concerned for a long time about the racial imbalance in American prisons." The issue is especially salient in Wisconsin, where African-Americans constitute only six per cent of the population but thirty-seven per cent of those in state prison. ***According to a study from the University of Wisconsin-Milwaukee, as of 2010 thirteen per cent of the state's African-American men of working age were behind bars—nearly double the national average, of 6.7 per cent.*** The figures were especially stark for Milwaukee County, where more than half of African-American men in their thirties had served

time in state prison. How, Chisholm wondered, if the work of his own office contributes to these numbers? Could a D.A. do anything to change them [The New Yorker, pp.24-32]?

A study found that in Milwaukee County more than half of African-American men in their thirties had done prison time [NY, p. 24].

The recent spate of deaths of unarmed African-Americans at the hands of police officers has brought renewed attention to racial inequality in criminal justice, but in the U. legal system prosecutors may wield even more power than cops. Prosecutors decide whether to bring a case or drop charges against a defendant; charge a misdemeanor or a felony; demand a prison sentence or accept probation. Most cases are resolved through plea bargains, where prosecutors, not judges, negotiate whether and for how long a defendant goes to prison. And prosecutors make these judgments almost entirely outside public scrutiny [p. 24].

Chisholm decided to let independent researchers examine how he used his prosecutorial discretion. In 2007, when he took office, the Vera Institute of Justice, a research and policy group based in New York City, had just begun studying the racial implications of the work of the Milwaukee County District Attorney's office. Over several years, Chisholm allowed the researchers to question his staff members and look at their files. ***The conclusions were disturbing.*** According to the Vera study, prosecutors in Milwaukee declined to prosecute forty-one per cent of whites arrested for possession of drug paraphernalia, compared with twenty-seven per cent of blacks; in cases involving prostitution, black

> female defendants were likelier to be charged than white defendants; in cases that involved resisting or obstructing an officer, most of the defendants charges were black (seventy-seven per cent), male (seventy-nine per cent), already in custody (eighty per cent of blacks versus sixty-six per cent of whites) [p. 24].

I ask the question: How does your work interact with your soul to uplift humanity? Chisholm's work resonates with an answer: "Measure me in my success in reducing mass incarceration and achieving racial equality."

> Chisholm decided that his office [p.25] would undertake initiatives to try to send fewer people to prison while maintaining public safety. "For a long time, prosecutors have defined themselves through conviction rates and winning the big cases with the big sentences." Nicholas Turner, the president of the Vera Institute, told me. "But the evidence is certainly tipping that the attainment for safety and justice requires more than just putting people in prison for a long time. Prosecutors have to redefine their proper role in a new era. Chisholm stuck his neck out there and stared saying that prosecutors should also be judged by their success in reducing mass incarceration and achieving racial equality." Chisholm's efforts have drawn attention around the country. "John is a national leader in law enforcement, because he is genuinely interested in trying to achieve the right results, not only in individual cases but in larger policy issues as se..," Cyrus R. Vance Jr., the Manhattan District Attorney, told me [NY, p.26].

Current data in periodicals

Jed S. Rakoff, "**Mass Incarceration: The Silence of the Judges**," *The New York Review of Books*, May 21, 2015/ Volume LXII, Number 9, pp.14–17.

"Silence of the Judges"! This title, alone, is a prelude to change. Dr. Martin L. King Jr. would describe it as the consciousness of the soul with the morality of the heart involved on a journey between life and death, seeking to use God-given gifts to uplift humanity to make this a better world. When bold and resourceful individuals apply their talents in the spirit of love, caring, sharing, and forgiving, a powerful example becomes a paragon for others to emulate. We thank *The New York Review of Books* and Jed S. Rakoff, for this article, "Mass Incarceration: The Silence of the Judges." Blessings to you as you continue your work to uplift humanity.

A time to speak out for justice:

> For too long, too many judges have been too quiet about an evil of which we are a part: the mass incarceration of people in the United States today. It is time that more of us spoke out.
>
> **The basic facts are not in dispute. More than 2.2 million people are currently incarcerated in US jails and prisons, a 500 percent increase over the past forty years.** Although the United States accounts for about 5 percent of the world's population, it houses nearly 25 percent of the world's prison population. The per capita incarceration rate in the US is about one and a half times that of second-place Rwanda and third-place Russia, and more than six times the rate of neighboring Canada.

> Another 4.75 million Americans are subject to the state supervision imposed by probation or parole.
>
> Most of the increase in imprisonment has been for nonviolent offenses, such as drug possession. And even though crime rates in the United States have declined consistently for twenty-four years, the number of incarcerated persons has continued to rise over most of that period, *both because more people are being sent to prison for offenses that once were punished with other measures and because the sentences are longer.* For example, even though the number of violent crimes has steadily decreased over the past two decades, the number of prisoners serving life sentences has steadily increased, so that one in nine persons in prison is now serving a life sentence (p. 14, New York Review of Books, May 21, 2015, Volume LXVII, Number 9, p. 14).

When more voices are heard, when more consciences are aroused, a difference will be made to right the wrong, hopefully, before the final trumpet sounds.

CHAPTER 13

Two Largest Prison Corporations in America

The prison privatization boom began in the 1980s, under the governments of Ronald Reagan and Bush, Sr., but reached its height in 1990 under William Clinton, when Wall Street stocks were selling like hotcakes.

VICKY PELAEZ.

Corrections Corporation of America (CCA) and George Wackenhut (GEO GROUP)

CCA was incorporated in 1983 but originated in the late 1970s. To understand how this prison industry began, let us look at the founders of CCA. One of the founding members is Tom Beasley. During the 1970s, Beasley served as chairman of the Tennessee Republican Party. His vision was to transform prisons into a profitable enterprise. Another founding member was Doctor ("Doc") Crants. Crants and Beasley had been roommates in West Point. The third founding member was Terrell Don Hutto.

> Corrections Corporation of America (CCA) owns or operates jails and prisons on contract with federal, state and local governments. CCA designs, builds, manages and operates correctional facilities and detention centers for the Federal Bureau of Prisons, Immigration and Customs Enforcement, the United States Marshals Service, as well as facilities across the United States.
>
> CCA houses approximately 90,000 offenders and detainees in its more than 60 facilities and employs more than 17,000 nationwide.[1]

What skills and talents did these founders bring to CCA?
Having served as chairman of the Tennessee Republican Party, Beasley brought political skills and connections. Crants was born on a Seneca Indian reservation. He was a graduate from West Point, trained as an Army Ranger, and served two tours in Vietnam. He has business and law degrees, both earned from Harvard University. While at Harvard, he became acquainted with Tom Beasley. It was this friendship that brought them together to form a business partnership to develop Correctional Corporation of America—the largest private prison corporation in America. Crants directed two state prison systems and served as president of the American Correctional Association. T. Don Hutto had a history of serving the prison system for more than twenty years.

The three men, Crants, Beasley, and Hutto, wrote and presented their business plan to a venture capital firm, Burch Investment Group. On February 14, 1983, Correctional Corporation of America became a reality. In 1985, *Financial World* printed summarized the approbation of Beasley. "We're on the ground floor of a multibillion-dollar industry." The prison troika had invested heavily in the privatizing business. Vicky Pelaez reflects on this privatizing boom of the 1980s:

> The prison privatization boom began in the 1980s, under the governments of Ronald Reagan and Bush, Sr., but reached its height in 1990 under William Clinton, when Wall Street stocks were selling like hotcakes. Clinton's program for cutting the federal workforce resulted in the Justice Departments contracting of private prison corporations for the incarceration of undocumented workers and high security inmates.[2]

Some serious questions should be drawn from Ms. Pelaez's notes on privatizing prisons. What was the political expediency of privatization? Who were the benefactors of this political process? How did this act make inmates vulnerable to serving as a human labor product in a prison economic industry?

Ms. Pelaez references the economic success of the two largest prison corporations in America:

> Private prisons are the biggest business in the prison industry complex. About 18 corporations guard 10,000 prisoners in 27 states. The two largest are Correctional Corporation of America (CCA) and Wackenhut [currently, GEO Group], which controls 75%. *Private prisons receive a guaranteed amount of money for each prisoner, independent of what it costs to maintain each one.*
>
> According to Russell Boraas, a private prison administrator in Virginia, "the secret to low operating costs is having a minimal number of guards or the maximum number of prisoners." The CCA has an ultra-modern prison in Lawrenceville, Virginia, where five guards on dayshift and two at night watch over 750 prisoners. In these prisons, inmates may get their sentences reduced for "good behavior," but for any infraction, they get 30 days

> added—which means more profits for CCA. According to a study of New Mexico prisons, it was found that CCA inmates lost 'good behavior time' at a rate eight times higher than those in state prisons.[3]

Another important assessment is the application of psychological supervision to increase profits. The prison system thrives as a lucrative prison industry to create profits.

There is a guaranteed amount for each inmate, no longer a human being, but a profit commodity. We can compare this proliferation of growth to the slave market as that "pot of gold."

George Wackenhut (The GEO Group)

George Wackenhut was the founder of the second-largest private prison corporation in America. He received his education from West Chester University and earned a BA degree from University of Hawaii and a MA degree in education from Johns Hopkins University. He was Director of Physical Education at Johns Hopkins University from 1946 to 1950.

George Wackenhut had five board members to render services to his corporation: Richard G. Capen, a publisher and US Ambassador to Spain, 1992–1993; Frank Carlucci, who worked in the government as the US Secretary of Defense, 1987–1989; Bobby Ray Inman, a military man who served as an admiral, NSA Director, and Deputy CIA Director; Paul X. Kelley, a military person who served with the 28th USMC Commandant, 1983–1987; and Thomas P. Stafford, an astronaut with Gemini 6 and 9, Apollo 10, Apollo-Soyu. Wackenhut and his board made his prison corporation a reality.

A closer look at the director provides a clearer picture of his work in the prison–industrial complex. Born George Russell Wackenhut on September 33, 1919, he grew up outside of Philadelphia, Pennsylvania, in the small community of Upper Darby. Upon completing high school in his town, he served in the US Army Corps of Engineers during World

War II. He was an eyewitness to the Japanese bombing of Pearl Harbor. Upon earning his degree from John Hopkins University, he assumed a position teaching physical education and health. His greatest change took place when he began his work with the FBI in 1951 as a special agent in Indianapolis and Atlanta. On this assignment, he handled cases related to counterfeit money, bad-check writing, and following up on Army deserters.

Wackenhut then added new dimensions in his life. In 1954, Wackenhut entered business for himself. He opened his office as Agent Investigations in Coral Gables, Florida. He began this office with three other men who worked together. A year later in 1955, because of dissension, Wackenhut bought out his partners and renamed the company after his name. In 1965, the Wackenhut Prison Corporation became a reality. He was very successful with his company. The profits afforded him the opportunity to lead a lavish lifestyle, owning several homes throughout the nation. "Prior to his move to Vero Beach, Florida, in 1995, his primary residence was 'Tyecliffe Castle,' in Coral Gables, near Miami."[4]

George Wackenhut died January 31, 2004. After his death, Wackenhut Prison Corporation was renamed, the GEO Group.

CHAPTER 14

Privatizing: Prison Support Base

How To Grow Prisons

In 2012, CCA (Correctional Corporations of America) sent a letter to prison officials in 48 states, offering to buy prisons from these states in exchange for a 20-year management contract and a guaranteed occupancy rate of 90%.[9] Federal Register March 3, 1993

What factor spiraled the growth of prisons from 1990 to 2010?

Two Colliding Objectives

- Hire more policemen to increase prison inmates
- Increase the inmate population to mandate an ongoing prison-construction industry

IRONY: Reduce the federal budget, surreptitiously, to foster the way for prison privatization.

In 1992, Bill Clinton campaigned on a presidential platform to reduce the federal budget. After inauguration, he was obliged to make this goal a reality. But in truth, he showed two images, one for the public and one behind closed doors.

The dismissal of the federal prison staff had a two-fold purpose. It dismissed a large percentage of federal prison employees while simultaneously making the prison population available for privatizing. It made a federal prison population available for corporations to develop a private prison industry.

These prison corrections companies were modern-day prison designs for profits. Just as Hospital Corporations of America (HCA) pioneered a hospital design for profit, the newly created prison corrections corporations were designed for profit.

The popular concept of humanitarianism in America was displaced by the profit motive. No more Hippocratic Oath, displacing a love and care for humanity. Hospitals became a model for the design of prison privatizing and profit. This was the brain child originally developed by multi-millionaire Ed Massey of Tennessee.

How do we grow the prisons?

STEP-BY-STEP DESIGN

- Prisons/facilities are built to meet the increasing prison population.
- The police force is increased to make drug arrests.
- Drug cartels are used in specified communities to validate the need for increased police force.
- The drug cartels and the increased police force increase arrests to grow the prisons.
- Growing the prisons, mandating prison construction, and hiring staff increased the number of workers for a cheap labor force for corporate growth with trade and commerce.
- Work by inmates, as a cheap labor force, inhibits labor demands for mainstream workers that will require corporations to pay regular wages.

Concepts To Explore In Prison Privatization

A farce was used to dismiss federal workers to reduce the federal budget. In disguise, the federal reduction budget made Federal Bureau of Prisons (BOP) inmates available for prison privatization. There is an insensitivity factor hidden in this agenda.

To dismiss federal workers is to send these people away as unemployed workers, who are from mainstream America. These people, more than likely, have to support their families, send their children to school, and be examples for decent community living.

When organizers of correctional corporations seek to become correctional companies, a fiduciary trust has been violated with the government and those who seek to engage in prison privatization. There are no studies to show that prison privatizing can reduce the government budget or provide more efficient services for BOP inmates. The obvious truth is how the old-age back-door think tank plan manipulates the government tax dollars to subsidize prison privatization corporations, where a few individuals grow their corporations at the expense of the taxpayer. This insensitivity lends itself to nepotism for future long-term profits.

This concept is further exploited, politically, by making appointments to persons who in return would serve as a conduit to grow the prison system by funneling contracts to these penal corporations.

> Although many rightly decry the Bureau's burgeoning inmate populations since 2000, a striking number of the sixteen privately managed Bureau facilities more than half (ten, to be precise) were awarded contracts beginning in the 1990s. That the Bureau began contracting in earnest with private corrections companies in the mid-1990s matters.[1]

The goal is not efficiency. We can forget that myth. The goal is to empower individuals to design and to grow these corporations into financial empires at the expense of the taxpayer and the government.

Justifying Prison Privatization [Reducing the Size of the Federal Workforce]

There is a built-in mechanism to justify prison privatization. The debate as to whether or not prison privatization is more efficient and less costly to tax payers has not been proven. Today, there is a great rise in awarding prison contracts to prison corporations across the nation. These penal institutions proclaim their services to be more cost effective than what BOP operated prior to the privatization period of the 1990s.

> Contrary to popular belief...the initial justification for privatizing the Bureau's facilities was not the result of economic necessity, but instead the indistinct outcome of a number of intersecting political (electoral) imperatives.[2]

A Close Look at the Prisons in the Clinton White House Years (1993–2000)

Bill Clinton's 1992 presidential campaign put him in a bind.

Clinton was confronted with fulfilling his campaign promises. His financial obligation upon assuming his responsibilities as president was to reduce the budget. In response to this goal, his challenge was to adjust the budget by reducing the federal workforce. Achieving this objective would placate the conservatives. The pseudo-mood of *Get tough on Crime* had become the nation's theme to fulfill operatives behind the think tank wall to allow for the growth of a furtive prison industry across the nation. How would the powers of his office avail him to accomplish these two objectives?

> Both aspirations emerged from Clinton's 1992 campaign promises to shrink the size of the government while, simultaneously, incarcerating more individuals in federal prisons for longer sentences.[3]

Clinton's White House years were devoted to fulfilling these objectives as discreetly as possible. The idea of prisons for profit mushroomed in the mid-1970s and took growth in 1983 to grow prisons as a financial industry in the nation. *To put the prisons on a solid foundation, legislation was enacted to impact sentencing laws to perpetuate the prison industry.* Clinton was responsible for two of these laws, the *Truth in Sentencing* bill and the *Violent Crime and Law Enforcement Act.*[4]

The "Truth in Sentencing" Bill

What in fact does this bill say? How did this bill affect the inmates? What impact did this bill have on the inmates and their families and/or the children of the nation connected to victims behind the prison wall? In some cases, with prison inmates, a sentence may be reduced based on positive modified behavior. In such a case, the inmate may have the opportunity to apply for an earlier release time. If reconciliation has occurred in this person's life and he/she realizes the consequences of the offense and seeks rehabilitation, this person can return to mainstream society and to his family for community adjustment. But, the *Truth in Sentencing* bill counteracts this vision of recovery. This bill does not provide for rehabilitation. In truth, it is a cruel bill designed to stifle the growth and preparation of an inmate to return to society.

This *Truth in Sentencing* bill "required offenders to serve at least 85 percent of their sentence before becoming eligible for parole."[5] In truth, this bill is a ploy to grow and to expand the prison industry. How does this occur? The best model to share with you to shed light on this bill is to review the institution of American slavery. The foremost goal of the bill was designed to validate the prison workforce by ensuring the years of an inmate to prevent [too much of] an interruption for the prison labor force.

When Europeans immigrated to America, they often hired themselves to the London and Plymouth companies to pay for their transportation. In this contractual arrangement, these indentured servants, as they were called, worked from five to seven years to indemnify their voyage to America. After this tenured period, they were able to live their lives as free persons. However, the colonial think tank engaged in economical thinking to conjure a way to prevent interruptions to their economic system. In essence, the plan was to find a permanent workforce. In 1661, this think tank introduced a bill in the House of Burgesses to make blacks permanent slaves. With this "property," the slave master had power to do as he pleased.

With the introduction of slavery in the American colonies, the South had a continuous workforce with no interruptions. As with Clinton's *Truth and Sentencing* bill, a similar economic principle was embedded in this law—less interruption in the prisons' cheap labor force!

In the *Truth in Sentencing* bill, inmates are mandated to spend at least 85 percent of their sentence in prison, regardless of model behavior. In this conceptual framework, the inmate's family suffers, and children are denied an earlier reconnection with parents and left vulnerable to street models. When Clinton signed this bill, he demonstrated loyalty to the prison growth model as an industry across the nation by enacting laws that would perpetuate a corrupt economic system resting in the hands of a few financial giants.

Congressional Prison Legislation

Violent Crime and Law Enforcement Act (Signed by Clinton on Sept. 13, 1994)

Like the Truth in Sentencing bill, the second law Clinton signed into effect was the Violent Crime and Law Enforcement Act. Our prisons should do more than incarcerate a person; they should be designed to provide rehabilitation. Sociologically, society would partake in preparing inmates to return to society in a saner state than when they were first isolated from the mainstream population. Failure to teach, train, and nurture the inmate who has been incarcerated simply increases the recidivism rate. For the individual, the prison becomes a revolving door.

> The crime bill provides that funding for its programs is to come from savings resulting from reductions in federal personnel recommended by the Vice President's National Performance Review. These savings are predicated on reducing 270,000 federal employees, which would result in almost $30 billion in savings.[6]

Now let us take a look at Clinton's *Violent Crime and Law Enforcement Act*. If, in fact, our concern is rehabilitation, the legislature should labor to enact laws that will address the issue and concern for rehabilitation. But this legislation is the antithesis of a rehabilitative model. This act "created over sixty new death penalty offenses, rendered prisoners ineligible from receiving Pell grants to participate in post-secondary degree programs while incarcerated, and *provided funds to hire an additional 100,000 police officers to enforce drug-related crimes*."[7]

This act *prohibited Pell Grant usage for career preparation* upon return to mainstream. This act set in place a legal plan to increase the recidivism rate and to provide continuity in the prison workforce. This act verifies the use of policemen to grow prison population—*the hiring of 100,000 policemen*. In summary, the act contributes to growing the prison population and to maximizing prison occupation for the corporate industrial industry. We summarize this scenario: drugs, policemen, and legislation to design laws with longer sentencing to perpetuate an economic prison industry.[8]

The power of the prison–industrial complex is so great that it boldly demands prisons be maintained at maximum capacity—contractual guaranteed occupancy rate.

> In 2012, CCA (Correctional Corporations of America) sent a letter to prison officials in 48 states, offering to buy prisons from these states in exchange for a 20-year management contract and a guaranteed occupancy rate of 90%.[9]

Human products and prisons for profit corporations are thriving on the stock market in 21st century America.

> In a 1990s report, Prudential Securities was bullish on CCA but noted, "It takes time to bring inmate population levels up to where they cover costs. Low occupancy is a drag on profits...company earnings would be strong if CCA succeeded in ramping up population levels in new facilities at an acceptable rate."[10]

The prisons are indeed as Vicky Pelaez said in "The Prison Industry in the United States: Big Business or a New Form of Slavery." Let us peer into some prison contractual dialogue in Ohio.

> In 2011, responding to an initiative from the State of Ohio to reduce "overhead costs by saving $130 million annually while adding 700 beds to house inmates in the overcrowded system," Corrections Corporation of America agreed to buy the Lake Erie Correctional Institution for $72 million. This represents a change of policy for CCA,

> which previously always constructed their own prisons the State offered for sale was taken as good news by the Ohio Civil Service employees Association, the union for prison guards.[11]

When prison corporations call for a **contractual guaranteed occupancy rate**, this in itself fosters a political mood to "create criminals" in an effort to fulfill the economic requirement. No wonder there have been bitter complaints from neighborhoods.

> Community organizations have criticized the proposals arguing that the contractual obligations of states to fill the prisons to 90% occupancy are poor public policy that could force communities into creating criminals, and that these contractual clauses end up costing taxpayers more than state-run prisons would.[12]

We need to ask a more vital question: *If Americans cannot trust leaders in a democracy to do that which is right for its citizenry, then where are the grounds for redress?* Should a democracy serve a few or all of its citizenry? This act contaminates the soul of America. The tax payers' dollars were used to establish and provide for an economic industry built on one segment of the population to grow the wealth of a select few individuals to make them corporate giants—in a democracy!

Statistics vividly reveal a decrease in violent crimes, but a growing increase in nonviolent crimes. These stats reveal a contrived growth rate using a controlled substance to inflate the prisons. Who is the culprit? The sad phenomenon is the use of the American government to abuse its own citizenry. When unveiling the jigsaw puzzle, one is able to view the political conundrum to make a prison industry a reality. First, reduce federal workers to make inmates available for prison privatization and pour wealth into the hands of a few selected individuals to allow them to build their corporate empires on the tax dollar. Second, destroy families across the nation by snatching federal jobs from BOP workers in order to make inmates available for prison privatization. Third, pass legislation to perpetuate prisons as an economic industry with power and control in the hands of a few political individuals.

Let us look further at Clinton's financial and political manipulation to disguise the prison privatization plan. First, private companies were to be used to manage new federal prisons. The key to all of this is to devise a means, in disguise, to issue private prison contracts. These contracts would be issued to individuals who had designed and constructed prisons. The shrewdly written privatization plan under Clinton's administration "embraced the concepts behind the National Performance Review, Vice President Al Gore's 1993 study to reinvent governments so that it 'works better and cost less,' especially the commitment to cut between 100,000–250,000 federal employees from the payroll."[13] In essence, in the public eye, this administration was created to reduce the budget, but in reality, finances were being used in a creative way to advance prison privatization. The jargon would give the illusion of great government innovations. In truth, the public was being robbed of federal workers in their community to be replaced by political kickbacks to individuals to allow for the development of a perpetual economic prison industry.

> Clinton's hypothesis was that after reducing federal personnel, Washington, DC, would then turn to private contractors to do their work.
>
> It's more than a bit ironic, for instance, that in early 1993, Michael Quinlan, Director of the Federal Bureau of Prisons from 1987–1992, was recruited to work for the Corrections Corporation of America (CCA), the nation's largest private prison firm. Since Quinlan's arrival the Bureau has awarded contracts to private corrections

> firms nearly on a yearly basis. And the trend persists to this very day.[14]

In 2010, a current example of private prison contracts and appointments to solidify the power base of the prison industry may be seen in the United States Marshals Service (USMS) appointment. The second-largest prison in America is the GEO Group, formerly, the George Wackenhut Corrections Corporation. Upon his death in 2004, the name was changed to the GEO Group. Our focus is on the two largest prison corporations in the United States—CCA and the GEO Group. These two prisons, alone, control seventy-five percent of prisons in the United States. Prison privatizing contracts are the lifeblood of these penal corporations.

Privatization and Government Contracts Subsidize Prison Corporations

Our example will show how the relationship of prison privatization by the government can provide contracts—the lifeblood of prison corporations to sustain an economic prison industry. We will use the political appointment of Stacia Hylton as an example to show how these political appointments feed the prison industry.

Stacia Hylton [Began work with USMS January 2011] [R-Senator Grassley of Iowa]

In 2010, President Obama nominated Stacia Hylton as the new Director of the United States Marshals Service (USMS). What is the USMS? "The Marshals Service handles security for federal courthouses, apprehends federal fugitives and oversees the detention of federal prisoners awaiting trial or immigration proceedings."[15]

Who is Ms. Hylton, and what is her background?

Wright gives a terse summary:

> Hylton, a former Acting Deputy Director of the U.S. Marshals Service with a lengthy and distinguished career in law enforcement, was employed from June 2004 to February 2010 as the Federal Detention Trustee. Following her retirement she was nominated by President Obama on September 20, 2010 to direct the Marshals Service.[16]

Prior to this nomination, Hylton "had agreed to a consulting contract with The GEO Group—the nation's second-largest private prison operator—worth $112,500. This appointment required Senate confirmation. During this period, several Civil Rights and civic organizations wrote the President asking him to rescind his nomination of Stacia Hylton as Director of USMS. These pleas were ignored and on December 2010, Hylton became the first woman to be appointed to this position."

> On November 9, 2010, a coalition of human rights and criminal justice organizations—the Alliance for Justice, Human Rights Defense Center, Private Corrections Working Group, Grassroots Leadership, National Lawyers Guild, International CURE, Detention Watch Network and Justice Policy Institute—announced their opposition to President Obama's nomination of Stacia A. Hylton to head the U.S. Marshals Service.[17]

Despite these protests against Hylton's appointment, no one took heed to these community voices for justice. In fact, a different scenario emerged to ensure the Senate confirmation for this appointment would become a reality.

> The day after the campaign against Hylton's nomination was announced, the Senate Judiciary Committee

> scheduled her for a hearing the following week, on November 17, in an apparent effort to "fast-track" her nomination.[18]

The inlaid power under political influence to perpetuate the growth of prisons as an economic industry in a democracy solidified a conduit to ensure federal contracts would flow neatly into the prison corporations of America. Wright sheds light on how key appointments can create a financial flow to prison corporations:

> During Hylton's tenure as the Federal Detention Trustee, GEO Group, the nation's second largest for profit private prison company, was awarded a number of lucrative contracts to house federal prisoners. These included a sole-source ten-year contract at GEO's Western Region Detention Facility in San Diego, generating approximately $34 million in annual revenue; a 20-year contract to operate the 1,500-bed Rio Grande Detention Center in Laredo, Texas with an estimated $34 million in annual revenue; and a 20-year sole-source contract to manage the Robert A. Deyton Detention Facility in Lovejoy, Georgia, generating $16–20 million in annual revenue.[19]

What was Hylton's work while serving as the Federal Detention Trustee?

Wright expands on the financial contract flow to prisons:

> Also while Hylton served as the Federal Detention Trustee, Corrections Corp. Of America (CCA), the nation's largest private prison company, was awarded a 20-year contract to design, build and operate the $80 million 1,072-bed Nevada Southern Detention Center.

> Further, under Hylton's direction, the Office of the Federal Detention Trustee granted a sole-source 20-year contract to CCA to hold U.S. Marshals prisoners at the company's Leavenworth Detention Center in Kansas, and approved a sole-source contract for CCA to house U.S. Marshals detainees at the prison in Pinal County, Arizona. *Approximately 40 % of CCA's business comes from the federal government.*[20]

The political influence reaches beyond retirement or resignation. The connection button remains open over a lifetime to ensure political favors and kickbacks for being of service to the hidden strings of money, power, and control. Paul Wright sheds light:

> As reported by the Washington Times in an October 25 article, after retiring as the Federal Detention Trustee earlier this year, Hylton quickly accepted a consulting job with GEO Group through her Virginia-based company, Hylton Kirk and Associates, LLC, of which she is the president and sole owner. In her financial disclosure statement, Hylton reported income of $112,500 for "consulting services for detention matters, federal relations, and acquisitions and mergers." GEO Group is the only company listed in her disclosure statement in connection with those consulting services.[21]

What was the work of Stacia Hylton in the position as director of USMS? Immediately, she assumed her assignment. There were so many complaints about the work of the newly appointed director that she was finally brought before a Senate hearing. In reference to the case, Stacia Hylton resigned her position in 2015. However, her appointment played a very important role in funneling government contracts to the major prison corporations of America.

How do we summarize the government connection with fueling prison contracts—placing wealth in the hands of a few to perpetuate an economic prison industry in a democracy?

> A revolving door is inefficient, so too is cronyism. Cronyism, by its very preferential nature, is antagonistic to the notion of fairness in competition, supposedly the bulwark of modern capitalism. Despite the popular taken-for-granted ideology that privatization spawns efficiency, there is no evidence to suggest that the Clinton administration—the vanguard of federal prison privatization—believed that private firms were any more effective than the Bureau at containing and rehabilitating prisoners. Clinton's calculus was political, not empirical. My hope here is that a brief sweep of past privatization debates will help us to challenge the sweeping partisanship of those in the present.[22]

The conflicted standard for maintaining an equilibrium for justice tends to be antiquated or a modern-day Rip Van Winkle. Wright sheds light on this outdated concept of justice:

> "It is extremely worrisome that Ms. Hylton is nominated for a position where she would be directly involved with overseeing contracts with private prison companies to house federal detainees, given her cozy relationship with the private prison industry and her acceptance of more than $112,000 from GEO through her consulting work," said Ken Kopeczynski, director of the Private Corrections

> Working Group, a non-profit citizen watchdog organization that opposes prison privatization.
>
> Despite repeated requests to both the White House and GEO Group, neither responded to questions regarding Hylton's consulting relationship with GEO. Hylton could not be reached for comment as her phone number is not listed. [23]

Democracy pinned by the iron hands of oppression. Democracy slain and justice obliterated.

> "While Ms. Hylton indicated she had spoken with the Office of Governmental Ethics to resolve any potential conflicts, the fact remains that she formed a consulting firm before retiring as Federal Detention Trustee, and apparently the only company she consulted for is GEO Group—which had received multi-million dollar contracts from the federal government, including the U. S. Marshals," Kopezynski noted. "Given that she accepted money from the very industry she was overseeing as Detention Trustee, and will be overseeing again if appointed to head the Marshals, this is a conflict that cannot simply be waived. It serves the public for the Obama administration to nominate Ms. Hylton in light of such an obvious conflict of interest."[24]

Would the coalitions of Hylton's appointment be redeemed? She served as Director of USMS for four years.

On June 9, 2015, Iowa statesman Grassley responds to the resignation of Stacia Hylton.

USMS head

From Press Release

Senate Judiciary Committee Chairman Chuck Grassley of Iowa made the following statement regarding the announced resignation of U.S. marshals Service Director Stacia Hylton:

The U.S. Senate Committee on Judiciary press release on June 9, 2015. This proceedings, March 19, 2015 opened.

> Senate Judiciary Committee Chairman Senator Chuck Grassley of Iowa, is exploring allegations that U.S. Marshals Service (USMS) officials hired unqualified personnel in a high-level contract position in order to receive favorable consideration for a promotion.
>
> According to claims received by the Senate Judiciary Committee, then-Deputy Assistant Director of the Asset Forfeiture Division (AFD) Kimberly Beal allegedly influenced subordinates to waive qualification requirements in order to hire an unqualified person who was recommended for a highly-paid contract position by USMS Director Stacia Hylton. Beal allegedly did so while under consideration for her current position as Assistant Director, which is the highest-ranking post in the division. [Grassley Probes Quid Pro Quo Hiring Allegations at the U.S. Marshals Services. [Washington, March 19, 2015]
>
> In a letter to Acting Deputy Attorney General Sally Yates. Grassley requested a full explanation of the circumstances surrounding the hiring as well as material on the current and former qualification requirements for the contract position in question.

An March 19, 2015
VIA ELECTRONIC TRANSMISSION

The Honorable Sally Quillan Yates
Acting Deputy Attorney General
United States Department of Justice

Dear Acting Deputy Attorney General Yates:

I write with some concern regarding allegations of inappropriate hiring practices within the United States Marshals Services (USMS) Asset Forfeiture Division (AFD) Whistleblowers with specific knowledge of the process have alleged that the AFD improperly waived qualification requirements in order to hire Donald Lenzie as a Senior Forfeiture Financial Specialist (SFFS), a highly paid contractor position.

Information obtained by the Committee suggests that Director Stacia A. Hylton personally recommended Mr. Lenzie for this position and that Kimberly Beal, then AFD Deputy Assistant Director, influenced subordinates to waive contract qualification requirements in order to hire him. It is further alleged that Ms. Beal violated these contracting standards in order to receive favorable consideration from Director Hylton in Ms. Beal's effort to become the AFD Assistant Director, a position she now occupies.

This quid pro quo exchange of favors, if true, would raise serious doubts about the operational practices of the USMS AFD under Ms. Beal as well as, frankly, Ms. Hylton's leadership of the USMS.

Accordingly, please provide the Committee with a complete written explanation of the circumstances surrounding the hiring of Mr. Lenzie no later than March 26, 2015. Please also include in your response the following information:

1. The resumes of all individuals who have filled the contractor position of SFFS under the USMS AFD contract with Forfeiture Support Associates (FSA)

2. A copy of the current and all previous versions of the contract qualification requirements used to hire SFFS contractors from 2010 to the present.

Please mark each version with the date that it became effective.

Should you have questions, please contact DeLisa Lay of my Committee staff at (202) 224-5225.

Thank you,
Sincerely,
Charles E. Grassley
Chairman
Committee on the Judiciary
Cc:
The Honorable Michael E. Horowitz
Inspector General
Office of the Inspector General [25]

CHAPTER 15

Prison Rehabilitation Prior to the 1970s

James V. Bennett Prison Reform

> *I knew I would pursue the cause of prison reform as if it were a call. Within two years I was able to recommend, write, and help get passed the laws that led to the establishment of the first federal Bureau of Prisons. I was later to take charge of all the federal prisons and change most aspects of prison life.*
>
> James V. Bennett, *I Chose Prison*

Am I My Brother's Keeper?

I Chose Prison by James V. Bennett, published in *Reader's Digest Condensed Books*, Vol. 2, 1970, pp. 374–467. Edited by Rodney Campbell. An innovator in prison reform, chapter 1: My Brother's Keeper.

I got my honorable discharge, married my Pembroke girl, and went to Washington to see about that government career. I passed the civil service examinations and was assigned to the U.S. Bureau of Efficiency, a forerunner of the subsequent Hoover Commissions designed to help streamline the federal bureaucracy. I also attended law school at George

Washington University and received my degree in 1926. My first real opportunity in the civil service came when Herbert Brown, chief of the bureau, asked me if I would like to be assigned to the Department of Justice to study the federal prison system. The purpose of the study would be to show that the country could save money by putting idle federal prisoners to work. This was an important and controversial proposal, of which I was in favor, for fruitful work engenders self-respect and encourages a prisoner to redeem himself. But I was aware that organized labor was hostile to the idea on grounds that the products of low-cost prison labor, thrown on the market, could undercut the products of free men. I knew that the study I was asked to do would have to be expert and invulnerable; and that it would be likely to go all the way to the White House [Reader's Digest, p. 385].

Before accepting the job, therefore, I read every book about prison industries I could find. Then for additional insight, I set out on a tour of some typical state prisons, starting with the Ohio penitentiary at Columbus, one of the four largest in the country.* What I saw there was decisive to my early career.

When I first looked at that antiquated stone prison, with its high walls and its bristling towers patrolled by riflemen, I lost some of my desire to present my letter of introduction to the warden. Through the bars that surrounded the reception area I saw gray clad men marching about silently, each with large numbers inked on the back of his rough shirt. It was a depressing introduction.

After what seemed like an unnecessary delay, I was ushered into the office of Warden Thomas, who sat at a square oak desk as solid as the stones of the prison. Thomas checked my credentials and sent for a guide to take me around the workshops—a prisoner who was, I later learned, a former state treasurer who had put his hand in the till. "Show Mr. Bennett around and bring him right back here." I followed my guide into an interior courtyard, where I saw a line of men moving with a long, skating stride, each man with one arm on the shoulder of the man in front. This was the famous lockstep. The prisoners moved rapidly, with no sound but the shuffle of their shoes, and their eyes were focused on the ground.

My escort volunteered no comment. He showed me around the tailors' shop, the weavers' shop, and the machine shop, all poorly lit and filled with obsolete and worn-out equipment. Many of the workers were squatting against the walls of the rooms or loitering by the drinking fountains.

The prison officers in charge were positioned on platforms three feet above the floor, heavy clubs in their hands. Now and then a guard would pound his club on the platform and point at a prisoner, or shout an order, and the prisoner would seem to understand. I thought the prisoners looked dispirited and hopeless, but the guards could not be blamed.

The enormous cellblocks depressed me beyond measure. One [p. 387] of them housed more than nine hundred men, with two prisoners to each ten-by-five-foot stone cubicle. As we walked down one corridor, I saw several men pacing their cells with unusual intensity, jabbering to themselves, rattling their bars, shouting obscenities. An officer told me that these men were "psychos," kept in the cell-block because there was no other place for them. I wondered whether this was really a civilized country in the third decade of the twentieth century. But there was more to come.

Warden Thomas welcomed me back to his office and began to talk. He said that his was an extremely tough job, and that he was not too impressed by "softies" and "do-gooders." He did not see much point in prison industrial work, because there was not enough market for prison products. The unions had too much power. As for the prisoners, they were getting what they deserved. I asked Thomas how prison officials maintained discipline and how they punished offenders.

He said, "Come with me. I'll show you."

We strolled back across the courtyard to a small brick building. Thomas handed on the door, which swung open, and we walked into a small, dark room with a high bench at the far end. This was his courtroom, Thomas said, where he and his deputies sat in judgment upon prisoners who violated the rules. The punishments were loss of visiting and correspondence privileges, loss of good behavior credits, and "the hole."

"Open up, officer," Thomas said. "I'll show Mr. Bennett." A barred steel door was unlocked, and after that, a steel boilerplate door. We went through into a narrow corridor lined with [p. 388] more steel doors, and Thomas motioned to a guard to open one. There stood a pathetic creature, his eyes staring vacantly, handcuffed to a bar halfway up the wall.

"What are you here for?" the warden asked.

"I put in a cop-out [request] to see you, sir," the man replied.

"How long have you been in here?"

"Five days."

"I don't believe you," Warden Thomas said. He hurried me on down the corridor to the cells reserved for prisoners who refused to work or were otherwise recalcitrant. These men stood for hours or days in tiny strap-iron cages, in which there was no room to sit down, until they agreed to go back to work. I did not argue with the warden or ask any more questions. I had seen enough, and I never wanted to get out of a place so badly in my life.

After this experience, I canceled the rest of my inspection schedule and so was spared the sight of the Minnesota State Prison and the Leavenworth Penitentiary in the mid-1920s. I went home and spent the weekend wondering whether I could accept this kind of assignment and whether I could be of any assistance.

My wife had few doubts, however, that I ought to persevere. Marie had done social work in Harlem and she was excited by the concept of prison reform. She did not see why prisoners were treated like wild beasts, or why, so degraded, they should be turned loose upon society only to commit new crimes. She was concerned about the plight of prisoners' wives and families, who were penniless, shamed, and shunned. Nor did she understand why prison labor could not be utilized constructively, perhaps to make products for sale to state agencies, so as not to compete with private markets.

Finally, Marie asked a question, **"Why not be your brother's keeper?" [p. 388]**

On the following Monday morning I reported to Herbert Brown at the Bureau of Efficiency and told him about my visit to Ohio State Penitentiary. He was a considerate man, and after I had finished, he asked if I still wanted to undertake the prison-study [p. 389] assignment. I could, if I'd rather, investigate the supply procurement systems of the Veterans Administration.

"Thanks," I said, "but I'll stay with the job you gave me."

So I chose prison.

Chapter 2. 1700 Lashes, p. 389

My entry into the prison service thus came about more or less by happenstance; but once I had made my decision, I knew I would pursue the cause of prison reform as if it were a call. Within two years I was able to recommend, write, and help get passed the laws that led to the establishment of the first federal Bureau of Prisons. I was later to take charge of all the federal prisons and change most aspects of prison life. As I saw it, my obligation was plain: *I was in prison and ye came unto me...Inasmuch as ye have done it unto one of the least of these my brethren, ye have done it unto me.*

It was therefore not naïve for me to study the lives of past prison reformers and to frame recommendations in the light of the torch they had placed in my hands. There was Cesare Beccaria, for example, a young nobleman of Milan who visited the horrifying dungeons of his native state and in July 1764 published what is perhaps the most influential single essay in the history of justice. He called it Essay on Crimes and Punishments and his words are pertinent today:

> The countries most noted for the severity of punishments are always those in which the most bloody and inhuman actions are committed—for the hand of the assassin

> and the hand of the legislator are directed by the same spirit of ferocity…The end of punishment…is to prevent the criminal from doing further injury to society, and to prevent others from committing the like offense. In order therefore that every punishment may not be an act of violence committed against a single individual, it ought to be public, speedy, necessary, the least possible in the given circumstances, proportioned to the crime, dictated by the laws. [Readers' Digest, p. 390]

Beccaria's Essay was a sensational success. Within six months of its translation into French, it went through seven editions. In the American colonies, John Adams, Franklin, Jefferson, and probably Washington read it, and in the new country punishment began to tend toward imprisonment instead of torture [Reader's Digest, p. 390].

James V. Bennett and Prison Reform [p. 390]

James V. Bennett began his prison reform work in the mid-1920s in the Bureau of Efficiency. He made many tours of prisons across the United States. In his visit to the state penitentiary in Atlanta, this system sent his mind to reminisce his reading on the Andersonsville Civil War prison camp. When the Justice Department requested a report on the prisons, Bennett had written his assignment. This report began with a history of the federal prisons.

> There were none until in 1891. Congress authorized the transfer of the military prison at Fort Leavenworth, Kansas, to the Justice Department for the housing of civilian prisoners. In 1896 the construction of the walled Leavenworth Penitentiary began. Subsequently, Atlanta and an abandoned marshals' jail on McNeil Island in Puget Sound were brought into the federal

> system under the management of a superintendent of prisons in Washington, with a staff of about a dozen people. The wardens were political appointees from the beginning. [p. 402]

The main body of his report summarized the appalling conditions in prisons. He used his experience leverage to outline recommendations for change. In these recommendations, Bennett called for "the establishment of a federal prison bureau within the Justice Department" [p. 402].

> The new bureau would have full control of the prisons and its first business would be to humanize prison life and to set an example to reformers in the states. I proposed the building of three new penitentiaries and experimental-type institutions, also two new "narcotics farms" in which addicts could be treated separately from the rest of the prison population, the whole system being keyed to a plan of rehabilitation [p. 402]

Bennett continued his prison review, while simultaneously holding fast to his mission and his wife's challenge, "I am My Brother's Keeper." Sanford Bates, prison administrator from Massachusetts had been asked by President Hoover "to find ways of overhauling federal prisons." Bates had read Bennett's report on recommendations for prison innovation and invited him to join him in the Justice Department to write recommendations for implementation in the federal prison system.

> My assignment was to help write the legislative proposals that Hoover would send to Congress. The first bill was to set up the new Bureau of Prisons. The second, a tougher proposition, authorized industries in the federal prisons and required federal agencies to buy our products. My

> strategy was to tie both the industries program and the compulsory-purchase clause to a broad statement of the purpose of prison reforms. This enabled President Hoover to throw his prestige behind us, and without undue delay the prison bureau was created and prison industries were under way. [RD, p. 403]

Bennett had a concern for preparing inmates with life skills to survive in returning to mainstream. The prisons, in his opinion should be rehabilitative, equipping them with skills to make a re-entry into society.

> Encouraged by this, we asked for and obtained authority to build two new prisons and a home for mentally ill prisoners. We established a full-time federal board of parole, and expanded the use of probation. We also brought about a significant change in the role of the U.S. Public Health Service. When we invited it to administer medical and psychiatric care in our prisons, we were awarding the PHS its first mission beyond the care of coast-guardsmen and the management of port quarantine. From this start the PHS extended its responsibility widely and today is involved in struggles to eradicate almost all forms of disease in the nation and abroad. [RD, p. 403]

Bennett concurred with Sanford Bates regarding criminality and rehabilitation. The current status of prisons was more active with stringent laws of regimental behavior with a high discipline code without resiliency.

> Bates believed that criminality could be cured in medical fashion, that punishment was out-of-date. And when Franklin Roosevelt moved into the White House in 1933

> he ratified Hoover's charters for prison reform and reappointed not only Bates but his three assistant directors, of whom I was one.

Roosevelt was confronted with providing a variety of work experiences for the American people during the Depression in 1929. Bennett and Bates were able to provide innovative changes in the prisons. Their business work-project industry met with great success. The two-fold goal was to equip the inmates with skills they could use in readjusting to life as well as to earn funds while they were completing their jail sentence. The World War II era provided opportunities for much growth within the prison industry.

> We made bomb fins, gun brushes, and in a variety of armament and support goods. The prison work week went from forty to forty-eight hours, and the men were paid overtime. By 1943 we had forty-nine plants in operation. We even had an airplane mechanics school at the Chillicothe, Ohio, reformatory, and our graduates were in demand in the Air Corps and, after the war, in civilian airlines and aircraft companies. [RD, p. 405]

"Am I My Brother's Keeper?" became a reality for Bennett when he was appointed to succeed Sanford Bates as director of the Bureau of Prisons.

> President Roosevelt called me to his office and expressed his concern with prison reform, offering to do everything he could to help. With FDR's engaging smile and warm handshake, I went off to my new duties.

> Thus heartened and empowered, I resolved to make a drastic start. I struck first and hardest at what would now be called the [p.405] gut issue of prison reform—brutality. In my first administrative order I ruled that prison guards were no longer permitted to carry nightsticks, trucheons, or blubs. I knew that corporal punishment was not allowed in federal prisons, but also that it was secretly practiced. I made it plain that there was to be no lashing, no use of the strap, no handcuffing of men to bars, no improper solitary confinement. Further, I ordered that prisoners could not be punished by removal of good-conduct credits or denial of important privileges without approval by my office in Washington.

Bennett was apprised of some results of his innovations in the prisons. Visitors were surprised to observe a new prison environment.

> The working relationship between the guards and the prisoners improved as mutual fear diminished. One Tennessee warden, on an inspection tour of a federal prison, told his guide: "O.K. I've seen all your showplaces. Now show me where you whip'em." When the federal officer replied that there was no whipping, the visitor laughed. "You come work for me any time, boy," he said. "You know how to keep your mouth shut." [RD, p. 406]

The innovative disciplinarian techniques were more humane, less of a beastly punishment but to define role changing behavior to make the violators responsible for their own behavior and more susceptible to developing a positive conscience.

> In fact, the standard punishment was administrative segregation, known as "seg." Prisoners who disobeyed orders were isolated in cells for several days. They were given the standard prison ration. They could not receive letters but could write them, and were allowed books and tobacco. If a prisoner still was obstreperous he was removed to punitive segregation, where he was deprived of all privileges. The idea was to cool off offenders, and it worked for most. [RD, p. 406]

Bennett paid close monitoring of the progress and effectiveness of changes implemented in the prison system. When positive progress was observed, he introduced layers of his program to reflect the entire prison system.

> With the issue of cruelty resolved, my associates and I felt free to promulgate new orders. The bureau ruled, for example, that every prisoner should get a stand ration of five pounds of food per day. Cafeterias were installed, replacing the hoary old food buckets, and varied menus introduced. Mealtime silence, with its overtones of Cherry Hill and Auburn, was abolished. Instead of marching in to their benches, the men were allowed to go to meals at any time the mess hall was open, and to eat at four-man tables with whomever they chose. In the first of several moves to desegregate the federal prisons, we urged Negro and white prisoners to sit at meals together, work together, and share cells and dormitories. [RD, p. 407]

Contributing to the whole being of an inmate was a major concern for Bennett. He wanted to introduce activities to inspire the inmates to grow and to change. He thought of various means and ways to realize this idea.

> Next, we expanded recreational facilities—baseball, football, volleyball, and indoor games such as table tennis. Our prison baseball leagues soon reached comparatively high standards. We supplied books, magazines, newspaper, radios, and, in time, television. There were libraries and reading rooms in which there was a rule of silence. The grim screens and barriers through which prisoners and their families had peered at each other during visiting hours were torn down.
>
> We re-equipped the visiting rooms with sofas, tables, and arm chairs, while several of our wardens arranged outdoor visiting areas where people could picnic together. I lengthened the visiting hours and, mindful that men had once been locked in their cells "from sundown to sunup," I set back the hour for lights-out, scheduling vocational and academic activities in the evenings. Finally, to prisoners who demonstrated good behavior we assigned individual cubicles or semiprivate unlocked rooms. [RD, p. 407]

A major concern for Bennett was related to the indolent population which was confronted with health challenges and with mental health issues. He did not waste time in addressing these concerns.

> So we placed full-time Public Health Service medical officers at each institution. Incredibly, this had never been done before. We enlisted part-time specialists and consultants to help the doctors, and we brought in trained medical orderlies. Many forgotten, undernourished,

> malformed citizens of the Depression era were now helped toward better health. Then we added to the system new medical centers at Springfield, Missouri, and Fort Worth, Texas. And before World War II began I succeeded in obtaining a hospital for narcotics offenders at Lexington, Kentucky. [RD, p.408]

Bennett moved his prison reform to address the issue of the drug population. He was thoroughly encouraged with the idea of designating a farm to combat this problem.

> I had been urging from the beginning that we create a farm where addicts could be treated as sick people and taken out of the prisons, both for their own sakes and because they would slow down the new programs I wished to introduce. In the mid-1920s, when I entered government service, drug users amounted to one in a thousand of our population. They were mostly white men in their late twenties, from well-off families, and from cities. After World War II drug convictions began climbing sharply and the percentage of Negroes, all from large cities, rose from thirteen percent in 1946 to fifty-three percent in 1957, and on up, I felt compelled to plead anew do perspective. To the end of my career I opposed those who wanted to lock addicts up for life. As I kept repeating, addiction is illness; and the true fight against narcotics is in the slums, in all of our moves against poverty and despair.

The prison reform had come a long distance of years from Bennett's beginning in the 1920s. As new programs were introduced, he continued his search to make prisons a true system of rehabilitation—a milestone for preparing inmates for return, capable and able to start life with a new beginning and using their prison acquired skills to prepare a new walk of life for them. This improvement was enough to keep Bennett's heart inspired to continue his search to resurrect inmates to rediscover their lives. The year of his retirement in 1964 gave him kudos for the great service he had given in working to achieve the mission he realized with an affirmative response, "Yes, I Am My Brother's Keeper."

We are in the 21st century and we need to review the work of James Bennett and how he addressed the prisons during his era. A look into the profile of a man, who pursued his work with a mind and a mission, made outstanding differences and provides insight into what our role should be by asking a similar question, "***Am I My Brother's Keeper?***" A greater question to ask, is what sociological problems must society innovate to answer and to understand why a prison industry is thriving in a democracy in the 21st century is so ineffective?

When James V. Bennett retired in 1964, the American prison system was much improved. This great work was reflected in showing how the prison populations had decreased. In fact, in the State of New York, statistics show "In January 1973 there were 12,500 persons in the State prison system" (The Correctional Association of New York).

Part II

The African American Lantern

Voice From Across Jordan

What happened to the community?
Questions to be answered!
A Charge to Keep

What happened to the community spirit that we cultivated in you? Why have you turned from the Faith tradition? Why have you given up God's law for the world? Why have you neglected to teach the children? Why are there so many divorces? Why are there so many children having children? Why is the teenage pregnancy rate so high? Why is there so much violence in the community? Where are the Christian models for youth?

Why are so many or our men locked behind the prison walls? Is this a new form of slavery? Why have so many of you run to the suburbs with your economic gains and left the "diamonds in the rough" to perish without role models to inspire and lift them up to realize their gifts and talents?

Why have you thrown away God's gifts? Remember your heritage, your Negro Spirituals of old, your family prayer hour, your dinner table and the nurturing of children, family living and building community! Remember your charge! Your charge from the Lord is to teach each generation about the goodness of the Lord. Have you thrown away your Faith Tradition?

Have you forgotten the Faith Story? The Faith Story is the song that you keep in your heart. Always remember you were slaves in America from 1661 to 1865, but you were brought out of bondage by the strong arm of God. Remember the promise the Lord made to us as a people: "If you keep my laws and my commandments I will bless you and your children. If you disobey my laws and my commandments, the curse will be on you and your children." You do remember, don't you? You do remember Deuteronomy 11:26-27? Well, from my view, life looks awfully dim down there, but I charge you to go back and remember your Faith Tradition. You can turn around while God has not removed his breath from the land.

We Dropped the Ball!

African Americans at the Crossroad

We African Americans had a golden ball in our hands.

About 40 years ago, we dropped it. When people come to this country now and view our current state of being, they cannot believe 40 years ago we had a golden opportunity. They laugh at us, engage in private buzz groups, and wonder why we let our children self-destruct!

Ah, come on, I know we sit with our fineries, six figures, investments, top-of-the-line vehicles, techno-savvy stuff and more. Of course, you are saying, "She's not talking about us." Well, the truth of it is, yes, I am; I am talking about all of us—the not-so-well-off and the well-off!

You see, we come from a people who served as a pillar of strength to this nation. No work was too hard for the strong African American women and strong African American men who worked from sun up to sun down! With little or no education, they bound themselves together "to make something out of nothing" to enable the race to survive! They had work ethics! **They transmitted these work ethics to their children**—father to son, mother to daughter. Today, if we called a service repair person into our homes, we would have to pay this person, first for coming out and then for the work. Our children are not acquiring the skills they once were privileged to accrue. We cannot talk about economic empowerment unless we talk about our children. Our children are being abused and exploited in every manner possible. And we sit, quietly and complacently, not elevating the bar for our children. **Aunt Jemima did not do that to her children!**

Aunt Jemima had her children under control! She had the white and black children of the nation under control! Now, our children are walking around as if in some satanic daze, not knowing their purpose in life, without love in their hearts, doing anything. I dare not mention the dress code and the prisons and the early graves and the lack of critical thinking skills to raise them up out of the morass of degradation and human destruction.

Forty years! What happened? Why did you drop the golden ball? Why did you get out of the driver's seat? What was the glue that held the African American family together for almost a century, from 1865 to 1965?

Make no mistake about it! It was the faith tradition. It was the Good Neighbor Policy, the Golden Rule, the Ten Commandments, teaching manners, respect, and responsibility to self, their elders, and others that made the difference! It was our gathering around the meal table and nurturing the children on how to live in community, teaching, disciplining, training, and modeling for our children that shaped our children with loving, caring, sharing, and forgiving.

You see, when we fail to execute our role as African American parents, carrying out the faith tradition and the historic heritage, we fail our children and leave them as pawns to a society which claims to rehabilitate, but ultimately contributes to their destruction!

- Pawns to fashion designers
- Pawns to the movie industry
- Pawns to television
- Pawns to music industry
- Pawns on college campuses where credit cards are given
- Pawns to the prison industry
- Pawns to the courts

- Pawns to teen pregnancy centers
- Pawns to special education

Now is the time to rise up and reclaim our children! Now is the time to **get back into the driver's seat to teach, train, discipline, love, and nurture our children** so they can be all God will have them to be.

You, as progenitors of the African American heritage, have power to turn this nation around. Oh, I know Hollywood has you singing, ***Aunt Jemima is dead***, but you can revive her spirit to make a difference in teaching, training, disciplining, and loving our children.

What happened?

You see, this is what happened when we dropped the golden ball:

- We broke the tie with our parents and grandparents ("*Reconnect with Old School*").
- We severed the nurturing vine.
- We lost the proud heritage, where we specialized in teaching, training, loving, and disciplining our children.

And you know what we need to do to revitalize the spirit? We need to put some logs in the fireplace of America. Our foreparents kept the fire burning with logs of HOPE! Remember what Aunt Jemima [with her busy schedule] would stop and say to your sister or brother rocking the baby in a chair? "Gimme my baby. Let me take out time and give my baby some love—so he/she can thrive and grow, thrive and glow." And Aunt Jemima would cuddle her baby in her lap, sing tender songs, smile, and engage in small talk with her child, giving tender love, nurturing the heart and soul of her baby.

WE'VE LOST THE GIFTS GOD GAVE US TO NURTURE FAMILY AND TO BUILD COMMUNITY.

You know the gifts we received:

- Motherly wit, second to none
- Our Negro spirituals (instead of killing and stealing, we sang songs of hope)
- Our faith tradition: the Good Neighbor Policy, the Golden Rule
- Respect for our elders and the Ten Commandments
- Fireside chats and cultural heritage in the kitchen corners and the family prayer hour.

When we fail to execute our role as African American parents, carrying out the faith tradition and our historic heritage, we fail our children and leave them vulnerable to be pawns to society, unable to realize the greatness God meant for them. **We become everyone else's trash, junk, and prison dung!** God requires us to get up, get up now, and teach, train, nurture, and discipline our children!

WHEN DO WE BEGIN?

Now is the time to begin! Each of you can make a difference, right where you are. Even with your economic problems, you can make a difference. **Get back into the driver's seat! Get back to teaching your children!** Get back to teaching your children manners, the Good Neighbor Policy, the Golden Rule, the Ten Commandments, and respecting the elderly—the neighbors—and watchdog the schools, put the school into your schedule. Set rules and guidelines for children. Prepare warm, healthy meals for your children. Let your children know they do not have to imitate others, that they are beautiful people in their own right. Teach them camaraderie—how to get along and how to help each other.

Strategize and plan buzz sessions on how to prepare our youth for job preparation and open their eyes to the global system of free enterprise. Prepare them to develop and use their gifts. Once they have **developed their gifts**, nurture their hearts in the spirit that they will **return to empower their own communities**, a light to glow with a positive ray, block-by-block until each neighborhood has been restored.

- Get training at tech schools.
- Graduate from college in four years instead of five or seven years.
- Cultivate early business plans.
- Increase career and job awareness in local and national government, utilities, etc.
- Teach them how to amortize debt and to improve their credit ratings.

Be a watchdog to break the cancerous cycles thriving in our communities.

- Break the cycle of prisons.
- Break the cycle of teen pregnancy.
- Break the cycle of dropping out of school.
- Break the cycle of violence.
- Strategize for enlightening youth in careers that will allow them to compete in our global economy.

Economic empowerment is to teach our children to become economic leaders. I say ***wake up, African Americans***—we are in a stupor! **Society is siphoning wealth from our children."** Do your job of training your children and cut off the waste of human destruction! "Defuel" this human-draining machine: teach your children to bypass the prisons, teen pregnancy, dropping out of school, engaging in deviant behavior. Build character in your children by telling them that they are *born with a purpose to do a good work*. You empower them with positive teaching and by positive example. Stop letting Hollywood, television, and fashion designers do your work. These are your children! You have a duty and responsibility to mold, shape, teach, and watch their environment for the good of your child!

The failure to help each individual realize the power of his/her gifts to make a positive difference to humanity is to deprive an individual of the joy of being a whole person. **Teach them to contribute, to receive, and to give back to build positive community.**

Be a beacon for the Lord, and the Lord will bless you, your children, and your family.

Dorothy R. Swygert
Author of *Healing the Nation: An Indepth Study of African Americans*

Healing the Nation

The novel opens with a description of the *Family Steeple Church* which was symbolic of America's spirituality. The church was intertwined with the home and the school. These symbols are the theme of Dr. Swygert's book. We are taken down memory's lane. This journey helps to rekindle the minds of the African American who many of the youth have forgotten their roots, and have no idea of their heritage.

The novel then lays the foundation of the African American roots by comparing the birth of America which was founded on the same premise. America, too, has fallen from its roots or founding religious premise.

The discussion of work ethics was a trip down memory land. Quilting bees, corn-husking bees, hog-killings, and potato plowing showed how the rural African American family displayed responsibility and accountability to society and to each other.

Role models like Mrs. Lillie Bell Drummond Golightly who was a Black teacher during segregation were discussed. She was a motivation for many children who walked 5 miles or more to school to get the best education possible. Percy L. Julian, despite working many odd jobs to achieve a college education, graduated as valedictorian of his class and later developed his own laboratory.

Obstacles such as the Vietnam War and the Klu Klux Klan were discussed. Dr. Swygert's book contains a great deal of historical facts about the making and forming of the American society. It provides a vital insight into the understanding of the African American and his role in forming today's society.

Many African Americans as well as other groups have gotten away from the initial principles that caused our nation to become so great. Morality and belief in God is being lost today; however, Dr. Swygert's book demonstrates a need to *Heal the Nation.*

The reading of *Healing the Nation* is informative in understanding the African American roots. Teachers and people who will be working with this group could benefit. All America will be enlightened to review the humble origin of this nation.

Book Review
Lillie Davis
NYC Teacher and Librarian

Dorothy R. Swygert, **Healing the Nation** may be purchased at Barnes & Noble Book Stores. ISBN: 0-964-8737-2-9.

Fireside Love

Famous Quotations by Dorothy R. Swygert

From her book: ***Healing the Nation: A Trip Down Memory Lane***

1. It was around those hot logs and iron stoves that black children were steeped in the knowledge about the law of God.
2. The language of the children was monitored and their behavior was kept hot on the fire: "Excuse me," "I'm sorry," and "Thank you."
3. The social amenities of life were small things that were warmly enforced in the African American community.
4. There was a kindred spirit running through the community with a philosophy of "live and let live."
5. There was a spirit of love, caring, sharing and forgiving.
6. The tie that bind the community was "let us work together to help each other."
7. The application of the Ten Commandments contributed to the moral strength of the community,
8. Saturday night preparation for Sunday gave reverence unto God. "Sanctify the people, prepare Israel to come before God. (Ex. 19:10-11) African Americans used the #2 and #3 tin tubs for Saturday night baths in preparation for worship service on Sunday.

9. Building community was girded with a philosophy of *Makin' Somethin' out of Nothin'*. Grandparents knew how to survive with little or nothing.
10. Our grandparents knew how to search out herbs and spices from the forests.
11. The Grandparent Connection: "Adult members from the family and the community knew their role and responsibility and were accountable for their contribution to children, family and community.
12. When grandparents made visits to the homes of their children, they were cautious as they inspected the household and the child-rearing practices.
13. Grandparents listened and observed carefully to see if the home fires were still burning.
14. The extended family, these caretakers of the family history, had woven a fabric that would preserve future generations. They had tied a knot with the nexus of LOVE.
15. A victory with one child in the community was a success for the whole community. (camaraderie) They were mentors, not nerds!
16. Despite the fact that they were living under the law of segregation in the South, the extended family was able to gather their posterity around their knee and nurture them on fireside love.
17. The hearts of children swelled with pride when they realized their life played an important role in building America. They were not just children but they were important threads in the fabric that kept the flag of the nation solid and strong. (patriotism)
18. Parallel Modeling: The beauty of this system was that "the tie that binds" encouraged children from all levels to appreciate the gift of learning. They learned teamwork and camaraderie.
19. There was not a lot of "greenback-wealth," but the community was rich in love and had a rekindling spirit in building community. They shared their hopes and their dreams to build for a brighter tomorrow. No one committed suicide.

20. HOPE: These children were reared with vitality and a zest for living, an innocence that gave them a zest for life, living today with great hope for tomorrow. They progressed, properly, through the growth stages of life. No child was rushed through before time. They embraced the Benjamin Franklin wise proverbs.
21. Talking back and disrespect to adults was a "no, no!" Parents taught children to bring their concerns to them so they could identify the problem and solve it on an adult level.
22. African Americans were given freedom without compensation (Exo. 11:12): They had no welfare, but they had their faith, strength and a will to overcome. They would make this new freedom work and put their trust in God. They rolled up their sleeves and worked in spirit to "make somethin' out of nothin'."
23. Value of the Black Teacher: These black teachers knew the culture, shared the black experience and cherished the history of these children. They were aware of the shortcomings of parents from the institution of slavery. They knew most parents did not have command of the three "Rs". Consequently, they accepted the teaching profession as educational vanguards for the community. They were the progenitors of HOPE, the symbols of DREAMS, and the BUILDERS of a brighter tomorrow.
24. Each institution knew its role, assumed the responsibility and was accountable for their part (role)
25. As a democratic society, the core of our existence is rooted in the fact that we have basic principles that benefit all for the good of the nation.
26. African Americans provided a free labor force for the nation for more than two hundred years, 1661 to 1865, and received neither reparation nor compensation for this labor.
27. The intricate network of the African American family in the community allowed them to share their knowledge, pool their resources, and to give a helping hand to the various projects to build community.

28. The African American dinner table was a pleasant, nourishing experience that embraced the whole family. It was unity; it was love. It was strength in cultivating family life from one generation to the next.
29. Once a week the family came together in the *Family Prayer Hour*. The gathering was more than a prayer hour. It was a time to teach and reinforce morals, values and standards of the family and community. Children learned discipline, respect, chores, tasks and proper attitudes. The family's oral tradition was always an integral part of the family prayer hour.
30. Black Teachers: Teaching was heart and soul where they kept an eye opened to identify gifts and talents of their students to spearhead them into a new horizon and realized the fruit of their labor.
31. Black teachers cultivated an educational atmosphere that made youth identify their gifts and talents and involved them in programs and activities to nurture the growth and development of the same. Children were encouraged to participate in extracurricular activities.
32. The purpose of education and training our children to become productive citizens has almost become a forgotten cause. In this state of existence, we will, as a nation, destroy the plan for building a strong future for America.
33. Today, black uneducated and unskilled youths become pawns to drug dealers who care little about humanity and everything about a list that will fill their pockets. With the community pillars being weathered by forces from without and from within, the impact became too powerful for the traditional agents to withstand the blow.
34. Before 1970s: Age of Accountability. Parents felt accountable for the behavior, manners, growth and development of their children. This accountability was in some way attached to their belief that they received their children as gifts from God and they assumed the role and responsibility with accountability as found in Psalms 127:3-4. "Lo, children are an heritage of the Lord: and the fruit of

the womb is his reward. As arrows in the hand of a mighty man, so are the children of youth."

35. A victory with one child in the community was a success for the whole community. [camaraderie]
36. The Black Church nurtured a wealth of talent. There were the church offices, deacons, ushers, missionary societies, BTU, Junior Red Circle, Sunday School, drama and vignettes, Scouts, Vacation Bible school and building maintenance. These descendents of slaves with their faith in God, believed they could weather any storm. [They kept HOPE alive].
37. The African American community embraced family life near and far. The tie that binds was most visible in community living. The community was a network of families and children.
38. The black teachers knew the culture, the black experience, and the history of the children. They were aware of the short comings of parents from the institution of slavery.
39. The church, once upon a time, in our nation before the 1960s, was our moral institution – the guiding light for the community.
40. The children were reared with vitality and a zest for living – an innocence that gave them the fervor of life – living today and living with great hope for tomorrow.
41. Black Teachers: Their job was more than a teaching positions, it was a mission – a mission that would allow them to nurture the minds and hearts of a new generation to exhale the dreams of freedom with disbanded shackles, loosened to allow them to realize their gifts, skills and talents.

DS: Workshop Themes

*Nurtured on Fireside Love before the 1960s

*Educators: Gem of the Nation

*Develop a Spirit of Positive Competitiveness among Youth to Build Community

*Challenge Students to Develop their Talents to Uplift Humanity

*Create Modular Groups to engage youth in competitive projects to enhance school life
*Present Round Table Discussions and Debates by Departments [Social Issues]
*Involve PTA in supportive programs

Blame it on Yourself!

- We are the blame for our communities being in disarray
  - Vanguard the community
  - Monitor the children
- We are the blame for our schools being in the low performance category
  - Attend PTA meetings
  - Attend local, central and town hall meetings
- We are the blame for our children being disrespectful
  - Train/teach/model
  - Discipline/nurture
- We are the blame for our children not having up –to-date skills
  - God is going to blame you, too, at the time of Grace
  - Accountability
- We are the blame for the immoral movie producers who flood our communities with SDV (Sex, drugs, and violence)
  - Boycott power
  - Censure movies and TV
- We are the blame for our children growing up on "unhealthy fast foods."
  - Remember the Family Dinner Table
- We are the blame for our children producing a high percentage of babies out of wedlock
  - Remember God's law [Ten Commandments]
  - Positive role models
  - Model Christ
- We are the blame for our children developing false images

    - Teach them to have a "purpose in life"
    - Guide them in life value assessment
    - Cultivate in them a philosophy for living"
- We are the blame for our children seeking to mimic movie stars and athletes with negative behavior
    - Teach them to value all life
    - Teach them to make positive decisions/choices
- We are the blame for our children seeking to mimic and imitate the physiological image of others instead of appreciating their own God-given beauty.
    - Teach African American history
    - Teach an appreciation for African American culture and literature
- We are the blame for our neighborhoods becoming infested with crime, drugs and violence
    - Vanguard the community
    - Screen merchants prior to admission into community
- We are the blame for the high unemployment rate in our communities
    - Monitor schools; get on executive boards; attend all meetings
    - Make local officials accountable to the community
- We are the blame for the high percentage of youth who are neither high school graduates nor possess GED diplomas
    - Monitor community services
    - Watchdog the schools
    - Train parents and guardians to fulfill their role
- We are the blame for the profane and vulgar language that flourishes in our communities
    - Make residents accountable for the well-being of the community
    - Infuse the philosophy of nurturing a healthy environ for kids

- We are the blame for youths being disrespectful to parents, themselves and elders
    - Teach the social amenities and co-partner with community organizations and institutions to do the same
    - Do not accept this vile language as appropriate for this time/age
- We are the blame for the rapid growth of sexual immorality in our community
    - Ministerial accountability
    - Parental accountability
    - Community accountability
- We are the blame for having so many "non-contributing businesses" in our community (offer no jobs, no scholarships, negative appearance, etc.)
    - Vanguard the community
    - Make local officials accountable
    - Screen community leaders and make them accountable
- We are the blame for the dismantling of family life
    - Discarding law of God
    - Ministerial bland handling of community morality
    - Failure to preach, teach and live the unadulterated Gospel
    - We are the blame for degrading morality and taking prayer out of the school
        - Taking a stand—packing unity to save children
        - Accountability of political/legislative officials

Prison Awareness for Change

Table of Contents

- The financial debt of 1661-1865 has not been amortized to African Americans- God still holds the nation accountable as he held Egypt accountable for holding the children of Israel in bondage

Developmental history of the problem

- Low crime rate
- Vietnam War—drug use
- Drugs – an ugly blemish upon the nation: schools, homes, neighborhoods

The Pre-climate: Low prison statistics, Legislative response - 1970s

- Congressional approach
- Mental Health approach
- The Federal approach

The surreptitious "think tank" with an Idea

- Prior history of American slavery
- African Americans in bondage 1661-1865
    - A free labor force for Southern economy
    - Revisiting the past for future wealth

Development of the Idea

- Create a voice of dissension
- Create a climate of fear
- Use crime to increase the fear—"the Hype"
- Use powerful political voices against crime [Just a fanatical scheme to sack up the wealth from the people by using status quo to verify the need to incarcerate a populace as an economic tool for corporate wealth]

CREATE AN ECONOMIC REGIME TO PERPETUATE EXPONENTIAL WEALTH

- Exploit the Criminal Justice system
- Disregard Mental Health Services
- Ignore screening to identify need for educational services
- Deny opportunities for drug treatment and rehabilitation even if services would be less than the horrendous prison industry budget

CATEGORICAL CONNECTIONS TO SOLIDIFY PRISON INDUSTRY

- State legislative approval
- Criminal justice willingness to participate
- Congressional laws regarding privatizing for perpetuation of prisons
- Legal voices to substantiate need for long sentences
- Double Standards to ensure the incarceration of a specified populace

A DEMOCRACY DESIGNING AN ECONOMY WITH HUMANS AS A SLAVE LABOR FORCE IN THE 21ST CENTURY

- The Mario M. Cuomo Prison Pioneering Years
- The model perpetuated across the nation
- The Prison Industry proliferating in the South, resembling American Slavery 1661-1865
- The CCA (Correctional Corporation of America: its plan, design and governance board
- The George Wackenhut Prison Corporation [GEO GROUP]
- Wackenhut's plan, design and governance board

WHO ARE THE BENEFACTORS?

- Rural community affected by a downsizing economy
- Corporations across the nation

- New York Stock Exchange received the IPOs and quickly placed the prison industry on the stock market—modern day slave labor for exponential profits

PART II

What must the African American community do to detour their children from the belly of the beast?

- Watch dog the community in every club, activity, institution and commerce
- Use all agents to commence training to make them aware of this grave danger to enslave their children
- Use communicative efforts to get youth to: Stay in school to graduate, do not have babies out of wedlock, do not take drugs (not even if they are legalized) of any kind nor sell drugs. These are the main factors that lure and lead the children to the prison door where their gifts and talents will be misused as a cheap labor force to enrich the pockets of corporations.
- Return children and families to the Lantern of God: Teach the Ten Commandments, The Good Neighbor Policy, The Golden Rule, Respect for self and others, Respect for Elders, positive community spirit, good home membership, goals-oriented children, camaraderie, teach love and forgiveness, daily use to develop their gifts and skills

Watchdog politicians and elected officials

- Honesty and integrity of local, state and federal officials
- Watchdog Congressional Record for new bills

Organize ministries in the church to come out of the pulpit to work in the community

- Don't dress up the pulpit
- Dress up God's vineyard with work with wisdom to build positive community
- Design programs to compliment the community—to provide for the needs of children and parents in the community
- Design programs to compliment the neighborhood schools to insure that children will get quality education and not a corporate design program to influence the minds and hearts of the children to become robots
- Nurture the children on love, caring, sharing and forgiveness
- Teach them how to live harmoniously in community, building and help each other to be their best person and to do their best work with the talents God has given them
- Create a barrage of positive extracurricular activities for youth
- Provide venues to exhibit and exercise their gifts and talents
- Teach them creative use of technology—as career preparation, as useful statistics for innovations for neighborhood enhancement
- Screen all neighborhood services for give back to the community: scholarships, job training, apprenticeship and volunteer work—no exceptions—"You're in the community, you have to give back."

PART III

FROM PIC TO PAC: From Prison Industrial Complex to Prison Awareness for Change

You were born free, shake off the shackles! Let no one play in your flesh! At birth, you were given talents and gifts to take your journey in life—from birth to death. Let no one entice you with any substance (drugs, alcohol, immoral sex) to play in your flesh. Do not seek the pleasure of the flesh not described by God, seek to live your life according to the His guideline so that you will be able to fulfill your purpose for being placed on this earth and to use your talents to complete your mission before returning to God who created you. You are SOMEBODY! You are a child of God with an assignment to fulfill between birth and death. Prepare yourself by finishing school to develop your gifts so that your life will be fulfilled in divine order and not another number with a sign that says RIP. Let God be the one to receive you where he will say, "Enter into my rest, inherit eternal life of blissfulness and peace forevermore!"

IV Addendum

- Workshops
- Seminars
- Lantern of God
- Youth Pledge
- Schedule
- Poetry
- Parent Guide Sheet for Youth
- Prison Vignette
- Biblical Scriptures
- Educational Resources for Parents
- Career Resources for Youth
- Forms for Youth: Goals and Steps to Achieve Goals
- Seven-Step Character Building Concepts for Youth
- Book Reading Summary Form
- Youth Group Leaders
- Flyers
- Evaluation

I Am Somebody

Cultivating My Life With Hope

To all people living in this world, I have a message for you. Here is a world report from me to you. I would like all people in this world to know that I am an upbeat person. I have a positive personality. I do not believe anyone can keep me down if I want to be up. To all you readers out there, I want you to know that I am a person of quality. If you do not understand my language, keep your eyes on this page and you will understand. You see, I look into the mirror everyday and compliment myself. Do not get me wrong, that is not being narcissistic or being hung up on myself, it is just normal behavior. *Think about it! If you plan to succeed in this life on this planet, you must feel good about yourself.* Do not take away from the Creator. Give thanks for your blessing of life. Remember, you must do your part in strengthening your heart to realize the greatness of your being.

The first thing you need to do is to give yourself a good start by kissing the dawning of the day. Make good use of your image when you get up. Look into the mirror and compliment yourself in the morning. This is not a narcissistic act, this is simply motivation—you are motivating yourself to be a survival on your day's journey. To make this day complete, there are three things you must know about yourself. *Firstly, you must know that you are somebody going somewhere in life to make a positive difference.* And if you know that you are somebody, then act and carry yourself as if you are somebody. When you esteem yourself in high regards, then you do not embarrass your Creator by going into the world looking at other human copies and wishing you looked like them. You look into your mirror and appreciate what you see, smile with thanksgiving with what you see and give appreciation for the gifts you have been given to travel on this human pathway.

Secondly, you must know that you are going somewhere in life because you have been blessed with some gifts, skills and talents. You may not have the same talents as others whom you meet along life's journey, but you do have your gift package, that is, when properly used, will provide you with the means to not only survive but to help others in life. Help may be seen in different ways, not necessarily from the hip, but from your lips or with other gifts. You may be a creative artist or an inventor. *Whatever your talents, your responsibility is to identify and develop them in a positive way to help yourself and others.*

Thirdly, the goal that you are going somewhere in life to make a positive difference must be made a reality as you make this journey along the human pathway. *You do not know how much time the Creator has allotted for your life. Consequently, you must view your journey with a serious heart so that you can use each day to the fullest in developing and using your talents.* You do not have time to be a procrastinator, always putting things off for tomorrow. You must perceive everyday as an opportunity to promote your human package and share the wealth. You must count each day as a blessing. When you look at others, you should wear a smile on your face and your lips should utter words of encouragement.

As you give to others, you must not lose sight of your own goals and the steps and stages you must pursue in order to fulfill them. You must respect differences with hope that others, too, will respect you, but if they do not, you still have the responsibility to travel the road to fulfill the purpose the Creator has entrusted to you. By doing this, *you can become the greatest person you are capable of becoming, as well as to make a positive difference in building a better world.* Remember, you must stay focused on the prize!

TAKE AWAY PACKAGE

QUESTIONS:

1. How would you describe the person in this article? What does it mean to be an upbeat person?
2. According to the writer, what is the first thing one should do in the morning? Why does the writer think this act is important?
3. Describe three things the writer says everyone should do.
4. What is the meaning of narcissism?
5. Describe the "human package" that one receives for his/her journey in life.
6. Have you ever wished that you were someone else or looked like someone else? Give an example.
7. Describe your human package. How are you using this package?
8. How does the writer feel about procrastination? Is this a good character trait?
9. According to the writer, the Creator plays an important role in preparing one for life's journey. Explain. Give examples.
10. How can human beings help each other to succeed in life? What is camaraderie?

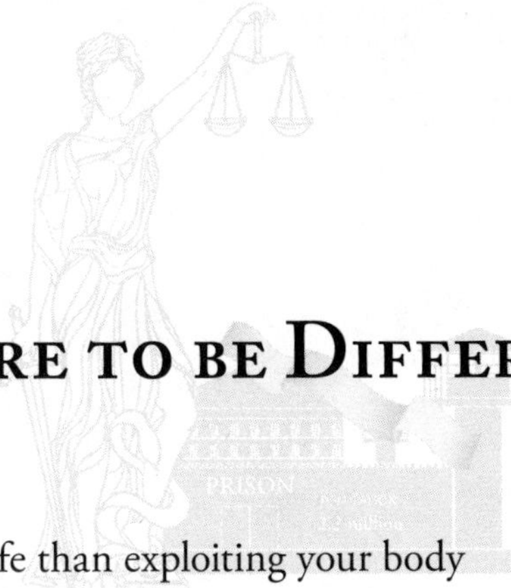

Dare to be Different

There is more to life than exploiting your body
by becoming a premature mother, an unequipped father.

There is more to life than being
an inmate behind a prison wall
where the dew drops of life never
rises to embrace that
magnificent person God
meant you to be.

There is more to life than having the sharpest tongue
rolling vulgar and profane language off your lips
that God made to be a great orator, singer or speaker.

There is more to life than being a conformist
ridiculing the "nerd" or
the "goody, goody" child,

Dare to be different—to be

Great in unison---in oneness

With God,

…………………Our Creator.

Courtesy & Reconciliation

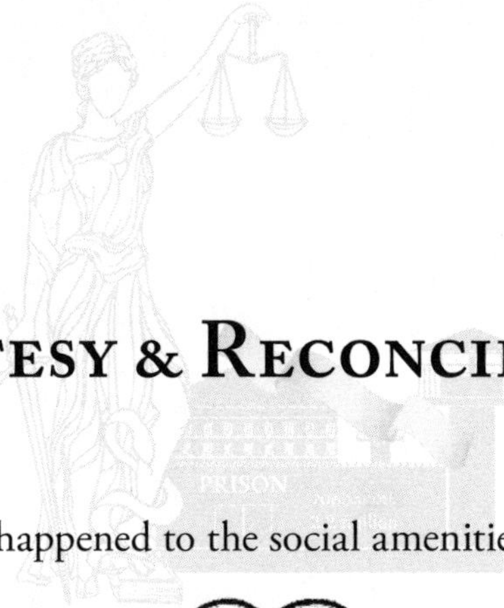

What happened to the social amenities of life?

A Request:	"Please"
A Favor:	"Thank you"
A Mistake:	"Excuse me"
An Error:	"I'm sorry"
A Bad Deed:	"Please forgive me!"
To Share:	"Would you like ...?"
A Kind Deed:	"A note expressing thanks"

Rekindle the

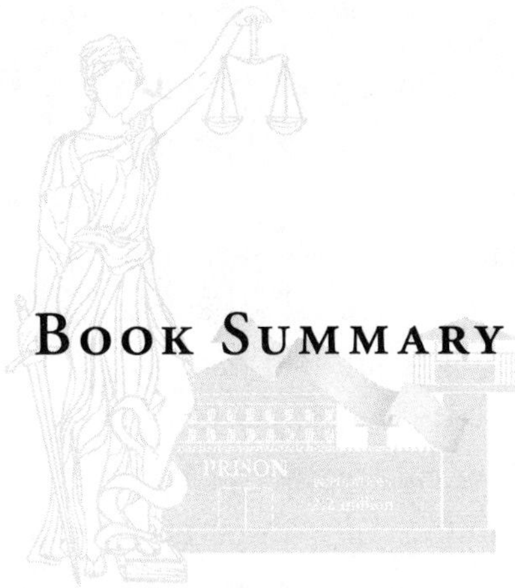

Book Summary

We, America, must remember our origin to ensure our ship is traveling in the right direction to sustain this nation. The thirteen colonies became thirteen states in 1783 when the Treaty of Paris was signed by England to recognize America as an independent nation.

Our origin reflects how ships tossed and turned to the coasts of Jamestown, Virginia, and Plymouth Rock made their beginnings on the shores of America. They were strangers and lacked survival skills in this new land. A friendly Indian tribe and one member in particular, Squanto, taught the new arrivals from Europe to survive in the wilderness. They were taught to grow crops, and during the harvest season, the settlers and some Indians came together for a great feast they called Thanksgiving.

What happened to that camaraderie between the Native Americans and the newcomers from Europe? A piece of the land was not enough; the new settlers wanted the entire continent and, with superior weapons, drove the Indians off the land and settled them on reservations in specified sections of what is now called the United States of America. When gold and other valuable minerals were discovered, this land, in many instances, was rescinded. What does God have to say about this behavior?

Another people came to America as early explorers from Africa and later as indentured servants. These people were harnessed as permanent slaves to work the agricultural system of the South to enhance the wealth of plantation owners. Upon receiving freedom from England in 1783, the thirteen states refused to grant freedom to African Americans.

They held on to this population as their free labor force to enhance their wealth and to sustain their pleasure of living a genteel life. The Civil War fought from 1861 to 1865 ended without compensating the slaves who worked for more than two hundred years. Instead, the nation, through creative means, designed a social system of segregation and discrimination. The African American, despite the passage of the 13th, 14th, and 15th Amendments, was confronted with perpetual deprivation of freedom, justice, and equality. Within their hearts, the wealthy failed to realize that they, too, were once economic slaves to the British Empire. The lesson was not internalized, and the perpetuation of humans as a cheap labor force continued. What does God have to say about this behavior?

Our concern here is how the nation once had an interest in the development of our children. The pendulum, since the 1970s, does not swing in the direction to our children. But let us look at the Founding Fathers' promise printed in the Constitution. Our children are charged high interest rates on college student debt, and despite the expense, a large population of our young people are unable to secure employment. We have a constitutional promise to our children.

The Promise

> "*We the people of the United States, in order to secure the Blessings of Liberty to ourselves and our Posterity, do ordain and establish this Constitution of the United States of America.*"
> —Preamble to the Constitution of the United States of America.

The fabric of the flag of the nation was a symbol of four great principles: Love of God, family, community, and the nation.

- Pride in training and leaving a legacy for our posterity
- The oneness of keeping hope alive for all people
- A sense of morality and ethical living
- The Good Neighbor Policy

There is nothing mystical about teaching children. Children learn in various settings and in a myriad of ways. With this postulation, we view the carriers and communication networks as having an obligation to adhere to legislation and methodology for nurturing children. Our children should be placed on a higher scale than the dollar. In essence, we should not sacrifice morality for the dollar. We must be aware of the negative impact television and movies have on the growth and development of children, if uncensored.

The value placed on education was established on two basic beliefs. Education was the core of society for it provided for the "welfare, the progress, and the perpetuity of a nation." It was further viewed as the vehicle by which the "individual could realize his potentialities in happiness and in accomplishment through education" [Ward G. Reeder, A First Course in Education, The Macmillian Company, NY, 1958, p. 9].

They were as the fabric of the American flag into which each thread was meticulously woven to create a symbol for states bound in unity. Any thread torn from the fabric would alter the appearance. Like the flag, any weakness in one of these basic institutions would distort the foundation of the nation.

- Write the message
- Publish it
- Run with the correct message

Three-fold message

- WARNING: Prison growth as an economic industry—using human products.
- MESSAGE: Spread the message to God's people to bring the children back into the fold of God: guide them away from the prison door.
- RE-TRAIN them by God's Manual: 10 Commandments, Good Neighbor Policy. Don't use drugs of any kind, have no babies out of wedlock, do not live together, marry the person you love, don't drop out of school, and teach camaraderie in community living. (Each helps one to live by God's law.)

Addendum

Corrections Corporation Of America

Chronological History of CCA

January 1984	Management of First Facility
April 1984	CCA Opens First Facility
October 1984	Assuming Management
Spring 1985	Connecting Communications [Newsletter]
February 1986	ACA (Americans Correction Association) Accreditation Houston Processing Center and Tall Trees
May 1986	First Private Juvenile Facility
October 1986	CCA on NASDAQ stock exchange (CCAX) at initial price of $9.
August 1987	Awarding CCA Leaders {T. Don Hutto-ER Cass]
January 1989	Company Store Established
May 1989	Employee Recognition Day
June 1989	First CCA Women's Facility New Mexico Women's Correctional Facility—first women's prison operated by a company in the USA.
Fall 1989	Working Safe

March 1990	First Medium-Security CCA Facility First medium-security prison in the US in Winnfield, LA-Winn Correctional Center
May 1990	Assuming Management of Winn Correctional
September 1990	West Tenn. Detention Facility opens in Mason, TN
December 1990	Torrance County Detention Facility opens in Estancia, NM
February 1992	CCA assumes management of Metro-Davidson County Detention Facility in Nashville and South Central Correctional Center in Clifton, TN
June 1992	CCA opens Leavenworth Detention Center in Leavenworth, Kansas, maximum-security facility under direct contract with a federal agency, managed by a corrections company.
January 1993	CCA celebrates a decade as a prison industry
October 1994	CCA opens Central Arizona Detention-Center in Florence, Arizona
December 1994	CCA lists its stock and warrants on New York Stock Exchange (CXC) at $16 per share.
January 1995	CCA acquires TransCor America, LLC—nation's largest long-distance inmate transportation company. 646 Melrose Ave, Nashville, N 37211, 615.251.7008. Transporting detainees since 1990—been the nation's leading provider of prisoner and detainee transportation services to federal, state, and local governments. Mission: To be an innovative and cost saving solution to government agencies seeking safe and secure transportation of prisoners and detainees by well-trained corrections professionals. Pledge: To recruit and train the industry's best, dedicated to maintaining a workforce fully one-third comprised of retired, reserve and active duty military,

	offering a paramilitary command structure and generous benefits package which includes a safe harbor matching contribution retirement plan. Uses Rand McNally for Mobile Fleet Management Solution.
August 1995	CCA acquired industry competitor Corrections Partners, Inc.
August 1995	CCA assumes management of Bay Correctional Facility in Panama City, FL, after winning a contract to build and manage from the State of FL.
September 1995	CCA opens Eden Detention Center in Eden, TX.
October 1995	CCA assumes management of Bartlett State Jail in Bartlett, TX, and Citrus County Detention Facility in Lecanto, FL.
April 1996	CCA assumes Correctional Facility in Las Animas, CO
January 1997	CCA assumes management of Elizabeth Detention Center in Elizabeth, NJ
February 1997	Facility named for T. Don Hutto Correctional Center in Taylor, TX; also assumes management of Lake City Correctional Facility in Lake City, FL.
May 1997	CCA opens Cimarron Correctional Facility in Cushing, Oklahoma, and Northeast Ohio Correctional Center in Youngstown, OH. CCA also opens Correctional *Treatment Facility*—specializing in substance abuse treatment for adults, in Washington, DC.
June 1997	CCA assumes management of Hardeman Correctional Facility in Whiteville, TN
July 1997	CCA assumes management of Dawson State Jail in Dallas, TX.

November 1997	CCA moves into new corporate headquarters in Nashville, TN. CCA also assumes management of Marion County Jail II in Indianapolis, IN.
1998	CCA high record—opens 11 facilities this year.
January 1998	CCA assumes management of Wilkinson County Correctional Facility in Woodville, MS.
April 1998	CCA opens Lee Adjustment Center, Marion Adjustment Center and Otter Creek Correctional Center in Beattyville, St. Mary and Wheelwright, KY, respectively. CCA also opens Cibola County Correctional Center in Milan, N.M.
May 1998	CCA opens San Diego Correctional Facility in San Diego, CA.
July 1998	CCA opens Whiteville Correctional Facility in Whiteville, TN.
December 1998	CCA opens Kit Carson Correctional Center in Burlington, CO and Coffee Correctional Center and Wheeler Correctional Facility in Nicholls and Alamo, GA, respectively.
July 1999	CCA opens Crossroads Correctional Center in Shelby, Montana.
August 1999	CCA opens Webb County Detention Center in Laredo, TX.
December 1999	CCA becomes the 6th largest corrections system in the country, contracting with 26 states and the District of Columbia.
April 2000	CCA opens Tallahatchie County Correctional Facility in Tutwiler, MS.
June 2000	CCA assumes management of Idaho Correctional Center in Kuna, Idaho.
August 2000	John Ferguson joins CCA as President and CEO and Willliam Andrews becomes Chairman of the Board.

October 2000	CCA's ticker symbol on the NYSER changes to CXW.
October 2001	CCA initiates the incident Management Team (TMT) program.
December 2002	CCA opens McRae Correctional Facility in McRae, GA
January 2003	CCA celebrates its 20th anniversary.
January 2003	CCA opens Crowley County Correctional Center in Olney Springs, CO
August 2003	CCA's J. Michael Quinlan receives the Edward R. Cass Correctional Achievement Award from the American Correctional Association (ACA)
November 2003	CCA is awarded 7 contracts from the State of Texas with a total of 8,315 beds.
January 2004	CCA Way is launched, defining the company's vision, mission and guiding principles.
May 2005	CCA implements its first Residential Drug Abuse Program (RDAP) at select facilities. (Rehabilitative Model)
June 2005	CCA approved for organizational membership in the National Association of Alcohol and Drug Abuse Counselors (NAADAC)
May 2006	CCA redesigns the T. Don Hutto Residential Center in Taylor, TZX, for detention of immigrant families.
June 2006	CCA opens Red Rock Correctional Center in Eloy, AR.
July 2006	CCA Assist Fund is founded as a 501c(3), tax-exempt charity through which "employees help employees" in times of need.
August 2006	CCA's Warden Mike Samerg receives Warden of the Year Award from the North American Association of Wardens and Superintendents (NAAWS)

October 2006	CCA contracts with California to house 1,000 inmates in out-of-state facilities, a first for the state CCA opens Stewart Detention Center in Lumpkin, FA.
November 2006	G.I. Jobs magazine for the first time names CCA one of the nation's "Top 50 Military-Friendly Employers."
January 2007	Forbes magazine names CCA the nation's "best managed company" in the business services and supplies category.
June 2007	CCA opens Saguaro Correctional Center in Eloy, Ariz.
August 2007	CCA breaks ground on its fourth Mississippi facility in Natchez-Adams County Correctional Center.
December 2007	CCA operates 66 facilities in 19 states and the District of Columbia, a designed capacity of more than 75,000 beds and over 16,000 employees.
February 2008	CCA is named one of the "100 Best Corporate Citizens" in the U.S. by Corporate Responsibility Officer magazine.
July 2008	CCA's largest project ever, la Palma Correctional Center opens, in Eloy, Ariz., two months ahead of schedule.
July 2009	CCA opens Adams County Correctional Center in Natchez, MS.
September 2009	CCA's assumes management of North Georgia Detention Center in Gainesville, GA.
October 2009	Damon Hininger, who started with the company as a correctional officer after graduating from Kansas State University, becomes President and CEO of CCA.
January 2010	CCA's tagline and logo change to "America's Leader in Partnership Corrections."

July 2010	CCA's 501c (3) fund for employees and their families, CCA Assist, passes the $million milestone in distributions.
August 2010	CCA's Warden Ralph Kemp receives Warden of the Year from the North American Association of Wardens and Superintendents (NAAWS)
September 2010	CCA opens Nevada Southern Detention Center in Pahrump, NV.
October 2010	CCA establishes the Courage Award, an annual recognition of employees who perform acts of extraordinary bravery, even at the risk of their own personal safety.
July 2011	CCA establishes the Pete Spackman Volunteer of the year Award, **honoring faith-based** volunteers at CCA facilities.
August 2011	Richard P. Seiter, CCA's executive vice president and chief correctional officer, is honored with the Edward R. Cass Correctional Achievement Award from the American Correctional Association (ACA)
December 2011	CCA operates 66 facilities, 45 of which are company-owned, with approximately 90,000 beds, in 19 states and the District of Columbia.
December 2011	CCA provides an annual review of the progress of our organization.
January 2012	CCA purchases and assumes ownership and operation of Ohio Department of Corrections facility, Lake Erie Correctional Institution, a milestone transaction in the industry.
March 2012	Jenkins Correctional Center opens in Millen, GA, making it the 6th CCA facility in the state of Georgia.
May 2012	CCA's Board of Directors declares a quarterly dividend to be paid to shareholders of record.

August 2012	CCA's 501c (3) fund, CCAssist, passes the $2 million milestone in distributions.
October 2012	CCA hosts the 21st Annual Chairman's Charity Golf, breaking all records by raising $290,000 and donating to more than 25 charities in the Middle Tennessee community.
November 2012	G.I. Jobs magazine names CCA one of the nation's "Top 50 Military-Friendly Employers" for the 6th year.
January 2013	CCA celebrates its 30th anniversary. (http://cca.com/media/default/documents/misc/30th_anniversary_edition-web.pdf.)

George Wackenhut/GEO Group

The GEO Group Inc. operates facilities in the United States, Canada, South Africa, Australia, and in the United Kingdom

Historic Milestones

1984 – Inception

Wackenhut Corrections Corporation (WCC) was formed as a division of the Wackenhut Corporation (TWC) in 1984. George C. Zoley was instrumental to the development and marketing of detention and correctional services to government agencies.

1987 – First Contract Award

Received first contract award, the Aurora Processing Center, providing secure care, custody, and control of 150 immigration detainees for the federal government.

1988 – Incorporation

WCC incorporated as a wholly-owned subsidiary of TWC.

1992 – International Presence

Entered the international market through the development of wholly owned subsidiary, Australasian Correctional Management PTY Ltd. (ACM) (later renamed GEO Australia).

1992 – United Kingdom

Entered the correctional services arena in the United Kingdom through a joint venture to form, Premier Custodial Group Ltd. (PCGL). The cooperative enterprise provided clients with prisoner transportation, court custody, home detention services, and correctional and immigration detention services. (The joint venture was discontinued by mutual agreement in 2003.)

1993 – Australian Milestone

Wholly owned subsidiary, ACM, was awarded its first contract, the Junee Correctional Centre, to design, build, and operate for the New South Wales Department of Corrective Services. This contract was the first privately operated correctional center in New South Wales.

1993 – Breakthrough Rehabilitation

Opened the world's largest in-prison therapeutic community chemical dependency treatment programs at the Kyle Correctional Center in Texas. The program provided intensive chemical dependency treatment.

1994 – Initial Public Offering

In July, WCC went public with an initial public offering (IPO) of 2.2 million shares on the NASDAQ.

1996 – NYSE

Through a secondary public offering, WCC is listed on the New York Stock Exchange under ticker symbol WHC. Now trading under ticker symbol GEO.

1997 – Residential Treatment Services

Atlantic Shores Healthcare Inc. (later renamed GEO Care) is created. This former wholly owned subsidiary was formed to provide premier behavioral and mental health care services to state and local government agencies.

1997 – Bureau of Prisons

Received award for the first privately operated facility by the Bureau of Prisons (BOP) The 2,048-bed Taft Correctional Institution opened in December 1997.

1998 – Design Services Inc.

Wholly owned subsidiary WCC Design Services Inc. (later renamed GEO Design Services) is formed, becoming the only company in the corrections industry to have an in-house design team.

1998 – First Private State Psychiatric Hospital in US

Received award to manage the first comprehensive privately operated state psychiatric hospital in the US. Takes over the operation and management of the 335-bed South Florida State Hospital November 1998.

1998 – CORRECTIONAL PROPERTIES TRUST

Co-created Correctional Properties Trust (later known as CentraCore Properties Trust), a real estate investment trust. Formed to support the growing trend towards utilizing privately sourced capital in the corrections industry.

1999 – ENTERS SOUTH AFRICA

Established, via joint venture, South African Custodial Management (SACM) an operating arm of South African Custodial Services (SACS) in order to remedy overcrowding conditions for the government corrections system.

1999 – SOUTH AFRICA CONTRACT

SACS awarded the first privatized correctional center in South Africa. A 25-year contract for the design, construction, financing, operation, and maintenance of the Kutama Sin humule Correctional Centre in South Africa began July 1999.

2002 – WACKENHUT CORPORATION ACQUIRED

Group 4 Falck (now G4S) merged with The Wackenhut Corporation (WTC) and became the indirect owner of majority stake in WCC.

2003 – SALE OF UK JOINT VENTURE

Completed sale of interest in UK joint venture PCGL as a means to facilitate the opportunity to pursue further independent growth in the UK.

2003 – INDEPENDENCE DAY

Completed repurchase of majority stake, 12 million shares of WCC common stock, from G4S. This historic transaction transformed WCC from a corporate subsidiary into a fully independent company with full access to the capital markets.

2003 – WCC TO GEO

Officially changed name to The GEO Group Inc. (GEO).

2003 – Florida Top Public Company

GEO is named a Florida Trend Magazine's Top 250 Public Company, a position still proudly held today.

2003 – International Standards

GEO's Kutama Sinthumule Correctional Centre in South Africa became the first prison on the continent to obtain the International Standard. Organization 9001:200 certification for the South African Bureau of Standards.

2004 – GEO UK

GEO reestablished subsidiary, the GEO Group UK Ltd, in order to pursue new business opportunities in England, Scotland, and Wales—the second-largest private correctional market in the world.

2005 – CSC Acquisition

GEO acquired Sarasota-based Correctional Services Corporation (CSC) Acquisition added 15 adult correctional facilities and others under development with a design capacity of approximately 8,000 beds in North America.

2007 – CentraCore Properties Trust (CPT) Acquisition

GEO acquired CPT. This merger resulted in the ownership of 13 correctional facilities totaling over 8,000 beds.

2007 – Secure Transport

GEO established in-house transportation division, GEO Transport Inc., to help meet its customers' increasing need for secure transportation services for offender and detainee populations.

2009 – Just Care, Inc.

GEO's former wholly owned subsidiary, GEO Care, acquired Just Care Inc., a medical and mental health service provider.

2010 – Cornell Acquisition

GEO acquired Cornell Companies. This merger resulted in a combined company with approximately $1.5 billion in annual revenues and approximately 78,000 beds under management, development and/or ownership.

2011 – ACQUISITION OF BI INCORPORATED

GEO acquired BI Incorporated, a private provider of innovative compliance technologies, industry-leading monitoring services, and evidence-based supervision and treatment programs for community-based parolees, probationers, and pretrial defendants.

2013 – REAL ESTATE INVESTMENT TRUST

GEO began operating as a Real Estate Investment Trust having completed all the necessary restructuring steps, including the divestiture of its healthcare facility operations under its former wholly owned subsidiary, GEO Care, on December 31, 2012.

Correctional Corporation of America

1. Wikipedia. http://en.wikipedia.org/wiki/Corrections Corporation of America - mw-navigationhttp://en.wikipedia.org/wiki/Corrections Corporation of America – p-search. Southern Changes, The Journal of the Southern Regional Council, 1978–2003, Volume 8, Number 3, 1989.
2. Wackenhut/The GEO Group. Wikipedia. Follow up biography: The Quiet American: A Biography of George R. Wackenhut, 1994, By: John Minahan.http://www.wackenhut.com/

A statistical view of American prisons by state

Prisons per 100,000 by State - Retrieved 4/1/2015

1. Louisiana 887
2. Mississippi 686
3. Oklahoma 654
4. Alabama 648
5. Texas 648
6. Arizona 572
7. Florida 556
8. Arkansas 552
9. Missouri 508
10. South Carolina 495
11. Georgia 479
12. Idaho 474
13. Nevada 472
14. Virginia 468
15. Kentucky 458
16. Ohio 448
17. Michigan 445
18. Colorado 445
19. Delaware 443
20. California 439
21. Indiana 434
22. Tennessee 432
23. South Dakota 416
24. Pennsylvania 403
25. Maryland 387
26. Wyoming 385
27. Montana 378
28. Connecticut 376
29. Illinois 373
30. North Carolina 373
31. Wisconsin 366
32. West Virginia 363
33. Oregon 361
34. Alaska 340
35. New Mexico 323
36. Kansas 317
37. Iowa 309
38. Hawaii 302
39. New York 288
40. New Jersey 286
41. Washington 269
42. Vermont 265
43. Nebraska 247
44. Utah 238
45. North Dakota 226
46. New Hampshire 209
47. Massachusetts 200
48. Rhode Island 197
49. Minnesota 185
50. Maine 148

NOTES

INTRODUCTION

1. John Hope Franklin, *From Slavery to Freedom*, (New York: Alfred A. Knopf, 1967), 128–29.

CHAPTER 1: PEACE CORPS: A GOOD IDEA IN A DEMOCRACY

1. Barbara Laming, *The Education of a Statesman*, (W. W. Norton & Company, Inc., 1961), 61.

CHAPTER 2: AMERICA'S FAITH IN EDUCATION

1. Reeder, Ward W. *A First Course in Education*, (New York: The Macmillan Company, 1958) 31. "New England's First Fruits," printed in London, England in 1643, 12.
2. Ibid, 12 First Schools
3. Ibid, 12 Old Deluder Satan Act
4. Ibid, 31 *Statesmen Views on Education*: Governor DeWitt Clinton
5. Ibid, 31 Daniel Webster,
6. bid, 31–32 Thaddeus Stevens
7. Ibid, 31 Governor Alfred E. Smith of New York
8. White House Conference, *White House Conference on Children 1952*: see Eisenhower Library, Abilene, Kansas, Records, 1930–70. Accessions 85–14. Processed by LKS, JWL, TB, PAN EB. Date completed May 1992.

9. Ibid, 51 America's abiding in education
10. Ibid, 6. The most powerful ambition of man
11. Ibid, 8 Impact of Federal Communication Commission on educating children
12. Wikipedia, June 19, 1934, FCC Act of 1934 (147 U.S.C. 151 et. Seq.)
13. Ibid, June 19, 1934
14. Erik H. Erikson, *Eight Stages* by Erik H. Erikson, summarized by Midcentury White House Confer: The records of the White House Conference on Children and Youth, a component of National Archives Record Group 220: Records of Temporary Committees, Commission and Boards, were transferred to the Eisenhower Library from the National Archives in July 1985.] and Life, pp. 60–63) Reference (Witmer and Kotinsky, 1952, White House Conference) Floyd Ruch, Psychology.
15. John Perkins, *Confessions of an Economic Hit Man*, (California: Plume Publishers: Berrett-Koehler Publishers, 2006) 211–12. "*The New Image of American Soldiers.*"
16. Eisenhower Presidential Library, Abilene, Kansas. Eisenhower.archives.gov The Farewell Address, 1961.
17. Annie Jacobsen, *Operation Paperclip: The Secret Intelligence Program that Brought Nazi Scientists to America* (New York: Little, Brown and Company, 2014), 123.
18. *Eisenhower's Farewell Address*, January 1961.
19. Ibid..

Chapter 3: Review Hypocrisy in a Democracy

Slavery: Dunmore Proclamation, Declaration of Independence

1. Eugene D. Genovese. *The Political Economy of Slavery.* (New York: Random House, 1961), 4.
2. Dorothy Swygert, *Healing the Nation*, 218. Virginia House of Burgesses, Journals of the House of Burgesses of Virginia 1659/60–1693. slave status unchanged.

3. Earl Conrad. *The Invention of the Negro*. (New York: Paul S. Erikson, Inc., 1966), 2. Vatican and slave trade.
4. Ibid, 2
5. Ibid, 2
6. Ibid, 1–2
7. Alfred & Ruth G. Blumrosen. *Slave Nation: How Slavery United the Colonies & Sparked the American Revolution*. (Naperville, Illinois: Sourcebooks, Inc., 2005), xiv. Pro-slavery compromise.
8. John Hope Franklin, *From Slavery to Freedom*. (New York: AlfredA. Knopf), 127.
9. William Henry Yarbrough, A *History of the United States for High Schools*. (New York: Laidlaw Brothers, 1941), 212. Topic: Original Declaration of Independence. Also, John Hope Franklin, *From Slavery to Freedom*.
10. John Hope Franklin, 131. Also blackloyalist.info. Lord Dunmore. 12/9/15.
11. Ibid, 132–133
12. Ibid, 132
13. Ibid, 133
14. Ibid, 133
15. Ibid, 133
16. Robert Starobin. *Slavery and Industry in the Old South*. (New York:Oxford University Press, 1970) 3.
17. Ibid, 3 Topic: Agricultural South
18. Ibid, 4 Topic: Slave population, four million
19. Kenneth M. Stampp, *The Peculiar Institution: Slavery in the Ante-Bellum South*. (California: University of Berkeley, 1956). Stampp "held that the national debate over the morality of slavery was the focal point of the U.S. Civil War. Prior to the Civil War southern slavery was America's most profound and vexatious social problem. More than any other problem, slavery nagged at the public conscience: offering no solution . . ."

The book was for Stampp not only about 19th century history but a necessary examination for Americans in the 1950s because 'it is an article of faith that knowledge of the past is a key to understanding the present,' and one must know what slavery meant to the Negro and how he reached to it before one can comprehend his more recent tribulations.. Wiki, retr. 1/29/16

Martin L. King quoted *The Peculiar Institution*; He describes Stampp's "fascinating depiction of the psychological indoctrination that was necessary from the master's viewpoint to make a good slave."

Stanley M. Elkins, *Slavery: A Problem in American Institutional Intellectual Life*. (New York: Grosset and Dunlap, 1963), Introduction by Nathan Glazer. xi. "The special virtue of this book is that Mr. Elkins, unconcerned by the formal boundaries between the disciplines, has made himself at home in all the fields of scholarship that help to explain the peculiar American form of slavery—peculiar, indeed, in more ways than Northern and Southern opponents realized, for it was unique in the history of the world, and thus peculiar in its consequences" (xi).

Elkins is also known for his controversial comparison of slavery in the United States to Nazi concentration camps. Ulrich Bonnell Phillips. *American Negro Slavery: A Survey of the Supply, Employment and Control of Negro Labor* (Forgotten Books, 2015). Phillips was the most powerful voice in defense of slavery. His descriptions of slavery mirrored a glorified living for slaves viewing slave masters as taking good care of their slaves, "adequate food, clothing, housing, medical care and training . . ." wiki, 2/28.16, 8:11 am.

Williaml W. Freehling, *The South vs. The South: How Anti-Confederate Southerners Shaped the Course of the Civil War*. (New York: Oxford University Press, 2001). In this book, Freehling "argues that anti-Confederate Southerners—specifically, border state whites and southern blacks—helped cost the Confederacy the war. White men in such border states as Missouri, Kentucky, and Maryland, were divided in their loyalties—but far more joined the Union the Union (or simply stayed home) than marched off in Confederate gray."

20. Ibid.
21. John Hope Franklin, From Slavery to Freedom, 206–207.
22. Wikipedia. Abigail Adams.

Chapter 4: Rescinding Civil Rights Gains: Part I and Part II

Part I: Dr. Martin L. King, Letter from Birmingham Jail

Part II: Post Civil War, Reconstruction, Election of 1876

1. Dr. Martin Luther King, *Letter from Birmingham Jail, April 16, 1963*
2. Course-notes.org. 2/3/16, 3:227 PM.
3. Ibid.
4. Ibid
5. Ibid.
6. .270towin.com; 1/31/16. 1:39 PM.
7. Wikipedia
8. Course-notes.org, 2/3/16, 3:27 PM.
9. Wikipedia
10. Ibid.
11. Randall Robinson, The Debt., p. 221.
12. course-notes.org
13. .historyhouse.gov
14. Ibid
15. Wikipedia
16. Ibid.
17. Ibid.
18. Ibid.
19. Ibid.
20. en.m.wikipedia
21. senate.gov
22. Ibid.

23. Ibid.

Chapter 5: A Bad Idea Destroys the Principles of a Democracy

Growing Prisons in a Democracy is a Bad Idea

1. Eric Schlosser, *The Prison Industrial Complex.* The Atlantic, December 1998. http:www.theatlantic.com/magazine/archive/1998-the-prison-industrial-complex/304669/.4.
2. *Social Reform: Mental Illness and Prisons*, Cambridge, MA. US History. internet, 1/28/15.
3. Vicky Pelaez. *The Prison Industry in the United States: Big Business or a New Form of Slavery?* March 31, 2014. EL Diano-LaPrensa New York and Global Research 10 March 2008, 1.
4. Ibid, 1.
5. Ibid, 1
6. Ibid, 2
7. Ibid, 2
8. Ibid, 2
9. Ibid, 2
10. Eric Schlosser, 4
11. Ibid, 3.
12. Leo Damrosch. *Tocqueville's Discovery of America.* (New York: Farrar, Strauss and Giroux, 2010).

Chapter 6: The Developmental Stages of the Idea to Grow a Prison Industry

1. William Martin and Andrew Pragacz, *Education and Incarceration in NYS, Recalculating the fate of New York's Youth, from Cuomo to Cuomo*, June 5, 2013, Binghamton Justice Projects.
2. Ibid, June 6, 2013 Andy Pragacz is a PhD student in the Sociology Department, Binghamton University. Apragc1@binghamton.edu. Binghamton Justice Projects Brief: June 6, 2k013. Citation: 4-page report. [13] Fiscal Policy Institution (2009) demonstrates that

community colleges have suffered the most from education cuts over the past 20 years. [14] "State budget calls for TAP cuts", Buffalo Law Journal, August 12, 2010, (http://www.lawjournalbuffalo.com/newsarticle/current/2010/08/12/102484/atate-budget-calls-for-tap-cuts, accessed June 1, 2013) reports how the state cut TAP spending by directly reducing aid by $75 a year, and limiting enrollment. New York State Division of the B. 2011-12 Executive Budget, Higher Education Section.

3. Robert Gangi, Vincenat Schiraldi, and Jason Ziedenberg, *New York State of Mind?: Higher Education vs. Prison Funding in the Empire State*, paper presented. [Descriptors: (eric.ed,gov). Correctional Institutions, Drug Legislation, Educational Finance, Government School Relationship, Higher Education. Resource Allocation, State Aid State Legislation. Trend Analysis. Retrieved 12/23/15, 3:38 PM].

Chapter 7: "Get Tough on Crime:"
The First New York Prison Builders.

Nelson A. Rockefeller

Drug Laws Set the Foundation for a Prison Industry in New York

1. Wiki; en.m. Wikipedia.org; 12/29/15, 8:29 AM
2. *Rockefeller Drug Laws*, Wiki, 12/26/15, 3:29 EST PM. References: Murray Rothbard (1979-03-05), Nelson Rockefeller, R.I.P., LewRockwell.com; Clyde Haberman.
3. *Rockefeller Drug Laws*, Wiki, 12/26/15, 3:29 EST PM. (References: Murray Rothbard (1979-03-05), Nelson Rockefeller, R.I.P., LewRockwell.com; Clyde Haberman (2002-11-05) "NYC; Proud of the Name. Not the Laws". The New York Times. Retrieved 2014-02-22).
4. NPR, "*The Drug Laws that Changed How We Punish.*" Brian Mann, North Country Radio, Feb. 15, 2015.
5. Ibid, Brian Mann
6. Ibid, Brian Mann

7. Ibid, Brian Mann
8. Ibid, Brian Mann.
9. Ibid, Brian Mann. This story is produced by NPR in cooperation with *North Country Public Radio's Prison Time Media Project,* a year-long investigative series looking at the national impact of Rockefeller-style laws. (retrieved 12/25/2015).
10. Wikipedia, Nelson Rockefeller, 3/5/16.
11. The Telegraph, 6:58 PM 09 Aug 2011.
12. William Lynch III, addresses an age-old question, *"I Am My Brother's Keeper, Why We Must Change the Code."* March 03, 2014; updated May 03, 2014. William Lynch III Vice President, New Business Initiatives. Bill Lynch Associates, LLC. Retrieved 12/25/2015.
13. Madison Gray, Rockefeller ADDEND [Racial Justice; Feb. 3, 2009 – NYCLU: *Sentencing Commission Report Squanders Historic, Opportunity on Drug Law Reform* 12/26/15, "A Brief History of New York's Rockefeller Drug Laws" in the Time]
14. Ibid.
15. Citation, Zimmerman, Joseph F. (2012) *State-Local Governmental Interactions.* SUNY Press, p. 127. ISBN 978-1-4384-4169-6. OCLC 2011018383, p. 127. [In its early years the UDC was responsible for "the last significant program of publicly assisted housing in the United States. [19] Citation [19]. http://www.arch.columbia.edu/index php?pageData=8882/23/4/1652.
16. Ibid.
17. The Telegraph, 6:58 PM 09 Aug 2011"
18. Ibid.
19. *Public Authorities by the Numbers: Empire State Development Corporation* (PDF) Office of the New York State Comptroller. February 2015, p. 3. Christian Science Monitor, Sun 1/4/16.
20. EIR, Investigation, *Executive Intelligence Review Investigation*, Volume 13, Number 33, August 22, 1986, p. 56.

21. *A New $500 Million Prison Bond Issue, But Why and For What?*, The Week in Review with Thomas A. Coughlin 3d, Commissioner of the State Department of Correctional Services, State Senator Ralph J. Marino, chairman of the Crime and Corrections Committee, and Donald J. Newman, Dean of the School of Criminal Justice at the State University of New York at Albany, to discuss prisons and prisoners with Richard J. Meislin, Albany Bureau Chief of T he New York Times, and Richard Levine, an editor of The Review. Excerpts from this dialogue. nytimes.com, Week In Review. 3/5/16, 5:53 PM.
22. Eric Schlosser, *The Prison-Industrial Complex*, The Atlantic, p. 5/9.

Chapter 8: Mario M. Cuomo: A Prison Model for the Nation
Massive Expansion of the State Prison
The Mario Cuomo Prison Building Empire (Jan. 1, 1983 – December 31, 1994)

1. Greater Ossining Chamber of Commerce. Archived from the original on 2008-02. Retrieved December 21, 2008.
2. EIR Investigation. Aug. 22, 198d6, p. 55.
3. Willkie Farr and Gallagher LLP; Wiki, 1/5/2016, 10:56 AM.
4. Steve Kornacki, *The Mario Effect*: Last time a group of presidential challengers was this unimpressive, there was a reason". Capital New York, Retrieved March 7, 2013. [Cuomo described his experience in that dispute in the book Forest Hills Diary, and the story was retold by sociologist Richard Sennett in The Fall of Public Man]. [Citation: Charles J. Hynes, Bob Drury, Incident at Howard Beach, 2011, p. 86.] [Citation: nycourts.gov 1/6/2016, 12:30 PM; "Charles F. Murphy, Tammany leader, "Adrian Paul Burke (Oct. 2, 1904–Sept. 3, 2000) Court of Appeals 1954–1973].
5. *Executive Intelligence Review*, Investigation, Aug. 22, 1986, p. 55. National Governors Association, Hall of States, 444 N. Capitol St. Ste. 267, Washington, DC 20001-15; 202.624.5300. Wikipedia, 1/5/2016.
6. Wikipedia, 1/6/15, Wed.; 9:50, Wikipedia on Cuomo.
7. Ibid, Mary Anne Krupsack.

8. Judicial Directories New York Courts; Judges of the Court of Appeals nycourts.gov.
9. Elizabeth Kolbert, *As Inmates Pour In, Cuomo Plans 3,000 Beds in Prison Gymnasiums,* Special to the New York Times, June 3, 1989, 1.
10. Ibid, 2
11. Ibid, 1
12. Ibid, 1
13. Ibid, 1
14. Ibid, 1
15. Ibid, 1
16. Warden Wilson J. Walters [105]
17. Elizabeth Kolbert, 1
18. Ibid, 2
19. Ibid, 2
20. Ibid, 2
21. Ibid, 2
22. Ibid, 2
23. Ibid, 2
24. The Correctional Association of New York, Nov. 1994.

Chapter 9: ***The Prison Industrial Complex*** **by Eric Schlosser**
Nonviolent Offenders Responsible for Prison Growth
Do we rehabilitate or do we incarcerate, that is the question?

1. Eric Schlosser, *The Prison Industrial Complex*, The Atlantic, December 1998.
2. Ibid, 1
3. Ibid, 2
4. Ibid, 2
5. Guide to Drug Enforcement; The Drug Enforcement formed July 1, 1973.
6. https://www.youtube.com/watch?=pWr_GOhZVc; [Charles Rangel]
7. Ibid. [Jackson]

8. Elizabeth Kolbert, 1

Chapter 10: Prisons on the Stock Market

The Big Question: Who Benefits from the Prison Industry?

1. Vicky Pelaez and El Diano-La Prensa, Prison Labor, 1
2. Ibid, 1
3. Annie Jacobsen, Operation Paper Clip, 122
4. Vicky Pelaez and La-Prensa, 1
5. Ibid, 1
6. Ibid, 1
7. Ibid, 1
8. Ibid, 1
9. Ibid, 1
10. Ibid, 2
11. Ibid, 2
12. Ibid, 3
13. Ibid, 3

Chapter 11: States Use Bond Issues to Support Prisons in the 21st Century

1. New Jersey Bond Issue, nytimes.com, 1/10/2016; NY and *NJ Setting a Financial Prison Rock!*
2. Eric Schlosser. *The Prison Industrial Complex*, p. 2; California prisons.
3. Leo C. Wolinsky, Los Angeles Times Staff Writer. Sacramento, California Bond Issue Dialogue. *Presley Plans to Push $500 million Prison Bond Issue* February 27, 1987.
4. California Prisons. "articleslatimes.comd, retrieved 1/11/2016, 10:58 AM.[Los Angeles Times, February 27, 1987].
5. Texas Bond Issue. *Private Prisons are Rotten to the Core*: 2/25/2010. Texas: Private prison fraud plays major role in campaign. [http://www.dallasnews.com/sharedcontent/dws/newstexassouthwest/stories/DN-Trailmix_24TEX.aart.State Edition 1.4c2aO1f.html. 12:00 AM

CST on Wednesday, February 24, 2010. The Associated Press, Perry blasts Hutchison law firm on prison deal]

6. The Correctional Association of New York, January 1995.
7. *Forbes On Bond Process*, retrieved 1/11/2016, 2:09 PM. Tax-Savings Bonds, Top Municipal Bonds, Bond Yields Today, Top 10 Government Bonds, Municipal Bond Funds, Best Municipal Bonds, Treasury Bond Rates and Best Bonds to Buy.
8. Ibid.

Chapter 12: Sentencing to perpetuate a prison industry

Borders open, Drugs flourish, and Prisons remain at maximum capacity
Black Man: Target for Destruction
Stats are self-explanatory from The Correctional Association of New Yor

1. E. Ann Carson and William J. Sabol, *Prisoners in 2011*,"(Washington, DC: US Dept. of Justice Bureau of Justice Statistics, Dec.2012), NC1239808, p. 8. http://www.bjs.gov/content/pub/pdf/p11.pdf
2. The New Yorker, May 11, 2015, ***The Milwaukee Experiment*** by Jeffrey Toobin. John Chisholm, District Attorney in Milwaukee County, Wisconsin: Racial imbalance in American prisons takes a stand to make a difference: Racial inequality in Criminal Justice
3. Jed S. Rakoff, ***Mass Incarceration: The Silence of the Judges***, The New York Review of Books, May 21, 2015/ Volume LXII, Number 9, pp. 14–17.

Chapter 13: Two Largest Prison Corporations in America

1. Wikipedia
2. Vicky Pelaez, 3.

Chapter 14: Privatizing: Prison Support Base

Prison Privatization: Pathway to Grow Prisons

1. Nation of Change, *Prison Privatization and the Efficiency Myth*, 92–93.
2. Ibid, 93.

3. Ibid, 94
4. Paula M. Ditton and Doris James Wilson, Bureau of Justice Statistics (BJS), *Special Report, U.S. Department of Justice*, Office of Justice Programs, pp. 1–16. *Violent Crime and Law Enforcement Act* signed in 1994 by Bill Clinton.
5. Nation of Change, 94.
6. Policy Brief. *The Federal Crime Bill: What will it Mean for California*? Figure 1 Section, "How the Programs are Funded." lao.ca.gov., September 27, 1994.
7. Ibid, *The Federal Crime Bill, Cops on the Beat*; Nation of Change, 94.
8. Huff Post, "When Congress Cut Pell Grants for Prisoners," Dec. 04, 2013. "Inmates of state and federal prisons became ineligible for Pell grants through a provision of the 1994 omnibus crime bill that President Bill Clinton signed into law. The House, then controlled by Democrats, approved the provision on a vote of 312 to 116 in April that year."
9. Federal Register, *National Partnership for Reinventing Government*, March 3, 1993. http://govinfo.library.unt.edu/npr/library/status/ex.sum.html.
10. "Prison Privatization and the Efficiency Myth." http://www.nationofchange.org/print/26476SHARE.
11. Paul Wright, *The Case Against Stacia A. Hylton*, November 12, 2010. counterpunch.org Director of the Human Rights Center.
12. Ibid, The Case Against Stacia A. Hylton. Tells the Facts and Names
13. Ibid, 127
14. Ibid, 127
15. Ibid, 127
16. Ibid, 127
17. Ibid, 128
18. Ibid, 128
19. Ibid, 128
20. Ibid, 128

21. *The Case of Stacia A. Hylton*. United States Senate, Committee of the Judiciary, Washington, DC, Oct. 1, 2015. VIA Electronic Transmission, total of 4 pages. Grassley.senate.gov
22. Ibid, 129

Chapter 15: Prison Rehabilitation prior to the 1970s

James V.. Bennett Prison Reform

James V. Bennett and Prison Reform 1925–1964: Am I My Brother's Keeper?

1. *I Chose Prison*, by James V.. Bennett, published in Reader's Digest Condensed Books, Vol. 2, 1970, 374–467. An innovator in prison reform.

Index

The author, Dorothy R. Swygert, ***Silence in a Democracy**: Prisons for Profit*, unveils prisons in the 21st century as modern-day slavery, with America cradling the highest prison population in the Western world. This prison economy is corporate America's cheap labor force, but the black man's secret annihilation. Nelson A. Rockefeller, governor of New York, held a press conference in January 1973 to announce his new policy on drugs—the Rockefeller Drugs Laws. These laws opened the door to the design and building of a prison industry in New York, and the model spread across the nation. The United States leads the prison pack and holds the largest prison population in the Western world—2.2 million people locked behind the prison walls, in a democracy!

Humanity, used as the product to fuel the prison engine, reveals the greed, lust, and ruthless political schemes to sustain this industry. Short of creating other economic enterprises, America has invested in a degraded prison–industrial complex. This paradigm resembles modern-day cannibalism, where young, strong, black males are incarcerated in their youth, used as a cheap labor force, to their fourth decade of life, debilitated, worn, and drained of any physical virility to realize their own purpose in life—and disposed as refuse.

Dorothy Swygert, who led a prison ministry in New York, unfolds the secret plan contrived in a 1970s design to implement an economic model—prisons for profit using drugs as a bait to perpetuate prison growth. The system has no respect for family, women, children, or community. The black family, furtively, is on a fast course to annihilation with their women and children. There is absolutely nothing sacred to the prison–industrial complex.

The prison–industrial complex is supported surreptitiously by public taxes and government contracts. A myriad of institutions contribute to fueling the prison system, including school dropouts, teenage mothers, and drug abusers.

The two largest prison corporations in America are Correctional Corporation of America and the GEO Group (formerly known as Wackenhut); combined. they control 75% of all prisons. To sustain these prisons, these two corporations spend millions lobbying in Washington to initiate and to sustain legislation to extend the prison sentences—to provide longevity and to prevent interruption in the cheap prison labor force, where stocks increase exponentially on the stock market. Lobbying takes place in Congress to insure these economic principles—longevity and consistency in the prison labor force—will be preserved.

On September 13, 1994, Bill Clinton signed two laws. The Truth in Sentencing bill requires an inmate to serve 85% of the jail sentence before becoming eligible to apply for parole. Regardless of good behavior or any other personality growth, the inmate must fulfill the 85% stipulation. The second act Bill Clinton signed was the Violent Crime and Law Enforcement Act. This act prohibits the inmate from receiving Pell grants to engage in post-secondary degree programs. But the key to this bill is how it appropriated funds to hire 100,000 police officers to enforce drug-related crimes. Over $30 billion dollars was the appropriation for this bill—monies that could have fueled historically black colleges and universities (HBCUs) that are in great need of funding. But prisons have priority over funds for colleges. Clinton must also be remembered for closing some federal prisons to make them available for prison corporations without any consideration for the 100,000 or more federal workers who lost their jobs because of this political action—privatizing prisons for profit. According to the Justice Policy Institute, Bill Clinton did, *Too Little, Too Late: President Clinton's Legacy.*

> The Justice Policy Institute released the report, "Too Little, Too Late: President Clinton's Prison Legacy," yesterday in honor of President's Day. The report reveals that more state and federal prisoners were added to the U.S. prisons during Clinton's eight years in office than during the term of any prior U.S. president, and more federal inmates were added under Clinton than under Reagan and Bush combined (the Justice Policy Institute. prisonpolicy.org; and democracy now).

Read the eleven-page policy report presented b: www.justicepolicy.org.

Bibliography

Beare, Emma. *501 Must-Know Speeches*. Great Britain. Octopus Publishing Group: Bounty Books, 2010.

Beckett, Katherine and Theodore Sasson. *The Politics of Injustice: Crime and Punishment in America*. London: Sage Publications, 2004.

Bernstein, R. B. *The Wisdom of John and Abigail Adams*. New York. Fall River Oress, 2002.

Bixel, Patricia Bells. *Seeing the New South: Race and Place in the Photographs of Ulrich Bonnell Phillips*. Phillips.

Blumrosen, Alfred W. and Ruth G. *Slave Nation: How Slavery United the Colonies & Sparked the American Revolution*. Naperville, Illinois: Sourcebooks, Inc., 2005.

Chua, Amy. World on Fire: Exporting Free Market Democracy. New York. Random House, 2003.

Commons, John Rogers. A *Documentary History of American Industrial Society*.

Cox, Jack. Nicaragua Betrayed by Anastasio Somoza. Massachusetts: Western Islands, 1980.

Damrosch, Leo. *Tocqueville's Discovery of America*. New York: Farrar, Straus and Giroux, 2010.

Davis, David Brion. *Slavery and the Post-World War II Historians*. Daedalus 103.2 (1974): 1-16. Web... Chicago: Davis, David Brion,

1974. Daedalus 103 (2. The MIT Press: 1-16. http://www.jstor.org/stable/20024201

Dubois, W.E.B. *Radical Reconstruction.*

Rabaka, Reiland. *Du Bois' Dialectics: Black Radical Politics and the Reconstruction of Critical.* Lexington Books, 7/15/2009. Product Dimensions: 6.1 x 1 x9.1 inches; 1.3 lbs.; 354 pp. ISBN: 0739119583; isbn13: 978-0739119587; Language: English

Eaton, Clement. *The Mind of the Old South.* Lousiana State University Press, 1964.

Elkins, Stanley. *Slavery: A Problem in American Institutional and Intellectual Life,* Chicago, 1976.

Elkins, Stanley M. *SLAVERY: A Problem in American Institutional & Intellectual Life.* Introduction by Nathan Glazer. New York: Grosset & Dunlap, 1963.

Engs, Robert Francis. *Educating the Disfranchised and Disinherited.* Knoxville: The University of Tennessee Press, 1999.

Franklin, John Hope. *From Slavery to Freedom.* New York: Alfred A. Knopf, 1964.

Freehling, William W. *The South vs. The South.* Oxford University Press, 2001.

Genovese, Eugene D. *The Political Economy of Slavery: Studies in the Economy* and Genovese, Eugene D. Roll, Jordan, Roll: *The World the Slaves Made.* Society of the Slave South. New York: Random House, 1967.

Goffman, Alice. *On the Run: Fugitive Life in an American City.* Chicago: The University of Chicago Press, 2014.

Goldwater, Barry. *The Conscience of a Conservative.* Stellar Books, 2013.

Jacobsen, Annie. *Operation Paperclip: The Secret Intelligence Program that Brought Nazi Scientists to America.* New York: Little, Brown and Company, 2014.

Jacobsen, Annie. *Area 51: An Uncensored History of America's Top Secret Military Base,* New York: Little, Brown and Company, 2011.

Johnson, Walter. *River of Dark Dreams:* Slavery and Empire in the Cotton Kingdom.
Journal of African American Studies
Journal of Family Theory & Review
Journal: DS: Reiland Rabaka, ass. Prof. Africana Studies/Dept. of Ethnic Studies at Univ of CO at Boulder; affiliate prof. of women and gender studies and a research fellow at the Center for Studies of Ethnicity and Race in America (CSERA). Recipient of the Cheikh Anta Diop Distinguished Career Award.
Korten, David C. *When Corporations Rule the World.* California: Berrett-Koehler Publishers Inc., 2015.
Leaming, Barbara. Jack Kennedy: The Education of a Statesman. New York: W. W. Norton & Company, 2006.
Mayer, Martin. The FED. New York: The Free Press, 2001.
Mayer, Martin. *The Greatest-Ever Bank Robbery.* New York: Charles Scribner's Sons, 1990.
Mayer, Martin. *Nightmare on Wall Street Salomon Brothers and the Corruption of the Marketplace.* New York: Simon & Schuster, 1993.
Perkins, John. *Confessions of an Economic Hit Man.* New York: A Plume Book, 2004.
Phillips, Ulrich Bonnell. American Negro Slavery: A Survey of the Supply, Employment and Control of Negro…
Phillips, Ulrich Bonnell. *Life and Labor in the Old South* (Southern Classics).
Phillips, Ulrich B. *Life & Labor in the Old South* (1st Paperback Printing) 1963.
Phillips, Ulrich *The Course of the South to Secession.*
Phillips, Ulrich Bonnell. *The Slave Economy of the Old South: Selected Essays in Economic and Social History.*
Phillips, Ulrich Bonnell. *The Course of the South to Secession* (American century series).

Phillips, Ulrich Bonnell. *A History of Transportation to the Eastern Cotton Belt to 1860.*

Phillips, Ulrich Bonnell. *Georgia And States Rights*: A Study Of The Political History of Georgia From The…

Posner,Gerald. *God's Bankers: A History of Money and Power at the Vatican*. New York: Simon & Shuster, 2015.

Potter, David M. *The Impending Crisis: America Before 1848-1861.*

Singal, Daniel Joseph. *Ulrich B. Phillips: The Old South as the New.* London: Oxford

University Press on behalf of American historians. DOI:10.2307/1893614. Stable URL: http://www.jstor.org/stable/1893614 ; Page count: 21.The Journal of American History 63.4 (1977): 871-891. Web…

Piketty, Thomas. CAPITAL: In the 21st Century. Cambridge, Massachusetts: The Belknap Press of Harvard University Press, 2014.

Reader's Digest Condensed Books. Spring 1970 Selections. Pleasantville, New York.

Ronald Stevens Journal of African American Studies.[racial/ethnic family studies scholars, family siciologists & critical race theorists.

Roper, John Herbert. U. B. Phillips: *A Southern Mind*. Georgia: Mercer University Press, 1984.

Schlesinger, Arthur M. *A History of America: The Rise of the City*. New York:

The Macmillan Company, 1933. "A critical inquiry into how American slavery differed radically from other slave systems and why its effects on Negro personality were so severe and lasting."

Sammons, Jeffrey T. and John H. Morrow, Jr. Harlem's Rattlers and the Great War: The Undaunted 369th Regiment and the African American Quest for Equality. University Kansas Press, 2014.

Smith, John David. *Ulrich Bonnell Phillips*: A Southern Historian and His Critics.

Starobin, Robert S. *Industrial Slavery in the Old South*. London:Oxford University Press, 1975.

Swygert, Dorothy R. *Healing the Nation: An Indepth Study of African Americans*. Virginia: Rekindle the Heart, 2005.

Talbot, David. *The Devil's Chessboard:* Allen Dulles, the CIA, and the Rise of America's Secret Government. New York: HarperCollins books, 2015.

Taylor, Albert. *Is Davis a Traitor?* Was Secession a Constitutional Right Previous to the War?

Washington, James. The Essential Writings and Speeches of Martin Luther King, Jr. New York. Harper Collins Publishers, 1991.

Welsing, Dr. Frances Cress. *The ISIS Papers: The Keys to the Colors.* Washington, DC: C.W. Publishing, 1991.

White, Deborah Gray. *Ar'n't I a Woman?* Female Slaves in the Plantation South.

York, Herbert F. York. *Making Weapons Talking Peace: A Physicist's Odyssey from Hiroshima to Geneva*. New York: Basic Books, Inc., 1987.

York, Herbert F. York. *Arms and the Physicist.* New York: American Institute of Physics, 1995.